# The Missionary's Catechism

Russell L. Ford

*Magnificat Institute Press*
*Houston*

*1997*

*Nihil Obstat:*
> Reverend R. Troy Gately
> Censor Liborm

*Imprimatur:*
> ✠Joseph A. Fiorenza, D.D.
> Bishop of Galveston-Houston
> December 9, 1997

The *Nihil Obstat* and *Imprimatur* are official declarations that a book is considered to be free of doctrinal or moral error. No implication is contained therein that those who have granted the *Nihil Obstat* or the *Imprimatur* agree with the contents, opinions, or statements expressed.

First Edition, 1998 by Magnificat Institute Press, P.O. Box 60591, Houston, Texas 77205.

Excerpts from the English translation of the *Catechism of the Catholic Church* for use in the United States of America Copyright © 1994, United States Catholic Conference, Inc. -- Libreria Editrice Vaticana. Used with permission.

Excerpts from the English translation of the *Catechism of the Catholic Church: Modifications from the Edition Typica* Copyright © 1997, United States Catholic Conference, Inc. -- Libreria Editrice Vaticana. Used with permission.

Cover design by Sallie Saltzman, Saltzman Design

Printed in the United States of America.
ISBN     0-9657125-1-6
Library of Congress Card Catalog Number: 97-75593

*To The Blessed Trinity*

# Contents

# Preface

I GREW up in unenlightened days. We learned our catechism —from a catechism, of all things. The propositions of the faith were set out in memorizable if dry answers that echoed equally dry questions. I still recall the first and most important pair: "Why did God make you?" "God made me to know him, love him, and serve him in this life and to be happy with him forever in the next." No two dozen words ever contained more truth. That simple exchange remains, I think, the best answer to *Why?* ever printed.

Long years after reading the *Baltimore Catechism*, I came across *Radio Replies*, three volumes in which Frs. Leslie Rumble and Charles M. Carty collected four thousand questions they had handled during their long years on the air. I found their spirited answers engaging, and the questions were authentic, just as one might hear them on the street. Unlike those in my child's catechism, the questions posed to Rumble and Carty expressed the ignorance, misinformation, and prejudice held by real people. That's why their volumes remain popular half a century after first seeing print.

As they did decades ago, today most Catholic magazines and newspapers have question-and-answer columns. The readers want them. Although self-styled pedagogical experts pooh-pooh such devices, the fact is that they work—they pass along the faith while keeping readers' attention. We like to see what others believe or don't believe (their problems often parallel our own), and we delight in quick-witted answers that bring closure. (Almost everyone likes detective stories. Question-and-answer books and columns are miniature theological whodunits.)

Russ Ford's *Missionary Catechism* might be called a streetwise version of the *Baltimore Catechism*, an updated version of Rumble and Carty, or a question-and-answer column with an attitude. No matter how it is characterized, it presents the Catholic faith in an approachable and understandable way, in little morsels that are digested easily. *Bon appétit!*

*Karl Keating*
*President*
*Catholic Answers*

# Foreword

JESUS chose a tall fisherman to build His Church. Peter tried to talk Jesus out of His holy sacrifice on Calvary, chattered nonsense during the Transfiguration, declared that Jesus would never wash his feet, fell asleep in the Garden of Gethsemane, and denied Jesus three times. Jesus could have chosen a learned man, perhaps Rabbi Gamaliel or his pupil Rabbi Saul of Tarsus. Jesus might have chosen Joseph of Arimathea or Nicodemus. For that matter, He could have come three hundred years earlier and chosen Alexander the Great, who conquered most of the known world. Alexander could have spread Christianity, rather than Greek culture. But if Alexander had carried Christ's teaching all over the world, everyone would remark on what a fine church Alexander had built. When a bumbling fisherman builds a church, we see Christ at work.

Jesus still works that way. He sent a cloistered nun to build a worldwide television network. Mother Angelica knew nothing of television technology or finance. He could have chosen Ted Turner, who knows a lot about these things. When a cloistered nun builds a worldwide network we see Christ at work. Compare Mother's Global Catholic Network with Ted Turner's Cable News Network. Which helps its audience reach eternal life in Christ? Which offers a clear and coherent worldview? Which shows beautiful images? Which brings peace in our hearts?

Russ Ford and I have unlikely origins. We would not have been friends as children because our backgrounds were so different. If anyone had suggested either of us would become a faithful Catholic, we would have said it was humanly impossible. But Jesus knew us both, and quietly led us along a path we ourselves could not see. Russ was baptized in an Alabama prison; I in a Virginia parish church, at nearly the same time. But if anyone had suggested that our paths would

*xiii*

cross, we would have regarded it as impossible. Russ was confined within prison walls hundreds of miles from my home.

Jesus continued His patient work. Back in 1994 I became active on a Catholic computer network then called CRNet, run by Jeff Mirus, a Catholic scholar whose name in Latin means "miracle." A friend on CRNet thought Paul Likoudis of The Wanderer might like to interview me to publicize my conversion experience. I had been born Jewish, and my conversion story was dramatic, but I didn't think it important enough to publicize. Paul telephoned me; we spoke for three hours, and The Wanderer published the interview over nearly an entire page on July 21, 1994. Russ saw the article and wrote to me. We both were working on books about the Catholic faith, and we both were writing magazine articles proclaiming the true Faith. We became good friends. There are prisons that hold the body, and prisons that hold the soul. Russ Ford was in a prison that held his body, but his soul could fly to heaven at Christ's command. The philosopher who said, "Man is born free, but everywhere he is in chains," meant chains that hold the soul. Today's culture of death, that seeks to drive Christianity out of public life, is such a prison; a soul chained to the culture of death here can be chained in hell for all eternity.

Many who read this catechism may think it impossible that they would become Catholic, that their souls could break out of the culture of death and soar to freedom with all the angels and saints. It is no more impossible than that a bumbling fisherman could build a worldwide Church, or that a cloistered nun could build a worldwide television network, or that an agnostic from Doniphan, Missouri, and a Jew from the Bronx, New York City, might end up as Catholic evangelists. Nothing is impossible with God.

The information in this catechism is more important than anything you have read so far. We buy life insurance and set up pension plans to prepare for a small part of our future, a few decades. This catechism will help you prepare for all eternity.

You have questions. The Catholic Church has answers. Russ has written them down so clearly that nearly anyone can see how it all fits together.

Read, and enter Christ's Light!

*Oremus Pro Invicem*
(Let us Pray for One Another)

Martin K. Barrack

# Introduction

In *Apostolicam Actuositatem* (Decree on the Apostolate of the Laity), the Fathers of the Second Vatican Council decreed to the faithful that we have a grave obligation to learn our faith well and share it with others. This decree, as with all the documents of Vatican II, demonstrates to us now a generation later how the Holy Spirit guides and protects His Church. In 1965, at the time this document was promulgated, Catholics the world over had lived for generations leaving the evangelization of peoples to bishops, priests, deacons, brothers, and sisters. It was a shock — a reality check — for the laity to learn that they too had a responsibility to share the immutable truths of Catholicism with non-Catholics. Indeed, the responsibility had always been there, but the laity simply failed to realize it. The Holy Spirit knew it, though. He eternally knew it.

Through Vatican II, the Holy Spirit began to prepare the faithful for the most glorious era of the Church's history. Our darkest era, on the other hand, began with the spread of godless Communism in 1917. Satan had embarked on almost a century of extraordinary activity. and thereby created an environment in which persecution of Christ's followers flourished. More Christians have died for their faith during the twentieth century than in all the preceding centuries of Christianity combined. A recent book by French authors, *Le Livre Noir* (The Black Book), has estimated the communists are responsible for the deaths of over one hndred million people.

Ever in control of His Church, the Holy Spirit then raised up an *alter Christus* in the office of St. Peter who had grown up under communist tyranny. He is known and loved the world over. He is Pope John Paul II. The

Polish Cardinal was elevated to the papacy by the Holy Spirit to usher the Church into the most glorious era of her 2000 year history. The Holy Father has unceasingly preached to us the need for evangelization, echoing the words of the Fathers of Vatican II, as we march boldly united into the Third Millennium. He has set the example for us with his biennial World Youth Day events, a prolificacy of encyclicals and pastorals, and evangelistic pilgrimages around the world. His evangelistic efforts have earned him the title *Pilgrim Catechist*.

It was roughly seven years into his pontificate that the efforts of Pope John Paul II began to bear substantial and noticeable fruit. Catholics who were holding their own and standing firm against the prevailing evils of the day began to take the offensive and move forward, resolved to work with the Holy Father to reassert the Church as the "pillar and foundation of the truth". Innumerable people began to experience re-conversion. Non-Catholics began to discover the immutable divine truths of Catholicism, drawn by their sublimity, holiness, and reasonableness. The new and glorious era of light had begun. Very soon Communism started to crumble in the Polish Pope's homeland and thereafter everywhere else around the world.

In the midst of these changes, a hate-filled and embittered agnostic found himself standing before an Alabama judge. When the judge's gavel fell, the agnostic faced having to spend the next twenty-five years of his life in prison. At the close of his first year in prison, the young agnostic met a man who had been inspired by the great pontiff, and had accepted the graces from the Holy Spirit to evangelize.

Because of that providential meeting, the young agnostic began the long and painful process to conversion. God stripped him down to nothing, and rebuilt a whole man where only the shell of a man had been. The most painful part of the agnostic's conversion process came when he told his father of his intention of becoming a Catholic during a telephone conversation. The ailing gentleman was enraged by his son's decision. The father said, "No son of mine is a Roman Catholic!" The line went dead. Those were the last words the son ever heard from his father. The father died two months later.

Not long before the young prisoner's reception into the Church on the feast of Our Lady of Lourdes in 1989, at his priest's insistence, the prisoner began to teach the Catholic faith to fellow prisoners. He also began to evangelize through the medium of print, having published scores of articles in many good Catholic publications. At this writing, God has used the prisoner to evangelistically teach the catechism to thousands of people, both one-on-one and in group settings; aid in the conversion of over one hundred prisoners, and many more in society; and to become the godfather to more than fifty souls. The prisoner has been called an expert in prison evangelization, and his work has been recognized as the most successful prison apostolate in the United States; however, he suffers no illusions as to who and what he is. The prisoner realizes that any of what others call success is nothing more than a cooperation with grace, and this cooperation comes because the prisoner has fallen helplessly, hopelessly, passionately in love with this living, breathing organism we call the Church. What all this means, in the most simple of terms, is this: The prisoner is just one man who is trying to work out his salvation in fear and trembling (cf. Philippians 2:12).

By now you must surely realize that the prisoner about whom you are reading is this author. I am not a great man. I'm not even a particularly good man, but I am a product of something in which God seems to relish. God has taken one of the lowly status of prisoner and given this convict a talent for teaching the truths of Catholicism evangelistically. It would be an injustice to God to deny that my work here in prison has been less than amazing in terms of conversions. But God did not give me methods and talents for evangelization for myself and those with whom I deal alone. These were given to me to share with the world.

*The Missionary's Catechism* is, to my knowledge, the only one of its kind. It is written in the tenor and method I have used to teach many people. The style is question and answer, and the posture is assertively evangelistic. This catechism provides not only a presentation of the deposit of faith, but also well reasoned answers to many of the most common objections to Catholicism. Based on the *Catechism of the Catholic Church*, this text provides answers from the writings of early Church Fathers, classical Christian literary works, numerous scriptural references, and an abundance of ecclesiastical and papal documents. *The Missionary's Catechism* is specially designed to satisfy any advanced intellect while simultaneously remaining basic enough for those occasional students who may have some trouble learning. There are even tests for each section so the student — whether studying this text alone, or by way of a catechist's direction — can chart individual progress.

If you are using this text for self-study, I implore you to precede each reading with a prayer to the Holy Spirit, asking Him to remove all distractions while enlightening your intellect to discern truth. Then move slowly through the text, taking time to think and meditate on the new things you will be learning. If you find yourself unable to grasp something in the text because I have failed to adequately cover an element of Catholic teaching, call or write Catholic Answers (P. O. Box 17490, San Diego, CA 92177. Phone: 619-387-7200). Because they are in business for this very purpose, the staff at Catholic Answers will be most pleased to help you.

To those of you who are using this text to teach others, I caution you to always remember one thing: It is *impossible* for you to convert anybody. Only the Holy Spirit can make conversions. It is your job to pray and present the immutable truths of the Catholic Church. It is the Blessed Virgin Mary's job to intercede for both you and your students to her divine Son for the necessary graces. And it is the Holy Spirit's job to give those graces. You are not at fault if your students reject the graces of conversion offered by the Holy Spirit. You cannot be true to the graces He gives others, but only to the graces He offers to you.

It is my most earnest prayer that all who use this book will be offered and accept many wonderful graces: To non-Catholics, the graces of conversion; to Catholics, the graces for continued interior conversion; to those who recognize the need for evangelization, the graces for that "fire in the belly" to share the faith with everyone! May God bless you, and may you experience the richness of His mercy.

In Mary's loving embrace,

Russell L. Ford

Solemnity of Mary Mother of God
January 1, 1998

## The Apostles' Creed

### First Article of the Creed

**"I believe in God the Father Almighty, Creator of heaven and earth."**

*The Existence and Nature of God*

**1. Who created us?**

God, who is the all-perfect Supreme Being, the Creator of all things, visible and invisible, and who keeps them in existence, is the One who created us (Genesis 1:27).

**2. How do we know God exists?**

There are several ways by which we know that God exists. First, we know He exists because He has revealed Himself to us (Hebrews 1:1-2).

Second, we know God exists because our reason tells us so. We can see from creation that all could only exist by the power of an infinitely wise, all-powerful, self-existing Being. He is a logical God who has created a logically functioning universe. As an example, look at the food chain. The smallest microscopic organism is food for the next largest organism, is food for the next largest organism, is food for the next largest organism. Eventually it becomes food for man, the highest form of natural creation. We eat a pork chop or chicken leg, and then we start the process all over again after the food has been digested.

Look at the trees. The trees inhale carbon dioxide and exhale oxygen. Now look at man. We inhale oxygen and exhale carbon dioxide. The trees cannot live without us, and we cannot live without the trees. What a logical God!

These are certainly proofs of God's existence, but sometimes we require reasoning that is more elementary and satisfying to the mind. For this reason, the following argument is presented.

It is a historical fact that the books of the Old Testament are ancient Hebrew literature. We take this as an established fact in order to present part of our argument; however, we will not (here) claim that anything in the Old Testament is true, but only that it is ancient Hebrew literature.

The second fact to establish is that Jesus of Nazareth was a real, historical person. Most people believe that only the Bible offers proof of Jesus' existence, but this is not true. We can mention at least four non-Christian historians who attest to the reality of Jesus as a historical person. They are Flavius Josephus (a Jew), and Pliny, Tacitus, and Suetonius (all pagans). These four ancient historians, none of whom were by any means friends of Christianity, all attest to the historical existence of Jesus.

With these two facts established, we can now present the argument.

First, we consider the Old Testament prophecies about the coming of the Messiah. The Old Testament is filled with such prophecies, particularly in books like Jeremiah, Isaiah, and the earliest promise in Genesis. We still do not yet claim these prophecies are true, but only that they exist.

If we were to take all of the prophecies regarding the Messiah and list them, then read all of the available accounts of the life of Jesus (whose existence and way of life are substantiated by Josephus, Pliny, Tacitus, and Suetonius), we find that only Jesus completely fulfilled those prophecies. But this, in and of itself, does not prove

He is the Messiah. The only logical conclusions we can draw about Jesus by His having fulfilled the prophecies is that He is either a bad man, a mad man, or who He says He is.

Could a bad man — that is, a criminal type — fulfill the prophecies? Could he wake up one morning and say, "Hey, if I fulfill these prophecies, I could have power by having lots of followers, and probably make a lot of money in the process"? Certainly he could, but there is a flaw to the argument that Jesus was a bad man.

Among the prophecies about the Messiah is that one which says he must die. A highly intelligent criminal could pull off all of the prophecies, but no criminal is willing to go to the extent of losing his life. By losing his life he necessarily loses all that he strove to gain. Since Jesus willingly went to his death — indeed, even repeatedly predicted it! — He could not possibly have been a bad man.

Since Jesus is not a bad man, could He have been mad, crazy? It is conceivable that a mad man could hear a voice he believes is God telling him he is the Messiah, and that he should begin to fulfill the prophecies. If a mad man really believed his "voice", he would even be willing to fulfill the prophecy about the Messiah's death. But when applying this argument to Jesus we discover yet another terrible flaw.

It is true that a highly intelligent mad man could possibly fulfill all of the prophecies, but the very nature of insanity is inconsistency. A mad man cannot maintain focus and stability long enough to do the job. Besides, a study of the things Jesus said and did prove that He was not only stable and consistent, but He was absolutely sane. So Jesus could not have been a mad man.

This leaves us with only one possibility. Jesus must be who He says He is. And who does Jesus claim to be?

He claims to be God! He repeatedly claimed to be God (cf. John 10:24-31). My personal favorite is His claim in John 8:58 when He said: "Truly, truly I say to you, before Abraham was, I am." This is the same phrase God used to describe Himself to Moses in Exodus 3:14. I AM: the statement of the all-eternal! The Jews understood by Jesus' words that He was claiming to be God, and they sought His death for it.

**3. What does "Supreme Being" mean?**

This descriptive term for God means that He is above all created things, is self-existing, and has all perfections without limit.

**4. What does "self-existing" mean?**

By "self-existing" we mean that no other being caused God to exist. He is eternal, which means that He had no beginning, and will have no end (Psalm 90:2).

**5. Does God have a body as we do?**

No. God has no body at all. He is *pure* spirit, with intelligence and free will. When Scripture refers to "the hand of God" or other bodily attributes, this is merely a method of teaching about God so the people could understand. People are better able to understand God's mercy and justice by attributing to Him certain physical characteristics.

**6. Does God ever change?**

Because He is perfect, God cannot change. If a thing is perfect, to add to or subtract from the thing alters its perfection. This means that it would no longer be perfect. God is all-perfect and can add nothing to his perfection.

**7. Is God all-powerful?**

Yes, God is all-powerful, which means He can do all things. We call this attribute omnipotence, which means all-powerful. (Omni = all. Potent = powerful. Omni + Potent = all-powerful).

**8. Is God everywhere?**

Yes, God is everywhere. There is no place that God is not (Psalm 139:8-10). We call this divine attribute omnipresence.

**9. Does God know everything?**

God knows everything: past, present, and future, our most hidden thoughts, desires, words, actions, and omissions. We are bound by the restraints of time and space; that is, we cannot relive what happened ten minutes ago, nor can we predict exactly what will happen ten minutes from now. God, on the other hand, sees all things, events, and people at the same time. Because He is eternal, everything takes place for Him in the present tense. This means He sees the creation of the world, the destruction of the world, and everything in between all at the same time. We call this God's omniscience. (Omni = all. Science = knowledge. Omni + science = all-knowing.)

**10. Why do we call God the Creator of heaven and earth?**

Absolutely nothing existed until God created everything by His almighty power. He created everything by an act of His will. Since He is free in all of His actions, nothing compelled God to create the universe. He simply willed it.

**11. Did God create only material things?**

God created material things, but He created the immaterial too. What we mean by the immaterial are those things which do not at all effect the five senses. He created the angels, which are pure spirits. He also created each individual human soul, which is also spiritual. Angels and the human soul arc examples of the immaterial creation of God.

**12. Does God care about us?**

Of course He does! God watches over us with fatherly care. We call His loving care Divine Providence.

**13. Can God ever do evil?**

God is all perfect. Since evil is an imperfection, God is incapable of doing evil. He permits evil because He respects the free will He gave us, and we often choose evil over good. He also permits our evil in order to show us His power and mercy, because He can draw a greater good from any evil. God is all-good, infinitely lovable, and all good comes to us from Him.

*The Blessed Trinity*

**14. Is there only one God?**

Yes, there is only one God (Isaiah 45:5).

**15. Then what is meant by the Blessed Trinity?**

The Blessed Trinity is one and the same God in three divine Persons: God the Father, God the Son, and God the Holy Spirit. God the Father is the first Person of the Blessed Trinity. God the Son is the second Person of the Blessed Trinity. God the Holy Spirit is the third Person of the Blessed Trinity. All three Persons are one God, but each is distinct.

An example would be the Smith family who live in one house. Many of us see the family as the single entity it is. The mortgage company will happily accept a check from any of them. You can invite the whole family by asking any one to come. You can borrow from anyone of them and repay another. Yet you can distinguish between them. They are distinct but not separate.

**16. Are we able to completely understand how the three divine Persons are only one God?**

No, we can never completely understand how this can be. This is the greatest mystery of our Faith. And by "mystery" we mean that it is a supernatural truth which we cannot completely understand, but which we firmly believe because we trust the authority of the one who revealed it, who is God Himself.

### *The Angels*

**17. Who are the angels?**

The angels are pure spirits who possess intelligence and free will. They have no body, but God has seen fit at various times throughout the history of man to allow the angels to assume a physical presence in order to deal directly with mankind (cf. Genesis 18 and 19). Also, the angels are more perfect than we are and more like God, because they are pure spirits. They are superior to us in the order of creation because of this.

**18. How do we know angels exist?**

We know angels exist through Sacred Scripture and Sacred Tradition, which is the totality of divine revelation. A few suggested quotations are from Luke 1:11-20, 2:9-13, and 22:43; Matt 1:20, 2:13, and 2:19; Acts 8:26, 10:3, and 12:7.

## 19. Are all the angels good?

God made all the angels good, but some became evil and rebelled against Him when God tested them ( II Peter 2:4). These rebellious angels are called devils, or evil spirits. God cast them into hell for their disobedience. Because they have become enemies of God, the devils' desire to harm us by tempting us to sin against God. We can resist the devils, though; not of ourselves, but with God's help (I Peter 5:8-9).

## 20. Did God reward the good angels?

Absolutely! God granted the faithful angels the same reward He will give to us if we persevere in serving Him well; that is, the reward of the eternal happiness of heaven where we will live with the angels to see God as He truly is, and to love and adore Him forever.

## 21. Do the good angels care for us?

Yes, the good angels pray for us, protect us, and serve us as guardian angels (Psalm 91:11). At the moment God creates each human soul, He assigns to us a guardian angel to be with us throughout all eternity. Our guardian angel protects us from spiritual and material dangers, guides our minds to know what is right, prays for us, and presents our prayers to God. Although our guardian angel is superior to us in the order of creation, he serves us in this life and will continue to be our servant in heaven. This is the way of God: that the least shall be first, and the greatest becomes the servant of all.

### *Man*

## 22. What is man?

Man is a creature composed of a physical body and a spiritual soul. The soul possesses intelligence and free will, and it is created in the image and likeness of God. The soul is also immortal, which means that it will live forever, and each soul is created by God.

The soul is what gives us life. This means that when we look at John Doe we are not really seeing John Doe, but rather we are looking at the house in which he lives. It is the soul which possesses the personality, free will, intelligence, and reasoning ability. This is why there is so much emphasis placed on the soul in Christianity.

### 23. Why did God create us?

This is the question that has baffled people of every age, but the Jews of old have known the answer from the beginning of their religion, and we Catholics — who are really nothing more than New Covenant Jews — have known it for 2000 years. God created us to know Him, to love Him, and to serve Him in this life, so we may be happy with Him forever in the next life. Once we come to know God we cannot help but love Him. After we learn to love Him we desire to serve Him. If we persevere in our service to God for love of Him, He will reward us with eternity with Him in heaven.

### 24. Why did God give us free will?

God created us with free will so we would love Him by our own choice. What good is the love of a robot who is programmed to love? It serves no purpose. By giving us a free will, He allows us to choose — with His help — to do what is good and to avoid evil. In this way He can reward us for our good choices.

### 25. Who were the first human beings God created?

The Bible tells us they were Adam and Eve, the first parents of mankind from whom the entire human race descended.

## 26. What gifts did God give our first parents?

The greatest of the gifts God gave our first parents was the gift of sanctifying grace; that is, a sharing in His divine life, which made them holy, and gave them a right to heaven.

Some of the other gifts God gave our first parents were superior knowledge, control of the passions by use of reason, and freedom from suffering death. By giving them superior knowledge, our first parents had dominion over all the earth. With control of the passions by reason, Adam and Eve were not driven by the desires of the flesh; in other words, they did not know lust or anger. Freedom from suffering and death means they were meant to live forever.

## 27. What are we to believe in regard to human evolution?

That human evolution exists, at least to some degree, is reasonable. Evolution, however, is just a theory. The actual proof of the descent of man's body from animals is inadequate, especially in respect to paleontology. The human soul could not have been derived through natural evolution from that of the brute animal, since it is of a spiritual nature. If evolution is ever proven to be a fact, we are to believe that only the *body* evolved — with God's help — and not the human soul. The soul cannot evolve, since each soul is individually created by God. The Catholic Church teaches that God created the world and all of its creatures but defers to science on when any particular creature appeared on earth. The Church firmly declares, however, that the appearance was by God's action.

## 28. What is original sin?

Original sin is the sin transmitted by Adam to all the human race. It is called original because it has been passed to all men from its origin, which is Adam. We know original sin is real from the Bible (cf. Genesis 3:1-24; Romans 5:12-19), and from the teaching of the Church.

## 29. If our first parents were created holy, how could they sin?

Our first parents were not yet in heaven, where a person sees God and cannot sin. They still lived on earth, so they lived by faith. Also, they had free will, meaning they could choose good or evil. When the devil tempted them, they knowingly (with superior knowledge) and willfully (with free will) disobeyed God.

Because of their sin, our first parents lost sanctifying grace and the right to heaven. They lost their other gifts too, becoming inclined to evil and subject to ignorance, suffering and death. This means that original sin, which has been passed down to us from Adam, causes us to enter the world (from the moment of conception) with the absence of sanctifying grace and the right to heaven. It also causes us, like it did Adam and Eve, to be inclined to evil and subject to ignorance, suffering and death (Romans 5:12).

However, original sin does not make our human nature *totally* corrupt. Our mind can still know truth and our will is still free; therefore, we can still do good and avoid evil, but with greater effort and God's help.

## 30. Is God unjust in punishing us for Adam's sin?

Not at all. Sanctifying grace was a free gift of God. No one has the right to a gift. When Adam sinned he forfeited his gift, thus losing it and God's other gifts for us as well.

Let's explain it this way. If your parents were very wealthy people, their wealth would be an inheritance intended to be left to you. You would have a right to that wealth because it had been secured to be left to you. But what if your parents made some bad investments and lost all their wealth? Would you still have a right to the lost wealth? Of course not! They lost their own wealth and, by necessity, lost what would have been yours.

**31. Is there any remedy for original sin?**

Yes, Jesus Christ, the God-man, died on the cross to redeem us from sin and restore sanctifying grace to us. The ordinary means of removing original sin from the soul is by way of the Sacrament of Baptism, which we will examine in a later lesson.

**32. Is there any remedy for the effects of original sin?**

The effects of original sin may be partially remedied. This is done by Scripture reading, religious instruction (such as this), prayer, devout reception of the sacraments, voluntary penance, and obedience to God's law.

**33. Was any human person ever preserved from original sin?**

Yes, the Blessed Virgin Mary was preserved from original sin from the moment of her conception in view of the merits of Jesus Christ. This privilege is called the "Immaculate Conception."

Because Jesus is God and could have no sin, and since original sin is passed to our descendants, it was necessary for the Blessed Virgin to be preserved from original sin. This made her a pure vessel, a worthy Ark of the New Covenant. So that we may better understand how God accomplished this, we will observe the following illustrations and commentary.

We will use the time-line on the following page to see how the Immaculate Conception was possible. First, we notice that the human race has a beginning and an end, just as each individual life has a beginning and an end. On the left end of the line is the creation of the universe. On the right end is the apocalypse, or end of time. The line itself represents all of time and human events between the two.

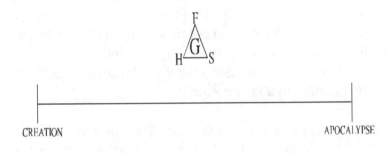

CREATION                                          APOCALYPSE

Above the time-line is a representation of God. From His vantage point, since He is not bound by the limitations of time and space, God sees all of human history from the beginning to the end, all at the same instant. Because He is infinite, there is no time for Him. Every thing is eternally present. He sees our history, our present, and our future all at the same time. This means that He also sees His Son's crucifixion and death at the same time that he sees the conception of His Son's mother.

It was on the cross that Jesus redeemed us. He won for us the graces to become heirs of heaven by the shedding of His blood. All human persons are dependent upon Christ's redemptive death for the possibility  of salvation, even Mary.

God looked down and saw the redemptive act of the cross at the same time He saw the conception of Mary in her mother's womb. In a manner of speaking, God reached down to His Son's cross and took some of the graces Jesus earned for us. Then He applied those graces to Mary's soul (I.C.) at the instant He created it and in-

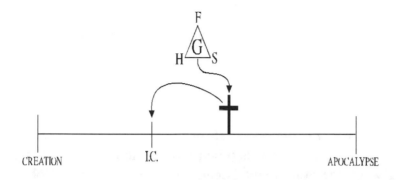

fused it into her newly conceived body. This is how Jesus was given a perfectly clean vessel to grow as He came into the world. This privilege God gave to Mary is the Immaculate Conception.

## Second Article of the Creed

## "Jesus Christ His only Son our Lord"

### *The Incarnation*

**34. What is the Incarnation?**
The incarnation is when God became man; that is, when the Son of God became man to redeem us (John 3:16-17). His very name as man, as foretold by the archangel (Luke 1:31), means "Savior".

### *True God and True Man*

**35. Why is Jesus Christ both true God and true man?**
Jesus is true God because He has the same divine nature as God the Father. He is true man because He was born of the Blessed Virgin Mary just like any man. Also, like any other man, Jesus has a human body and a human soul. Although Jesus is true man, He was still free from all sin, both original and personal, because He is also true God — and God cannot sin.

**36. How many Persons are there in Jesus Christ?**
There is only one Person in Jesus Christ. He is the second Person of the Blessed Trinity. That means that His Person is divine, or God Himself.

**37. How many natures are there in Jesus Christ?**
There are two natures in Jesus Christ. One of His natures is divine, the other is human.

**38. If Jesus possesses a human nature, how is it that we can call Mary the Mother of God?**

Did your mother give birth to a person or a nature? She gave birth to a person, of course. (A nature is merely something possessed by a person.) Since Jesus is a divine Person, the second Person of the Blessed Trinity, she conceived and gave birth to the second Person of God. This makes her the Mother of God. Mary's divine motherhood is the greatest privilege ever given to a human person.

**39. Was the Son of God always man?**

No, He was not. He became man at the Incarnation when He united a human nature to His divine nature. The Son of God is eternal; He has always existed. Jesus Christ, as God and man, has existed for only 2000 years.

**40. Do we owe worship to Jesus Christ?**

Yes, absolutely! We owe the same worship to Jesus as we owe to God the Father because Jesus is true God as well as true man.

## Third Article of the Creed

## "Conceived by the Holy Spirit, born of the Virgin Mary"

### *Son of God and Son of Mary*

**41. When did the Incarnation take place?**

The Incarnation took place on the day that the Son of God was conceived in the womb of the Virgin Mary. We call this event the Annunciation, because the archangel appeared to Mary to announce to her the opportunity to become the Mother of God by offering her this special privilege (Luke 1:26-38).

**42. Who is the father of Jesus Christ?**

The only true father of Jesus Christ is God the Father. St. Joseph was Jesus' foster father and the husband of the Blessed Virgin Mary. St. Joseph loved and cared for Jesus as any father would do, but God is His true Father.

**43. When and where was Jesus Christ born?**

Jesus Christ was born in Bethlehem nearly 2000 years ago in a small cave where animals are fed. Bethlehem means "House of Bread" and a manger (from the French verb "to eat"), where the Christ child was laid, was used to hold food for the animals.

It is important to realize that Jesus could have been born under any circumstances He chose. Because He is God and King of the universe, Jesus was deserving of being born into wealth and royal splendor; however, He chose to be born poor. He chose this because He wanted to teach us to be detached from earthly goods and to concentrate on the riches of heaven. There is nothing wrong with having a lot of money and wealthy possessions. It is only wrong to care more about them than the things of God, and that is what Jesus taught us by being born poor.

## The Blessed Virgin Mary

**44. Was Mary always a virgin?**
Yes. Mary was a virgin before, during and after the birth of Christ. This is called the perpetual virginity of Mary.

**45. If Mary was perpetually a virgin, why is it that Scripture speaks of the "brethren of the Lord"?**
The word "brother" in itself proves nothing, as it had a very wide meaning among the Jews. It is used in the Old Testament for relatives in general (Job 42:11; 19:13-14), nephews (Genesis 29:15-16), distant cousins (Leviticus 10:4), and first cousins (I Chronicles 23:21). Besides, there was no word in Hebrew or Aramaic for cousin, so that the Old Testament writers were forced to use the word AH, brother, to describe different degrees of kindred. For example, Jacob, speaking of his cousin Rachel, calls himself her father's brother, rather than style himself the son of her father's sister, the only way he could describe the relationship in Hebrew (Genesis 29:12). It is certain, then, that if Jesus had cousins, especially if they were born of the same mother, they had to be called His brother in the Aramaic tongue. Therefore, the phrase "brethren of the Lord" in no way threatens the doctrine of the perpetual virginity.

**46. Why is Mary the Mother of God?**
Sacred Scripture plainly declares in many passages that the Blessed Virgin Mary is the Mother of God. The angel Gabriel said to Mary: "And behold you shall con-

ceive in your womb, and bear a Son, and you shall call
his name Jesus ... The Holy Spirit will come upon you,
and the power of the Most High will overshadow you;
therefore, the Holy Child to be born will be called the
Son of God" (Luke 1:31,35). The saintly Elizabeth greeted
Mary with these words: "Whence is this to me that the
mother of my Lord shall come to me?" (Luke 1:43). St.
Paul says that "God sent His Son, born of a woman"
(Galatians 4:4, cf. Romans 1:3-4).

The Apostles' Creed professes: "And in Jesus Christ,
His only Son our Lord, who was conceived by the Holy
Spirit, born of the Virgin Mary." The belief was so firmly
accepted as divinely revealed, that the Council of Ephesus
(A. D. 431) made it the standard of orthodoxy.

**47. Why is Mary the Mother of the Church?**

The Church is the Mystical Body of Christ; we are its
members, and He is its head (cf. Romans 12:4; I
Corinthians 12:12; Ephesians 1:22-23; 5:23; Colossians
1:18). By the mere fact that the Church is a divine institution, and that a mother cannot give birth to a head without giving birth to the whole body, Mary is the Mother of
the Church.

Because Jesus is God, all of the events associated with
His crucifixion, particularly the words He spoke, were of
infinite value and were of great significance to all men of
all times in all places. "When Jesus saw his mother, and
the disciple whom he loved standing near, he said to his
mother, 'Woman, behold your son!' Then he said to the
disciple, 'Behold, your mother!' " (John 19:26-28). Since
these words were intended universally John was repre-
senting the Church while Mary was who she is — the
Mother of God. It was at this moment that our Savior
gave Mary as the Mother of the Church. We use this to
prove that Mary was ever-virgin, e.g., that James, the

"brother of the Lord" was not a second child of Our Blessed Mother. God had commanded, "Honor thy father and thy mother." If James had been a child of the Blessed Mother, Jesus would have given her into his care since he would have been obligated by law to care for her. Jesus' giving the Blessed Mother into the care of John who was not one of her children, shows us that her only Son would no longer be there to honor and protect her.

**48. What does Mary do for us?**

Mary is a true spiritual Mother. She takes loving care of us in a spiritual manner as our earthly mother cares for us in a temporal way.

**49. Does devotion to Mary diminish our devotion to Christ?**

Certainly not! Indeed, devotion to Mary has quite the opposite effect. No man is ever honored by failing to honor his mother! In honoring Mary we imitate Jesus Christ, who loved her as a Mother. We pray to her so that she will help us to know her Son, lead us to Him, and help all mankind to accept Him.

*Jesus' Knowledge*

**50. Did Jesus always know that He was God?**

Yes. How can an infinite God ever not know He is God? Even though Jesus has two natures, He is only one Person — the second Person of the Blessed Trinity, the Son of God. Because of this, Jesus knew He was God even while a zygote in His Mother's womb.

**51. Did Jesus know all things; that is, the past, present, and future?**

Again, Jesus is an infinite God. From the moment of the Incarnation and throughout His life He knew all things.

## *Jesus' Proofs of Divinity*

**52. Did Jesus say that He was God?**

He made this claim repeatedly (cf. John 8:58, et al.). It might be good to stop here and review the answer to question #2.

**53. Did Jesus prove that He was God?**

Yes. Jesus proved He was God by the miracles He worked through His own power (cf. John 11:1-44), by His prophecies (cf. Matthew 17:23), by His holiness of life, and by His sublime teachings. The crowning testimony of His divinity was that He rose from the dead by His own power.

## *Jesus' Private and Public Life*

**54. What did Jesus do during His private and public life?**

During His private life — that is, the first thirty years of His life — Jesus lived as any good Jew would. He prayed, worked hard, and took care of His family obligations; thus, giving us examples, for our own daily lives. During His public ministry, He showed us the way to heaven by teaching us to know, love, and serve God. To perpetuate His work until the end of time, He founded the Church to continue teaching us exactly the things He taught.

## 55. How can we follow Jesus?

In Matthew 5:48 Jesus told us to "be perfect as your Father in heaven is perfect." This was a command to become holy, a saint. We can obey this command and follow Jesus by trying to think as He did, imitating His virtues, and seeking always to grow in His grace. It is important to note, though, that Jesus — who is our Creator and knows us better than we know ourselves — realizes that we may sometimes fail when trying to follow Him. It is for this reason that He gave us the Sacrament of Penance. This means we need never become discouraged and give-up when we sometimes fail.

**Fourth Article of the Creed**

**"Suffered under Pontius Pilate, was crucified, died and was buried"**

*The Sufferings and Death of Our Redeemer*

**56. What do we mean when we call Jesus Christ our Redeemer?**

To say that He is our Redeemer is to say that He offered Himself to God the Father in sacrifice, shedding all His blood for the forgiveness of our sins. For love of us, Jesus suffered betrayal by one of His close friends (Matthew 26:20-25, 47-50), suffered an agony of spirit (Luke 22:39-44), was falsely accused by the very people He loved and came to save (Matthew 27:15-23), was scourged and mockingly crowned with thorns (Matthew 27:27-30), was forced to carry a heavy cross (the instrument of His death) through the streets of Jerusalem (Matthew 27:31), and He was finally crucified by having nails driven through His flesh and died with the humiliation of being stripped naked (Matthew 27:35-36).

**57. When and where did Jesus Christ die?**

Jesus was executed on Good Friday, outside Jerusalem on a hill called Golgotha, a Hebrew name meaning "place of the skulls". The same hill was called in Greek, Calvary. We know this to be true from the gospels, and from various historians of that time. In fact, St. John the Evangelist, who wrote the last gospel, was present at Jesus' crucifixion.

### 58. Did Jesus suffer and die as God or as man?

Jesus suffered and died in His human nature, because as God He could neither suffer nor die. It is important to note that Jesus died just like every man, as His human soul separated from His human body; however, His divine nature remained united to His body and His soul.

### *Jesus' Love for All*

### 59. Did Jesus die for everyone?

Yes. Jesus died for all people of all places and all ages — past, present, and future. Since all are conceived with the stain of Adam's sin, He died so that all could be redeemed (I Timothy 2:3-6).

### 60. Did Jesus *have* to suffer and die for our sins?

No. Nothing compelled Jesus to suffer and die. He did so of His own free will for love of us (John 10:17-18). Because Jesus is God the Son, He is infinite. This means that all of His sufferings have infinite value. The slightest suffering of God the Son (diaper rash as an infant? a scraped knee as a toddler?) could have been accepted by God the Father as adequate for the redemption of all mankind. However, Jesus chose to suffer the immense pains of His Passion and death because He wanted to make full reparation to the Father, teach us how evil sin is, and show us the depth of His love for us.

### 61. How can we respond to Jesus' love?

How does any child respond to the boundless love of a devoted parent? By affection and obedience! We should strive to obey His law, trust in His infinite mercy and forgiveness, receive the Sacrament of Penance often and with sorrow for our sins, take time to keep Him company in the tabernacle in the sanctuary at the local parish church,

and most of all  participate well in the Holy Sacrifice of
the Mass, in which Jesus perpetually offers Himself to
the Father for our salvation.

## Fifth Article of the Creed

**"He descended into hell, the third day he rose again from the dead."**

*Christ's Descent into Limbo*

**62. What does "He descended into hell" mean?**

When we say that Jesus descended into hell we mean that after His death on the cross, while His body remained in the tomb, Jesus' soul descended into the lower parts of the earth. Since the gates of heaven were closed with Adam's original sin, and could not be reopened until the Redemption, the patriarchs and other just of the Old Testament (i.e. Abraham, Issac, Jacob, Moses, David, etc.) who were not condemned to the hell of eternal punishment were sent to the so-called vestibule of hell, what Catholic tradition calls the limbo of the Fathers.

**63. Why did Christ descend to the dead?**

He descended into the abode of the dead to show Himself to the souls of the just who were waiting for their redemption. He told them that their time of waiting was over, and that the Redemption had been accomplished.

The doctrine of Christ's descent to the dead, which was defined by the Fourth Lateran Council, is explicitly taught in the Scriptures. "But God has raised him up, having loosed the sorrows of hell, because it was not possible that he should be held fast by it" (Acts 2:24; cf. 31). "Now this, he ascended, what does it mean but that he also first descended into the lower parts of the earth?" (Ephesians 4:9). "In which also he went and preached to those spirits that were in prison" (I Peter 3:19).

In the New Testament, Christ Himself refers by various names and figures to the place or state which Catholic tradition has agreed to call the limbo of the Fathers. In Matthew 8:11 it is spoken of under the figure of a banquet or in Matthew 25:10 under the figure of a marriage feast. He also calls it "Abraham's bosom" in his parable of Lazarus and Dives (Luke 16:22), and "paradise" when addressing the penitent thief on the cross (Luke 23:43).

## The Resurrection

**64. What do we mean when we say that on the third day Jesus rose from the dead?**

This means that on the third day Jesus reunited His human soul with His human body and rose from the dead, as He had predicted (cf. Matthew 17:23). We know that Jesus truly rose from the dead because this historical fact was witnessed by hundreds of Christ's followers and recorded in Sacred Scripture.

The most telling evidence of Christ's resurrection is the Apostles themselves. First of all, Christ's Resurrection was the central theme of their preaching. They preached His resurrection as proof of His divinity.

Secondly, the resurrection is proved by the Apostles' lives and deaths. All but one of the Apostles was martyred, that is, murdered for the Faith. At any given point, a renunciation of Christ's resurrection would have spared them horrible deaths. Besides, no reasonable person is willing to die for a lie. If the Apostles had made up the story of Christ's resurrection, it is reasonable that at least one of them would have admitted the resurrection was a lie to save his own life. The fact is that none did. They all had seen Him, touched Him, spoken with Him, and died for that truth.

**65. What did Jesus do after His resurrection?**

Jesus remained on earth for forty days after His resurrection to prove that He had truly risen and to complete the teachings of His Apostles.

**66. Why is Christ's resurrection important?**

The resurrection is important because it proves that He is God. Since He proved He is God, then we are obliged to obey all He had commanded us through His Church.

Another reason the resurrection is important is because of the way it inspires us. The resurrection strengthens our faith and gives us courage to suffer and serve for the love of Him. It is this way that we can one day join Him in heaven.

## Sixth Article of the Creed

### "He ascended into heaven, and sits at the right hand of God, the Father Almighty."

*The Ascension*

**67. What do we mean by the words "He ascended into heaven"?**

By this we mean that forty days after His resurrection, in the presence of many of His followers, Jesus ascended into heaven of His own power. It was not merely a spiritual ascension, but He actually ascended body and soul (Acts 1:9-11).

**68. Why did Jesus ascend into heaven?**

Jesus ascended into heaven to fulfill the promises He had made: to prepare a place for us (John 14:3); to be our mediator with God the Father (Hebrews 9:24); to send the Holy Spirit to the Apostles (John 16:7).

**69. Did Jesus ascend into heaven alone?**

No. Although they were not visible to those who witnessed the Ascension, the souls of the just who were in the limbo of the Fathers accompanied Him to heaven.

**70. What does "sits at the right hand of God the Father Almighty" mean?**

Since God the Father is pure spirit, we know that this phrase is symbolic rather than literal. It means that, as God, Jesus has the same power as God the Father, and that as man, He is King over all creation.

**71. Is Jesus now only in heaven?**

Of course not! Because He is God, Jesus is most certainly everywhere (omnipresent). As the God-man, Jesus has ascended into heaven to await His second coming, and He is present for our love, worship, and adoration in millions of tabernacles throughout the world in the most Holy Eucharist.

**Seventh Article of the Creed**

**"From thence He shall come to judge the living and the dead."**

**72. What does "from thence He shall come to judge the living and the dead" mean?**

This phrase refers to Christ's "second coming" (Acts 1:11). At the time appointed by God the Father, Jesus will return to earth to judge all people who have ever lived. For some this will be the most glorious and happy day they have ever known. For others it will be the most terrible day of their pitiful existence.

**73. How many judgments are there?**

There are two judgments. One takes place immediately after death. This one is called the particular judgment. The other judgment takes place at the end of time. It is called the general judgment.

*Particular Judgment*

**74. On what will we be judged in the particular judgment?**

Christ's judgment of us will be very exacting. Each individual soul will be judged on the good and evil we have done (all of our thoughts, desires, words, actions, and omissions) from the time we reached the age of the use of reason, that is, when we were old enough to know the difference between right and wrong.

Once each soul is judged, the soul will either be rewarded with eternal life in heaven, punished in purgatory until cleansed perfectly for heaven, or condemned to an eternal damnation in hell. The reward or punishment deserved by each soul will be carried into effect immediately after this particular judgment.

## The General Judgment

### 75. Why will there be a general judgment?

God is both perfectly just and perfectly merciful, and all mankind has a right to see the perfection of His justice and mercy. All will see that in His infinite mercy God wanted to save us all, and we will see that He was right in rewarding those who trusted in His infinite goodness. On the flip side, we will see how He was just in punishing those who rejected Him with their sins and refused to repent.

The same identical sentence levied in the particular judgment will be given in the general judgment. There are no second chances after death, so it is to our benefit to do as God asks us now. Throughout all eternity you will be reminded of the words you have read here. If you choose in favor of God because of these words you will be made happy by remembering them in heaven, because you chose to love God and live with Him in heaven. If you choose to reject God and condemn yourself to cternity in hell by your sins, these words will be remembered by you as a source of your torment.

### 76. On what will we be judged in the general judgment?

In all of Sacred Scripture there is only one time that our Lord gives us the criteria by which we will all be judged. This criteria, found in Matthew 25:34-46, is specific and deserves a brief treatment here.

Jesus gives six areas in which we will be judged. In each of these areas He tells us that we are (quite literally, the Church believes) treating Him in whatever manner we treat these six classes of people.

The first class of people is the hungry. We typically think of the hungry as those who are without food or money to get food. Although we would do well to show compassion toward such people and do whatever we are able to help them, this covers much more than what meets the eye. For example, if you get yourself a snack, take an extra moment to get one also for your spouse, parent, child, or guest. In this way, if you at least occasionally think to offer this little service to Jesus through the person whom you are feeding, He counts this to your favor.

The second criterion He lists is giving drink to the thirsty. The above example applies here, but there are still other examples to be given. How many times have you seen someone working in the sunshine who is hot, tired, and sweaty? Your postman? A construction worker? A ditch digger? How pleased Jesus would be if you took a few extra minutes to give someone like that a soft drink or a glass of water!

The next criterion is welcoming the stranger. This is commonly interpreted as serving the homeless. It is laudable of the state to desire to eliminate homelessness, but this is not the job of the state. It is the job of each Christian to do this work. When the state fulfills this role the Christian allows himself to be robbed of the chance to serve Jesus in the person of the homeless. We cannot claim to serve Jesus in the homeless by way of our tax dollars, because our taxes are involuntary contributions. Although the heroic act of charity is to help the homeless get back on their feet by personally taking them in, Jesus does not expect us to go this far ordinarily. However, there are many worthy charities established to help the homeless. You could give Jesus a home by contributing your time or money to those charities.

The fourth type of person Jesus mentions is the naked. Think twice before you throw out a piece of clothing you just replaced with a new item. I once knew a man who had a genuine need for a suit, but he had none. Another man who had been made aware of that need went out and bought the fellow a brand new suit. The benefactor bought the suit because of this command of Jesus, so the man actually got a chance to buy Jesus a suit of clothes.

Jesus tells us of the sick. Hundreds of thousands of people languish in nursing homes, hospitals, insane asylums, and hospices for the terminally ill. Many of them have no one to visit them. They are lonely, afraid, and sometimes abused. I once knew a fellow who went to a local nursing home once a week. He would spend half an hour visiting the lonely old people to make them feel happy and needed. Then he would spend another half an hour visiting the mentally disturbed and retarded who lived in another part of the home. He would take them snacks, toiletries, tobacco, or whatever they needed, then he would play his guitar and sing songs with them. You, too, can visit a sick Jesus in this or a similar way.

Finally, there are prisoners. When thinking about Jesus' life, it is easy to see that Jesus had been in all these situations at one time or another; however, we usually do not think of Him as a prisoner. He was, though. Jesus was a death row convict, and think of how brutally He was treated!

Crime is a terrible problem in our society. We all want to get tough on crime, but many advocate the mistreatment of prisoners as a way to do it. Some say that bread and water for their only food, the use of chain gangs, and treating prisoners like animals is justified by the crimes they commit. This is not Jesus' way. Indeed, He was always merciful to the criminal; such as the "good thief" on the cross, or the woman caught in adultery.

We, too, can serve Jesus in prison. Instead of going along with the crowd, which seems bent on social vengeance, we should reach out to prisoners. There are many ways to serve Jesus by serving prisoners, but the absolute best way is by teaching them about the Catholic Faith. In this way they can be truly rehabilitated, find hope, become productive citizens, and go to heaven.

Remember that Jesus Himself told us that we will be judged on the basis of how we serve Him by serving these others. In fact, He made it seriously binding on us when He said: "Truly, I say to you, as you did it to one of the least of these my brethren, you did it to me."

## Eighth Article of the Creed

## "I believe in the Holy Spirit"

### *The Divinity of the Holy Spirit*

**77. Who is the Holy Spirit?**

The Holy Spirit is the third Person of The Blessed Trinity and He proceeds eternally from the Father and the Son. The Holy Spirit is indeed God, completely equal to the Father and the Son. Like the Father and the Son, the Holy Spirit is almighty, eternal, and infinite.

**78. How do we know about the Holy Spirit?**

We learned about the Holy Spirit by way of divine revelation from Jesus Christ, who placed Him on an equal level with the Father and the Son.

**79. Are there other names for the Holy Spirit?**

Yes, there are many other names. He is called Soul of My Soul, Soul of the Church, Paraclete, Advocate, Sanctifier, and Spirit of Truth to name a few.

### *The Holy Spirit and the Apostles*

**80. When did Jesus promise to send the Holy Spirit?**

He made this promise on several occasions (cf. Luke 24:49; John 14:26; 15:26; Acts 1:8).

**81. When did the Holy Spirit come upon the Apostles in a visible way?**

The Holy Spirit first manifested Himself to the Apostles in a visible way as tongues of fire on the first Pentecost Sunday. Through this manifestation of the Holy

Spirit the Apostles received the light to understand all that Jesus had taught them. This new light, which is the power of the Holy Spirit, gave the Apostles the zeal to preach what Jesus taught without fear.

## *The Holy Spirit and the Church*

**82. What is the role of the Holy Spirit in the Church?**

The Holy Spirit is the soul of the Church, making her holy by the grace of Jesus Christ. The Holy Spirit enables the Church to teach all that Jesus taught without the possibility of error (this is called infallibility). Finally, He transforms the members of the Church into witnesses for Christ. The Holy Spirit was sent by the Father and the Son to live in the Church until the end of time (John 14:16).

**83. What is the role of the Holy Spirit in our lives?**

Provided we are in a "state of grace", that is, a state of friendship with God, the Holy Spirit dwells in our souls to make us holy with sanctifying grace. He enlightens our minds to know God, strengthens our wills to carry out God's will, and He sets our hearts on fire to love God and neighbor.

We should practice devotion to the Holy Spirit by praying to Him and asking Him to teach us to respond eagerly to His inspirations.

## Ninth Article of the Creed

### "The holy Catholic Church; the communion of saints"

*The Visible Church*

**84. What is the Catholic Church?**
The Church is the society of the baptized faithful who believe the same Faith, receive the same sacraments, and obey the Pope, who is the successor of St. Peter. She is also the communion of life, charity and truth and used by Christ to continue His work of redemption in the world until the end of time.

**85. Who founded the Catholic Church?**
Jesus Christ founded the Catholic Church. He brought it into being, structured it, and passed onto it His own mission to continue His work of redemption.

**86. How did Jesus found the Catholic Church?**
Jesus founded the Catholic Church on St. Peter. He set Peter as its rock and foundation, and to him alone did Jesus give in a special way the powers of binding and loosing everything on earth, of strengthening his brethren, and of feeding the whole flock (Matthew 16:18-19; Luke 22:31-32; John 21:15-17).

**87. Who is the head of the Catholic Church?**
Jesus is the head of all the Catholic Church. But the pope, who is the successor of St. Peter, is the head of the Catholic Church on earth.

**88. Is there any biblical evidence that Jesus made St. Peter the first Pope?**

Yes, the biblical evidence is overwhelming. Following the logical presentation of Karl Keating in his modern classical work *Catholicism and Fundamentalism*[1], we find the evidence to be irrefutable.

Keating notes first that St. Peter was almost always named first in the Gospels' listings of the Apostles (Matthew 10:1-4; Mark 3:16-19; Luke 6:14-16; Acts 1:13), and that sometimes the Apostles were referred to only as "Peter and those who were with him" (Luke 9:32). He points out that St. Peter was the first of the Apostles to preach, the first to perform a healing miracle, and one to whom the revelation came that Christianity was for Gentiles as well as Jews (Acts 2:14-40; Acts 3:6-7; Acts 10:46-48).

Keating goes on to tell us that "Peter's preeminent position among the apostles was symbolized at the very beginning of his relationship with Christ, although the implications were only slowly unfolded. At their first meeting, Christ told Simon that his name would thereafter be Peter, which translates as Rock (John 1:42). The startling thing was that in the Old Testament only God was called a rock. The word was never used as a proper name for a man. If one were to turn to a companion and say, 'From now on your name is Asparagus', people would wonder. Why Asparagus? What is the meaning of it? What does it signify? Indeed, why Peter for Simon the fisherman? Why give him as a name a word only used for God before this moment?

"Christ was not given to meaningless gestures, and neither were the Jews as a whole when it came to names.

---

[1] Karl Keating, *Catholicism and Fundamentalism*, (San Francisco: Ignatius Press, 1988) 205-214.

Giving a new name meant that the status of the person was changed, as when Abram was changed to Abraham (Genesis 17:5); Jacob to Israel (Genesis 32:28); Eliacim to Joakim (2 Kings 23:34); and Daniel, Ananias, Misael, and Azarias to Baltassar, Sidrach, Misach, and Abdenago (Daniel 1:6-8). But no Jew had ever been called Rock because that was reserved for God. The Jews would give other names taken from nature, such as Barach (which means lightning; Jos 19:45), Deborah (bee; Genesis 35:8), and Rachel (ewe; Genesis 29:16), but not Rock. In the New Testament James and John were surnamed Boanerges, Sons of Thunder, by Christ (Mark 3:17), but that was never regularly used in place of their original names. Simon's new name supplanted the old."[2]

St. Peter's name has been firmly established by Christ as a name synonymous with God. Throughout Jesus' and St. Peter's relationship the reason became gradually clearer, but it becomes crystal clear in Matthew 16:17-19. Immediately after St. Peter proclaims Christ's divinity, our Lord says, "Blessed are you, Simon Bar-Jona! For flesh and blood has not revealed this to you, but my Father who is in heaven. And I tell you, you are Peter, and on this rock I will build my church, and the powers of death[3] shall not prevail against it. I will give you the keys of the kingdom of heaven, and whatever you bind on earth shall be bound in heaven, and whatever you loose on earth will be loosed in heaven" (Matthew 16:17-19).

This passage seems obvious to most readers. As Keating points out, the verse could be rewritten as: "You are Rock, and on this rock I will build my church."[4] It

---

[2] Keating, *Catholicism and Fundamentalism*, 205-206.

[3] This is the text of the Revised Standard Version. Most versions read "and the gates of hell" instead of "and the powers of death."

[4] Keating, *Catholicism and Fundamentalism*, 208.

makes perfect sense that Jesus is here giving St. Peter supreme authority; however, those who desire to debunk the papacy, and the divine authority it possesses, prefer to claim the rock refers to Christ instead of Peter.

To settle this objection, we turn once more to Keating; "According to the rules of grammar, the phrase 'this rock' must relate to the closest noun. Peter's profession of faith ('Thou art the Christ, the Son of the living God') is *two verses earlier*, while his name, a proper noun, is in the immediately preceding *clause*. As an analogy, consider this artificial sentence: "I have a car and a truck and it is blue.' Which is blue? The truck, because that is the noun closest to the pronoun 'it'. This identification would be even clearer if the reference to the car were two sentences earlier, as the reference to Peter's profession is two sentences earlier than the term rock."[5]

Not only is the reference to rock clear, but we see also that Jesus is giving St. Peter more authority than God had ever given any man, along with some specific promises. Immediately after stating that He will build the Church upon St. Peter (the Rock), Jesus goes on to make a promise and explain why He will do this.

The promise is that "the power of death" (or the more common "gates of hell") will not defeat the Church built on St. Peter. This is a promise that the Church will not be destroyed by Christ's enemies, and that She will stand until the end of time, as we will more closely examine later.

Next, we find Jesus using the symbol of the keys. This symbol has always implied power and authority, and the giving of keys implies a transfer of power and authority. The symbol of the keys is not lost on us today. The owner and manager of a business possess both the keys to the

[5] Keating, *Catholicism and Fundamentalism*, 208.

business and the authority to run it. When the business is sold, the keys are passed to the new owner. Likewise, prison guards possess the keys to the cell doors, and they have the authority of law over the prisoners. When a fresh shift of guards arrive so the tired guards can go home, both the keys and the authority are transferred to the new guards. It is obvious, then, that He is giving St. Peter power and authority when Jesus gives him "the keys to the kingdom of heaven."

Finally, there is what we call the power of binding and loosing. Father Bertrand Conway writes: " 'Binding and loosing' among the Rabbis of our Lord's time meant to declare something 'prohibited' or 'permitted'. Here it plainly means that St. Peter, the Steward of the Lord's house, the Church, has all the rights and powers of a divinely appointed steward. He does not, like the Jewish Rabbis, declare probable, speculative opinions, but he has the right to teach and govern authoritatively, with the certainty of God's approval 'in heaven' ... A law giving power is certainly implied by these words."[6]

There is much more biblical evidence in support of St. Peter being the first Pope, but we will forego any additional references here. However, readers seeking a good treatment of scriptural evidence may read the following books: *Catholicism and Fundamentalism* by Karl Keating (Ignatius Press); *The History of the Church* by Fr. John Laux (TAN Books); *And on This Rock* by Stanley L. Jaki (Ave Maria); and *Fundamentals of Catholic Dogma* by Ludwig Ott (TAN Books).

### 89. Who is the Pope?

As already stated, the Pope is the visible head of the Church and the successor of St. Peter. He is the Vicar of

[6] Bertrand L. Conway, C.S.P., *The Question Box* (New York, Paulist Press, 1929) 146-147.

Christ, and he possesses the power of jurisdiction over the universal Church in matters of faith, morals, discipline and government.

### 90.  What is meant by the hierarchy of the Church?

According to the Vatican Council II document *Lumen Gentium* (18): "In order to shepherd the People of God and to increase its numbers without cease, Christ the Lord set up in his Church a variety of offices which aim at the good of the whole body. The holders of office, who are invested with a sacred power, are, in fact, dedicated to promoting the interests of their brethren, so that all who belong to the People of God ... may attain to salvation."

These "office holders" are the Church's leaders in different levels of authority. They are, in order of authority, first the Pope, then the bishops, priests, and deacons.

### 91.  Who are the bishops?

The bishops are the successors of the Apostles, just as the Pope is the successor of St. Peter. They take the place of the Apostles in the modern Church. Jesus made the bishops the authentic teachers of the Faith, and only the Pope's power is superior to theirs.

### 92.  Who are priests?

All baptized persons participate in the common priesthood of the faithful, but there is a difference in essence, and not merely degree, between the priesthood of the faithful and the priesthood of Holy Orders. "In what sense? While the common priesthood of the faithful is exercised by the unfolding of baptismal grace — a life of faith, hope, and charity, a life according to the Spirit —, the ministerial priesthood is at the service of the common priesthood. It is directed at the unfolding of the baptismal grace of all Christians. The ministerial priesthood is a *means* by which Christ unceasingly builds up and leads his Church. For this reason it is transmitted by its own sacrament, the sacrament of Holy Orders."[7]

The two most important tasks of a priest are to offer the Eucharistic Celebration (the Holy Sacrifice of the Mass) and to reconcile sinners to God by way of the Sacrament of Penance. Priests are also collaborators with their bishops, and they are subject to him.

### 93. Who are deacons?

Deacon comes from a Greek word which means "kicking up dust," which gives us some idea of the busy life a deacon leads. Deacons are men who truly live their Catholic faith, and they are ready for every good work that leads to the salvation of souls. They are ordained for a ministry of service to the Church and Her faithful. Deacons are helpers of bishops and priests, and they obey the authority of the bishops and priests by fulfilling the duties assigned to them.

There are two types of deacons. The more common among deacons are called *transitional* deacons. These are men who are studying for the priesthood. They are usually ordained to the diaconate one year before being ordained to the priesthood.

The second type of deacon is called *permanent*. Permanent deacons are just as the term implies, they intend to serve the Church in the life-long capacity of the diaconate. Permanent deacons may be married, if the marriage took place before ordination. If the wife of a permanent deacon dies the deacon cannot marry again.

---

[7] *Catechism of the Catholic Church*, 1547.

**94. Who are religious?**

Religious are men and women who live a consecrated state of life as members of religious orders, such as the Salesians, Carmelites, or Franciscans. They are neither clerical nor lay people, except those who are priests. They are called by God to live the evangelical counsels of poverty, chastity, and obedience. They renounce the world and dedicate themselves to life-long service to God and His Church. They imitate the poor, chaste, and obedient Christ, who founded the religious state (Matthew 19:10-11).

Regarding priests, like deacons, there are two types. The *religious priest* is a priest who is a member of a religious order, and he is subject to both his religious superior and the local bishop. The *secular*, or *diocesan* priest does not belong to a religious order, but rather serves the Church throughout his life in the diocese for which he was ordained.

**95. Who are the laity?**

The laity are all the baptized faithful who are neither bishops, priests, deacons nor members of religious orders. The laity possess the responsibility of aiding the bishops and priests in spreading and sharing the Faith, insofar as their God-given talents permit. They are also subject to the Pope, and the bishops who are in union with him, in matters of faith and morals.

*The Church as Mystery*

**96. When did the Church become known as Catholic?**

Although the name Catholic is not applied to the Church in the Bible, Christ and the Apostles had the concept of catholic in mind, as catholic comes from a Greek word meaning universal. The Catholic Church is certainly universal, that is, for all people.

St. Ignatius of Antioch (AD 107) writes in his *Letter to the Smyrnaeans*: "Where the Bishop is, there let the multitude of believers be; even as where Jesus Christ is, there is the Catholic Church" (Ad Smyr., 8:2). Notice that St. Ignatius did not write of the Catholic Church as if he were giving it a new name, but rather as though the name had long been in use. It is reasonably safe to assume, then, that the Church was probably called Catholic during the latter part of the first century. Indeed, it is likely that St. John the Apostle had heard the Church called by the name Catholic, since he died around the year AD 100. The Apostles' Creed, written in the first century, also refers to the "one, holy, catholic, and apostolic Church".

### 97. Are there other names for the Catholic Church?

Yes, the Catholic Church has many other names. Among them are the Church of Jesus Christ for Sinners, the People of God, and the Bride of Christ. The most common and best descriptive name of the reality of the Church is the Mystical Body of Christ.

### 98. Why is the Church called the Mystical Body of Christ?

St. Paul refers to the Church as the Body of Christ repeatedly (cf. I Corinthians 12:12), but in order to understand why he does so, as well as its significance, we need to focus on Paul's conversion (Acts 9:1-6).

St. Paul, who prior to his conversion is called Saul, was a Pharisee and persecutor of Christians. At the time of his conversion, Saul was on his way to Damascus to arrest Christians when Jesus appeared to him in His glorified state. "Now as he journeyed he approached Damascus, and suddenly a light from heaven flashed about him. And he fell to the ground and heard a voice saying to him, 'Saul, Saul, why do you persecute me?' And he said, 'Who are you, Lord?' And he said, 'I am Jesus, whom you are persecuting' " (Acts 9:3-5).

This encounter with Jesus apparently formed St. Paul's theology on the Church. Paul saw the Church as a divine institution, with Jesus as its head and we as its members. Indeed, Paul saw that Jesus Christ and His Church are one and the same. Notice that Jesus did not ask "Why do you persecute my followers?" or "Why do you persecute my Church?" He asked, "Why do you persecute *Me?*"

Jesus had ascended into heaven a long time before St. Paul met Jesus on the road to Damascus, so Paul could not have been persecuting Jesus. The persecution was of His followers. But that isn't what Jesus says. Christ's words are clearly indicative that to persecute the followers of Christ is to persecute Him. This is why St. Paul taught that we are the members of the Body of Christ — the Church — and He is its head. You cannot persecute any one part of a body without the entire body suffering. Paul understood that Jesus and His Church are one.

### 99. Who is the soul of the Church?

The Church is the Mystical Body of Christ. For a body to live — and the Church *is* a living, breathing body — it must have a soul. The Holy Spirit, then, is the soul of the Church. He remains with the disciples of Christ for all times (cf. John 14:16); He binds them in one body (cf. I Corinthians 12:13); He leads them to all truth (cf. John 16:13); He lives in them as in a temple (cf. I Corinthians 3:16; 6:19); He helps to preserve the Deposit of Faith entrusted to the Church (cf. II Timothy 1:14); He directs Church authorities in their activity (cf. Acts 15:28).

## The Church's Mission

**100. What mission did Jesus Christ give to His Church?**

Jesus gave His Church His own mission. He willed that the successors of Peter and the other Apostles, that is, the Pope, and the bishops, should preach His Gospel faithfully, administer the sacraments, and shepherd His people with love.

The mission of Christ is not left solely to the Pope, Bishops, priests and deacons. Although the laity cannot perform those functions that are specific to the offices of Pope, bishop, priests and deacons, we still are obliged to help bring souls into the Church as the Holy Spirit gives us aid. Since the laity are the Church, then we must participate in the Church's mission. "As the 'convocation' of all men for salvation, the Church in her very nature is missionary, sent by Christ to all the nations to make disciples of them [cf. *Mt* 28:19-20; *Ad Gentes* 2:5-6]."[8]

**101. From where does the Church draw her teachings?**

All of the Church's teachings are drawn from Divine Revelation.

**102. What is Divine Revelation?**

Divine Revelation is what God has spoken to us about Himself, the purpose of our life, and His plan for our salvation. He spoke to us first through the prophets of the Old Testament, then through His Son Jesus Christ. Jesus gave the totality of Divine Revelation to His Apostles, who continued to teach all that Jesus had taught them. Thus, Divine Revelation ended with the death of the last

---

[8] *Catechism of the Catholic Church*, 767.

Apostle, St. John. The Church does not and cannot accept a new public revelation as pertaining to the divine deposit of faith.

### 103. Where do we find Divine Revelation?

We find Divine Revelation in Sacred Scripture and Sacred (or Apostolic) Tradition.

### 104. What is Sacred Scripture?

Sacred Scripture is the Bible, the Word of God written down under inspiration of the Holy Spirit.

### 105. What is Sacred Tradition?

Sacred Tradition (also called Apostolic Tradition) is the Word of God entrusted by Jesus Christ and the Holy Spirit to the Apostles. The Apostles, in turn, handed those sacred truths down to their successors (the Pope and the bishops) in the fullness of purity (John 21:25; II Timothy 1:13-14; 2:2; II Thessalonians 2:15). The Apostolic successors, by proclaiming the Word of God handed down by word of mouth, preserve the truth faithfully, explain it, and make it more widely known.

The Fathers of Vatican Council II explained it more clearly when they wrote: "Hence there exist a close connection and communication between sacred Tradition and sacred Scripture. For both of them, flowing from the same divine wellspring, in a certain way merge into a unity and tend toward the same end. For sacred Scripture is the word of God inasmuch as it is consigned to writing under the inspiration of the divine Spirit. To the successors of the apostles, sacred Tradition hands on in its full purity God's word, which was entrusted to the apostles by Christ the Lord and the Holy Spirit. Thus, by the light of the Spirit of truth, these successors can in their preaching preserve this word of God faithfully, explain it, and make it more widely known. Consequently it is not from sacred Scripture alone that the Church draws her certainty about everything which has been revealed. Therefore both sacred Scripture and sacred Tradition are to be accepted and venerated with the same devotion and reverence."[9]

### 106. What is the Magisterium?

The Magisterium is the living teaching authority of the Church. It is exercised when the Pope and the bishops who are in communion with him authentically interpret the Word of God, whether written or handed down, guarding it scrupulously and explaining it faithfully in accord with a divine commission and with the help of the Holy Spirit. Therefore, the fullness of divinely revealed truth comes to us by way of Sacred Scripture, Sacred Tradition, and the Magisterium, which is the Church's teaching authority.

### 107. How many forms of the Magisterium are there?

There are two forms of the Magisterium. The most common is the *ordinary* Magisterium, which consists of the daily teachings of the Pope and the bishops in communion with him.

The second form is the *solemn* or *extraordinary* Magisterium, which consists of dogmatic definitions. It adds nothing to Divine Revelation, but only explains it and creates a new obligation to believe.

---

[9] *Dei Verbum*, 9.

*The Marks of the Church*

## 108.  How can we know that the Catholic Church is the church Christ founded?

We can know that the Catholic Church is the Church founded by Christ because it is the only one with the characteristics (marks) that Jesus Christ gave to His Church; that is, He made it one, holy, catholic, and apostolic.

We say the Catholic Church is *one* because all its members profess the same Faith, participate in the same sacraments, and obey the Roman Pontiff, the Vicar of Christ (Ephesians 4:4-5).

Jesus never spoke of a plurality of Churches, but of "my church", when He first promised Peter that He would make him the rock foundation of the Church He was about to establish (Matthew 16:18-19).  The Church is always pictured in the New Testament as visibly one, presided over by Peter, who represents Christ, telling all men until the end of time to *believe* only what He and His Apostles taught, to *obey* His and their commands, to worship as He ordered (cf. John 10:16).

Christ plainly foretold that the gates of hell would never prevail against His Church, and that He would provide for its unity by His own presence and the power of the Holy Spirit.  It is granted that the private judgment of the individual *naturally* brings about disunion in the Church, but Christ ensured its unity by a special *supernatural* grace, which He asked of His Father the night before He died.  His prayer for unity to the Father was: "That they may all be one; even as thou, Father, art in me, and I in thee, that they also may be in us.... The glory which thou hast given me I have given to them, that they may be one even as we are one, I in them and thou in me, that they may become *perfectly* one" (John 17:21-23).

St. Paul insists on the unity of the Church in all his epistles. Although he mentions individual local churches in certain cities, he teaches clearly that they are parts of the one Church in every place (I Thessalonians 1:8; I Corinthians 1:2; II Corinthians 2:14). The Church is not a mere organization that may be divided and subdivided like a nation or club, but a divine organism with its own inherent principle of life. It is Christ's Mystical Body, of which He is the head and all Christians are members. It is founded by *one* Lord, given life by *one* Spirit, entered into by *one* baptism, ruled by a *united* body of bishops, and having *one* aim, the glory of God and the salvation of men's souls (Romans 12:4-8; I Corinthians 12:12-27; Ephesians 4:3-16).

The Catholic Church is *holy* because Jesus, its Founder, and its Soul, the Holy Spirit, are holy. The Church teaches holy doctrine and gives its members the means of living holy lives, thus producing saints in every age (Ephesians 5:25-27). The founders of the other churches — Luther, Calvin, Zwingli, Wesley — were but men, and in no way remarkable for heroic virtue.

The Catholic Church is holy, because of her intimate union with Christ as His Bride (Ephesians 5:23-32) and His Mystical Body (I Corinthians 12:27; Ephesians 1:22; 4:12; 5:30). Catholics are a "chosen people" and a "holy nation" because they are branches of the true Vine, Jesus Christ (John 15:5). Although people outside her fold may, through invincible ignorance, be members of the Church in desire, and thus share in her divine life, their churches are "cast forth as a branch and withers" (John 15:6).

The Catholic Church is *catholic*, or *universal*, because it is for all peoples of all eras, because all mankind is called by the grace of God to salvation (Mark 16:15). The Catholic Church alone is universal in time, doctrine, and extent. She has existed in perfect continuity from the time of Christ, and she will last until His second coming. She teaches all His Gospel, and administers all His divine means of salvation. She is not confined to any particular region or nation, but is widespread among all the nations of the world. Indeed, until the year 1517 there was no other Christian religion beside the Catholic Church. All others are merely imitations of the real thing.

To say the Church is "apostolic" implies that the True Church is the Church which Christ commissioned His Apostles to establish under the supremacy of St. Peter. The True Church must trace its origin in unbroken line to Jesus and the twelve Apostles. Before giving His divine commission to the Apostles, Christ insists upon His divine commission from His heavenly Father. "As the Father has sent me, even so I send you" (John 20:21).

The only Church that can rightly claim that its origin is not due to a break with the past is the Catholic Church. The continental Protestants broke with the Apostolic Church at the time of Luther's revolt (1517-1520), and the English Protestants (1559), when King Henry VIII made Parker the first Protestant Archbishop of Canterbury.

When the early Catholics wished to use a most convincing argument to prove the true Church, they always appealed to the fact of its apostolic origin. We find them compiling authentic lists of legitimate bishops, especially with regard to the Apostolic See of Rome. As early as the second century we find the Syrian Hegesippus and the Greek Irenaeus, Bishop of Lyons, maintaining that the source and standard of the faith is the apostolic Tradition, handed down in an unbroken succession of bishops. "But since it would be very long in such a volume as this to count up the successions [i.e., series of bishops] in all the churches, we confound all those who in any way, whether through self-pleasing or vainglory, or through blindness or evil opinion, gather together otherwise than they ought, by pointing out the tradition arrived from the Apostles of the greatest, most ancient, and universally known Church, founded and established by the two most glorious Apostles, Peter and Paul, and also the faith declared to men which through the succession of bishops comes down to our times."[10]

## Indefectibility and Infallibility

### 109. What does indefectibility mean?

Indefectibility means that the Catholic Church will remain until the end of time, that it cannot be destroyed by any force in the world or from hell. Jesus said: "And I say to thee, thou art Peter, and upon this Rock I will build my Church, *and the gates of hell shall not prevail against it*" (Matthew 16:18). Since Christ promised that not even the gates of hell shall prevail against His Church, we have the steadfast assurance that the Church will continue until the end of the world.

### 110. What does infallibility mean?

Infallibility means the impossibility of falling into error. The perpetual assistance of Christ and the Holy Spirit guarantees the purity and integrity of the faith and morals taught by the Church.

Would a good God, "who desires all men to be saved and to come to the knowledge of the truth" (I Timothy 2:4), fail to provide His revelation with a living, infallible teacher? Would a just God command us to believe under penalty of hell (Mark 16:16), and at the same time leave us to the mercy of every false teacher and lying

---

[10] St. Irenaeus, *Adversus Haereses*, 3:3.

teacher, preaching a Gospel opposed to His (II Peter 2:1; Galasians 1:8)?

No, the Church Christ founded is everywhere spoken of in the New Testament as a divine, infallible teaching authority. Because Jesus and His Church are one, and because He is an infallible God, His Church must by necessity also be infallible.

### 111. Is the Pope infallible?

According to *Lumen Gentium* of the Vatican Council II: "The Roman Pontiff, head of the college of bishops, enjoys this infallibility in virtue of his office, when, as supreme pastor and teacher of all the faithful — who confirms his brethren in the faith — he proclaims by a definitive act a doctrine pertaining to faith or morals."[11]

This does not mean the Pope is infallible in all things. For example, the Pope would not be exercising the charism of infallibility if he were to predict the winner of the World Series. Karl Keating says that "the inability of the Church to teach error is infallibility, and it is a *negative* protection. It means what is officially taught will not be wrong, not that the official teachers will have the wits about them to stand up and teach what is right when it needs to be taught."[12]

The Pope is infallible *only* under the following conditions:

1. When he speaks *ex cathedra*, i.e., when he speaks officially as supreme pastor of the universal Church. He is not infallible when acting as supreme law maker, judge, or ruler. Nor is he infal-

---

[11] *Lumen Gentium*, 25.

[12] Karl Keating, *Catholicism and Fundamentalism*, 217 (emphasis added).

lible as a simple priest or as the local Bishop of Rome.

2. When he defines a doctrine regarding faith and morals. This means to settle a doctrine definitely, finally, and irrevocably. To omit defining a doctrine may cause great harm or be negligence on the part of a pope, but that would not nullify the charism of infallibility.

3. When he speaks of faith and morals, which includes the whole content of divine revelation. It follows that the Pope is also infallible in judging doctrines and facts so intimately connected with revelation that they cannot be denied without endangering revelation itself.

4. When he intends to bind the entire Church and the intention at binding all the faithful must be clearly stated. If he fails to express the intention to bind the consciences of the faithful, it is not infallible.

**112. Are the bishops infallible?**

Individually the bishops are not infallible. However, they do teach infallibly in an ecumenical council (such as Vatican II) when, with the approval of the Pope, they set forth teachings of faith or morals to be held by the entire Church. The bishops can also teach infallibly when, in union with the Pope, outside of an ecumenical council, they all teach the same doctrine of faith and morals.

**113. Does infallibility mean that the Pope can do no wrong?**

No, infallibility does not mean that the Pope cannot commit sin. He may commit sin like any other Catholic, and he is bound to seek forgiveness like any other Catholic through the Sacrament of Penance. Infallibility is not a personal charism, but rather a divine and official charism, given by Christ to Peter and his successors to keep them from error in defining the content of the deposit of faith.

**114. Why did Jesus make His Church infallible?**

Jesus made the Church infallible so that she would not compromise with the ideas of changing times nor yield to pressures within or without, but would teach always and only the Faith entrusted to her by her divine Founder, who is Christ.

Almost without exception, other Christian religions have changed their theological views, particularly as regards morals. For instance, fifty or sixty years ago some Fundamentalist sects did not teach that the use of tobacco was wrong. Today, however, they teach that the use of tobacco, even in moderation, is sinful. Does that mean that a modern Fundamentalist's grandfather smoked and went to heaven, but the modern Fundamentalist will go to hell if he smokes? That would seem to be the implication. The Catholic Church, on the other hand, teaches that using tobacco products *in moderation* is normally not sinful.

A more vivid example would be the events which have unfolded in Christendom since 1930. At one time, *all* Christian religions taught that artificial contraception is a sin worthy of eternal punishment. In England, at the Lambeth Conference of 1930, the bishops of the Anglican church were under immense pressure to rule that artificial contraception is acceptable. Although those Protestant bishops admitted artificial contraception is wrong, they granted permission for its use by Anglican followers. Resultantly, the flood gate of permissiveness was opened. Today, the Catholic Church stands virtually alone in condemning the use of artificial contraception.

Jesus made His Church infallible to protect the fullness of divinely revealed truth. Because Jesus, who is God, is the same yesterday, today, and forever (Hebrews 13:8), His moral laws and doctrines of faith must also remain the same.

### 115. How should Catholics feel toward the Church?

Jesus called for unconditional obedience to the Church (cf. Luke 10:16; Mark 16:16). Because of this, and the fact that Jesus and His Church are one, Catholics should allow themselves to be guided by the Church, assent to her teachings, love her, respect her priests and bishops, and pledge their fidelity to the Supreme Pontiff, who represents Jesus on earth.

### 116. What is heresy?

Heresy is the deliberate denial of one or more truths of the Catholic faith. If one intentionally holds to what one knows is heresy one risks eternal punishment.

### 117. What is schism?

Schism is the deliberate refusal of a Catholic to submit to the authority of the Pope. This, too, presents the risk of eternity separated from God.

### 118. What is apostasy?

Apostasy is the complete rejection of one's Catholic faith. Like heresy and schism, the apostate risks an eternity in hell.

## The Church and Non-Catholics

**119. Since Jesus Christ founded the Church to continue His mission of salvation, are all people obliged to belong to it?**

The Fathers of Vatican II explained it this way:

Basing itself on Scripture and Tradition, the council teaches that the Church, a pilgrim now on earth, is necessary for salvation: The one Christ is the mediator and the way of salvation; he is present to us in his body which is the Church. He himself explicitly asserted the necessity of faith and Baptism [Mark 16:16], and thereby affirmed at the same time the necessity of the Church which men enter through Baptism as through a door. Hence they could not be saved who, knowing that the Catholic Church was founded as necessary by God through Christ, would refuse either to enter it or to remain in it.[13]

However, those same Council Fathers went on to say:

Those who, through no fault of their own, do not know the Gospel of Christ or his Church, but who nevertheless seek God with a sincere heart, and, moved by grace, try in their actions to do his will as they know it through the dictate of their conscience — those too may achieve eternal salvation.[14]

[13] *Lumen Gentium*, 14.
[14] *Lumen Gentium*, 16.

## 120. What is the difference between the Catholic Church and all other Christian Churches?

Catholics and the members of other Christian churches are brothers who believe in Jesus Christ, are baptized, and possess in common many means of grace and elements of truth; however, our separated brethren are not yet blessed with that unity that Jesus Christ bestowed on His followers (John 17:20-21).

## 121. May a Catholic belong to a secret society?

Catholics are discouraged from seeking membership to secret societies, and the Church forbids membership to any secret society that in any way plots against the Church or state.

## *Church and State*

## 122. What does the Catholic Church claim from the state?

The Catholic Church claims religious freedom, which is necessary that she may be faithful to her divine commission (Matthew 28:19).

## 123. Should the state fear the Church?

The state should not fear the Church. "It is the duty of citizens to work with civil authority for building up society in a spirit of truth, justice, solidarity, and freedom"; however, "citizens are obliged in conscience not to follow the directives of civil authorities when they are contrary to the demands of the moral order."[15]

---

[15] *Catechism of the Catholic Church*, 2255-2256.

*The Communion of Saints*

**124. What do we mean when we say, "I believe in the communion of the saints"?**

The communion of saints is the spiritual union which unites the Church Militant (the faithful on earth), the Church Suffering (the souls in purgatory), and the Church Victorious (the saints in heaven) in the one Mystical Body, the Church and the participation of all in the one supernatural life. The saints, by their closeness to God, obtain from Him many graces and favors for the faithful on earth and the souls in purgatory; the faithful on earth, by their prayers and good works, honor and love the saints, and give relief to the suffering souls by their prayers and the Holy Sacrifice of the Mass; the suffering souls in purgatory also pray for those still on earth.

## Tenth Article of the Creed

## "The forgiveness of sins"

*Personal Sin*

**125. What does "the forgiveness of sins" mean?**

This means that in His infinite mercy Jesus Christ has given His Church the power to forgive all sins, no matter how serious they are or how often they have been committed, if the sinner is truly sorry (John 20:22-23).

**126. Doesn't Jesus speak of an unforgivable sin against the Holy Spirit (Matthew 12:31-32)?**

No sin is unforgivable, either by God or the Church that forgives in God's name. God wills all men to be saved (I Timothy 2:4), and His mercy is infinite. Matthew 12:31-32 refers to the sinner who refuses to repent, despite the graces God gives him. Such a person does not actually receive God's pardon because he neither asks for it nor is willing to fulfill the conditions necessary to obtain it.

The sin mentioned by Christ is the willful rejection by the Pharisees of the miracles he performed as proof of His divine mission. Instead, they credited Christ's miracles to Satan.

**127. What is actual (personal) sin?**

Actual (personal) sin is any sin we commit ourselves by any free and willful thought, desire, word, action, or omission that is against the law of God.

**128. How many kinds of actual sin are there?**

There are two kinds of actual sin: mortal (deadly) and venial.

**129. What is mortal sin?**

Mortal sin is any *serious* offense against God's law (i.e., murder, masturbation, abortion, adultery, etc.). It causes the soul to lose sanctifying grace, destroys the merit of all a person's good acts, and makes the person deserving of eternity in hell, unless the sinner repents.

**130. When is a sin mortal?**

A sin is mortal when three conditions are present: 1.) there is *serious matter* (the thought, desire, word, action, or omission must be seriously wrong or thought to be seriously wrong); 2.) *sufficient reflection* (the person knows it is seriously wrong); 3.) *full consent of a free will* to doing what the person knows is seriously wrong. All three of these conditions *must* be present for a sin to be mortal.

**131. What is venial sin?**

Venial sin is a less serious offense against God. It does not deprive the soul of sanctifying grace, but it does weaken the will toward mortal sin. Venial sin does not make the sinner deserving of eternal punishment; however, because God is infinitely just, punishment is still exacted, either in this life or in purgatory.

**132. What makes a sin venial?**

A sin is venial when it lacks one or more of the elements which constitute a mortal sin.

## Sources and Occasions of Sin

**133. What are the main sources of sin?**

The main sources of sin are seven vices called the "capital sins": pride, covetousness, lust, anger, gluttony, envy, and sloth (laziness). They are called "capital sins" because they are the chief sources of actual sins.

**134. What is the source of all the capital sins?**

Original sin is the source of all the capital sins.

**135. What are "occasions of sin"?**

Occasions of sin are persons, places, or things which lead one to sin. They are *near occasions of sin* when they will certainly, or almost certainly, lead a person to sin. They are *remote occasions of sin* when the danger of sinning is only slight.

**136. Are we obliged to avoid the occasions of sin?**

We are obliged to avoid all of the near occasions of sin as far as possible. Here is a practical example.

Let's say that Mike has confessed to his priest five weeks in a row getting drunk one time. The wise priest sees an obvious problem, and he resolves to help Mike work it out. When Mike confesses drunkenness the sixth week in a row, Father asks him why this is happening. Mike says, "Well, Father, I stop off after work on payday to have one drink. But there are lots of bars on my way home, and I get good and thirsty after one drink, so I end up stopping at many of the bars before I get home."

Father instructs Mike to get a map of the city, and to highlight the various routes he can take home from work. Mike brings Father the following map. On it the "H" represents Mike's home, the "W" represents his place of work, and the "A", "B", and "C" represent the three possible routes to and from work.

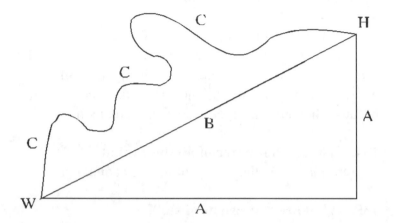

*Father*: Which route do you take to and from work, Mike?

*Mike*: I take "B", Father. After all, it's the closest and quickest.

*Father*: Apparently not on Friday nights, Mike. What is "A" like? Are there many bars?

*Mike*: Not quite as many, Father, but, uh ...

*Father*: What is it, Mike?

*Mike*: Well, Father, all of those places are where women stand up on a stage and...

*Father*: Oh! Well, we'll not have you driving down a lane like that! What's wrong with "C", Mike?

*Mike*: Aw, Father, that road will take me an extra twenty minutes each way.

*Father*: Which is better: an extra twenty minutes here, or eternity in hell?

*Mike*: Okay, Father. You've made your point.

For Mike, the route he took home from work on payday was a near occasion of sin. Listening to his wise confessor's advice will be pleasing to God, and can save Mike from eternal punishment. Drunkenness *is* a mortal sin.

### 137. What are temptations?

Temptations are inclinations to sin that come to us from the world, the flesh, and the devil. We can always resist temptations, but not by our own power alone. God gives us all the grace we need to resist temptation, so we should ask Him to do so with confidence (I Corinthians 10:13).

### *Situation Ethics and Fundamental Option*

### 138. What is "situation ethics"?

"Situation ethics" contends that moral decisions should not be based on universal moral laws, but on the specific particular situation in which a person finds himself. Since this situation is unique and unrepeatable, the person's conscience alone is to determine the right moral decision, apart from any principle or law. The fundamental error of situation ethics is that it is incompatible with the fact that God gave us an objective moral norm to judge what is right and wrong: the Ten Commandments. The Church has always taught that there are some acts which are intrinsically good and some which are intrinsically evil, apart from any circumstances.

An example of this would be for a married couple to use artificial contraception, because as newlyweds they are not yet financially capable of caring for children. Artificial contraception is always evil.

**139. What is "fundamental option"?**

"Fundamental option" is the theory of those who hold that a person commits a mortal sin only when he has the intention of rejecting God. An example of this would be when a couple engages in premarital sex, believing themselves to be expressing love rather than rejecting God. However, the Church teaches that when a person knowingly and willfully does anything which is seriously against God's law, a mortal sin is *always* committed no matter the sinner's intention.

*The Sacraments of Forgiveness*

**140. How does the Church forgive sins?**

Christ made His Church the "sacrament of salvation" and gave her two sacraments for the forgiveness of sins committed after Baptism: Penance and the Anointing of the Sick. These are called the sacraments of healing.

**141. What must we do to avoid sin?**

To avoid sin we must pray constantly, receive the sacraments often, remember that God sees us, recall that we are temples of the Holy Spirit, keep busy with work or legitimate recreation, promptly resist temptations, and avoid the near occasions of sin.

## Eleventh Article of the Creed

## "The resurrection of the body"

### Bodily Resurrection

**142. What does "the resurrection of the body" mean?**
It means that the bodies of all people — both good and evil — will rise from the dead at the end of the world and will be reunited to their souls for all eternity (I Corinthians 15:51-53).

**143. Why will our body rise?**
It is natural to the human person to be a material body and a spiritual soul. The body participated with the soul in all the good and evil done in life, so it is only just that both body and soul should share in the eternal reward or punishment earned in life.

**144. Will each of us have our own body when we rise from the dead?**
Yes, the body we will have at the resurrection is the same body we had on earth. Assuming we are judged worthy of heaven, the only difference between our earthly body and resurrected body is that the latter will be in a glorified state; that is, it will be exceedingly beautiful and forever free from pain and death (I Corinthians 15:43-44). We know that the Blessed Virgin Mary was at least fifty years old at the end of her earthly life, yet visionaries invariably describe her as youthful and exceedingly beautiful.

**145. Has anyone already entered heaven with a glorified human body?**

Yes, Jesus Christ is in heaven with His glorified body. Also, His Mother, the Blessed Virgin Mary, is living in heaven, body and soul. This is called the Assumption.

According to the Catechism of the Catholic Church, " 'the Immaculate Virgin, preserved free from all stain of original sin, when the course of her earthly life was finished, was taken up body and soul into heavenly glory, and exalted by the Lord as Queen over all things, so that she might be the more fully conformed to her Son, the Lord of lords and conqueror of sin and death' [*Lumen Gentium* 59; cf. Pius XII, *Munificentissimus Deus* (1950): DS 3903; cf. *Rev* 19:16]. The Assumption of the Blessed Virgin is a singular participation in her Son's Resurrection and an anticipation of the resurrection of other Christians."[16]

*Reincarnation*

**146. What is reincarnation?**

Reincarnation is the false belief that the souls of the dead keep returning to earth in different forms or bodies. Various Scriptural references show that reincarnation is not possible. Among the most striking is when Paul wrote that "it is appointed for men to die once, and after that comes judgment" (Hebrews 9:27).

---

[16] *Catechism of the Catholic Church*, 966.

## Twelfth Article of the Creed

## "And life everlasting"

*Eternal Life*

**147. What is meant by "life everlasting"?**
This refers to the eternal blissfullness of the saints in heaven, and the eternal torments of those damned to hell (cf. Matthew 25:34,41).

**148. What is meant by the immortality of the soul?**
This means that the soul will never die, that it will live forever. The soul can either live eternally in heaven (usually after a period of purification in purgatory) or hell.

*Hell*

**149. What is hell?**
Hell is a place of eternal punishment for those who refused to repent of their wicked ways during life. They will suffer forever with every sort of torment, with no relief. The worst of these torments will be eternal separation from God (cf. Mark 9:48; Matthew 13:41-42).

**150. How can a loving God send anyone to hell?**
In actuality, God does not send anyone to hell, but rather we send ourselves. He created us with free will, then gave us an objective set of moral norms by which to live. He respects the free will He gave us. If we choose to ignore Him and abuse the gift of a free will by way of unrepentant mortal sin, then we choose hell.

*Purgatory*

## 151. What is purgatory?

"All who die in God's grace and friendship, but still imperfectly purified, are indeed assured of their eternal salvation; but after death they undergo purification, so as to achieve the holiness necessary to enter the joy of heaven. The Church gives the name *Purgatory* to this final purification of the elect, which is entirely different from the punishment of the damned. [Cf. Council of Florence (1439): DS 1304; Council of Trent (1563): DS 1820; (1547): 1580; see also Benedict XII, *Benedictus Deus* (1336): DS 1000.]"[17] It is in purgatory that the last vestiges of love of self are transformed into love for God.

Purgatory is a testimony to God's mercy and justice. Because He is infinitely merciful, as well as infinitely just, purgatory is a necessity. If God were more merciful than just, He would be imperfect. He is perfectly merciful, but that mercy can be perfect only if it is balanced by His justice. Let's try to demonstrate this with an example.

You borrow your friend's car. You are very careful, but realize on the way home that you are running late. In your haste to return your friend's car, you take a corner turn a little too quickly and a little too sharply. The right front fender is creased by the corner fire hydrant when you drive over the curb.

When you return the car, you point out to your friend the damage you have done. You say, "I'm sorry. Will you forgive me?" Your friend is a good Christian. He replies, "Sure, I forgive you. Now, pay for my fender!"

This demonstrates the sense of justice God has given to us all. If we who are so imperfect must demand such

---

[17] *Catechism of the Catholic Church*, 1030-1031.

simple justice, as God has ingrained it into us, how can we expect that He should do less? Purgatory is the perfect reflection of both His justice and His mercy. Without purgatory to show His mercy, the slightest sin would by necessity condemn us all to hell.

Although purgatory is not explicitly mentioned by that name in the Bible, the concept of a place of purification is certainly implied. Jesus said, "I tell you, you will not get out till you have paid the very last penny" (Luke 12:59). Christ mentions the sin for which "there is no forgiveness, either in this world or in the world to come" (Matthew 12:32). This implies that venial sins can be forgiven in the next world. Where? Hell is eternal punishment. "Nothing unclean shall enter heaven" (Revelation 21:27), and even venial sin causes the soul to be unclean. The implication is clearly purgatory.

"Paul tells us that at the day of judgment each man's work will be tried. This trial happens after death. What happens if a man's work fails the test? 'He will be the loser; and yet he himself will be saved, though only as men are saved by passing through fire' (I Corinthians 3:15). Now this loss, this penalty, cannot refer to consignment to hell, since no one is saved there; and heaven cannot be meant, since there is no suffering ("fire") there. Purgatory alone explains this passage."[18]

The Church has always believed in purgatory. The Bible mentions the need to pray for the dead: "It is a holy and wholesome thought to pray for the dead, that they might be loosed from their sins" (II Maccabees 12:46). There are also the inscriptions of prayers for the dead in the catacombs, where Christians stayed largely hidden during the great Roman persecutions of the first three cen-

---

[18] Karl Keating, *Catholicism and Fundamentalism*, 193.

turies.  Finally, we have the writings of early Christians such as Tertullian (160-240), Cyprian (200-258), Cyril of Jerusalem (315-386), Ambrose (340-397), John Chrysostom (344-407), and Augustine (354-430) to tell us about purgatory and the need to pray for the dead.

**152.  Will purgatory last forever?**

No, purgatory will not last forever.  After the general judgment there will only be heaven and hell.

*Heaven*

**153.  What is heaven?**

Heaven is a place of everlasting possession and vision of God, in which the souls of the just will be filled with a complete happiness that is totally free from suffering or fear of loss (cf. I Corinthians 2:9; Romans 8:18; I John 3:2; Revelation 21:3-3).

**154.  Who will be eternally rewarded in heaven?**

The souls rewarded in heaven are those who did good works and died in a state of grace, and who are, after their purgatory, free from all venial sin and purified of all punishment due to sin (cf. Matthew 6:20; 16:27).

**155.  What must we do to attain heaven?**

To attain heaven we must fulfill the purpose for which God made us; that is, to know Him, to love Him, and to serve Him in this life.  For those who are aware that the Catholic Church is the Church Christ founded, this means they must become Catholic and live in obedience to Christ and His Church.

# Divine Grace and the Sacraments

## Grace

### *God's Free Gift*

**156. What is grace?**
Grace is a supernatural (above nature = divine) gift which God freely gives us for our salvation. All grace comes to us through the merits of Christ's Passion — His suffering from Holy Thursday night until His death on the cross — and is offered to us by His Church.

To say that grace is a supernatural gift implies two things. The first is that as a gift we have no right to it, but that God grants grace because He loves us. The second is that grace has a supernatural purpose, which is the attainment of heaven.

**157. How many types of grace are there?**
There are three primary types of grace. One type, *sacramental grace*, we will discuss when we study an overview of the sacraments. The other two, *sanctifying grace* and *actual grace*, we will discuss now.

### *Sanctifying Grace*

**158. What is sanctifying grace?**
Simply stated, sanctifying grace is God's life in us. It is a supernatural quality infused into our soul at baptism. Sanctifying grace gives us a share in the divine life and allows us to become a temple of the Holy Spirit, God's friend, and an heir of heaven. It also makes possible the ability for us to merit heavenly rewards for our good ac-

tions (cf. I Corinthians 6:11; II Peter 1:4; I Corinthians 3:16; John 15:15; I John 3:1; Romans 8:16-17; Romans 2:6).

**159. Why is sanctifying grace also called "habitual grace"?**

Because it inheres permanently in our soul, provided we are free of mortal sin.

**160. Is sanctifying grace necessary for our salvation?**

Sanctifying grace is necessary for our salvation because it makes us "pleasing to God,"[19] and this type of grace alone makes possible the attainment of heaven.

**161. What does it mean to be in a state of grace?**

To be in a state of grace means to be in a state of friendship with God; that is, to have sanctifying grace in the soul and be worthy of heaven.

**162. Can sanctifying grace be lost?**

Yes. We lose sanctifying grace each time we commit a mortal sin. One who's soul lacks sanctifying grace because of a mortal sin risks eternal damnation at death.

**163. Can sanctifying grace be recovered?**

Yes. The ordinary means of recovering sanctifying grace is by making a good confession and receiving absolution through the Sacrament of Penance.

**164. Can sanctifying grace be increased?**

Certainly! And we should strive always for its increase, because increased sanctifying grace makes us

[19] *Catechism of the Catholic Church*, 2024.

closer to God. Sanctifying grace can be increased by good works, prayer, and devout reception of the sacraments, most especially the Holy Eucharist.

### Other Divine Gifts

**165. Do we receive any other supernatural gifts along with sanctifying grace?**

Absolutely! Along with sanctifying grace God infuses into our soul the theological virtues of faith, hope, and charity (to be discussed in a later lesson), which makes us capable of performing ordinary acts of Christian virtue. God also infuses the gifts of the Holy Spirit, which allow us to respond easily and joyfully to actual graces and to perform heroic acts of virtue.

**166. What are the gifts of the Holy Spirit?**

There are seven gifts of the Holy Spirit: wisdom, understanding, counsel, fortitude, knowledge, piety, and fear of the Lord. You can find them in 1 Corinthians 12.

### Actual Grace

**167. What is actual grace?**

Actual grace is a divine enlightenment of our mind and strengthening of our will to help us to choose what is good and avoid evil (cf. Psalm 32:8; Hebrews 13:20-21).

**168. Is actual grace necessary?**

Yes. Without actual grace it is impossible for us to do anything that is pleasing to God. We respond to God's actual grace every time we do good and avoid evil. By the mere fact that you are studying this catechism you are responding well to God's actual grace (cf. Philemon 2:13; John 15:5).

**169. Does God give sufficient grace to all?**

Yes, God gives sufficient grace for the salvation of all. He gives enough grace for us to always keep His Commandments, and He gives enough grace for sinners to be converted (cf. Ezekiel 33:11).

**170. Can God's graces be resisted?**

God gave all people a free-will, and He respects the will He gave us. God will never force Himself on us. We can reject God's grace, but by doing so we reject His love.

**171. Is there any way we can dispose ourselves to respond positively to actual grace?**

To become attuned to actual grace we must become attuned to God. This is done by constant prayer.

## The Sacraments in General

*Grace-giving Signs*

### 172. What is a sacrament?

"The sacraments are perceptible signs (words and actions) accessible to our human nature. By the action of Christ and the power of the Holy Spirit they make present efficaciously the grace that they signify."[20]

### 173. How many sacraments are there?

There are seven sacraments: Baptism, Confirmation, Holy Eucharist, Penance, Anointing of the Sick, Holy Orders, and Matrimony.

### 174. Were all seven sacraments instituted by Christ?

Yes, all seven sacraments were instituted by Christ. As we shall soon see, there is ample Scriptural evidence of this.

### 175. Do all the sacraments give grace?

Provided they are received with the right disposition which means with the intent to receive grace, all the sacraments give grace.

### 176. Which graces do the sacraments give?

All of the sacraments give or increase sanctifying grace. They also give sacramental grace.

### 177. What is sacramental grace?

Sacramental grace is the special grace proper to a particular sacrament which gives us the right to those actual

[20] *Catechism of the Catholic Church*, 1084.

graces that will help us attain the sacraments' purpose. For example, the sacramental grace from Matrimony helps us to live always in fidelity to our spouse, to raise our children well, and to help our spouse to become holy.

### Kinds of Sacraments

**178. How may the sacraments be grouped?**

The sacraments may be divided into three groups. They are the sacraments of initiation, the sacraments of reconciliation, and the sacraments of vocation.

**179. What are the sacraments of initiation?**

The sacraments of initiation are Baptism, Confirmation, and Holy Eucharist. They are called sacraments of initiation because they are the sacraments through which we begin the Christian life.

**180. What are the sacraments of reconciliation?**

The sacraments of reconciliation are Penance and Anointing of the Sick. They are called sacraments of reconciliation because they reconcile us to God. The primary work of Anointing is to bring spiritual healing to the soul and often also the natural healing of the body.

**181. What are the sacraments of vocation?**

The sacraments of vocation are Holy Orders and Matrimony. They are called sacraments of vocation because the priestly state and the married state are life-long vocational commitments.

**182. Can some sacraments be received only once?**

Yes. The sacraments of Baptism, Confirmation, and Holy Orders can be received only once because they place an indelible mark, called a *character*, on the soul. This character is eternally visible to God, His angels and saints, and the demons. For those who persevere and win the crown of eternal glory, these characters will forever edify the angels and saints in heaven, and glorify God. They also increase our own capacity for joyfulness in heaven. For those who do not persevere, the demons will use these characters to add to the eternal punishment the damned deserve.

### Elements of a Sacrament

**183. What constitutes a true sacrament?**

Two elements are necessary to constitute a true sacrament. They are *matter* and *form.*

**184. What is "matter"?**

Matter is some sensible, concrete thing or action. Examples would be the pouring of water or anointing with oil.

**185. What is "form"?**

Form refers to the essential words used by the minister of a sacrament. For example, "I absolve you from your sins."

**186. Must the matter and form be united?**

Yes, they must be united. The matter must be used at the same time that the words of the form are spoken, and both must be done by the same minister.

**187. Who is the minister of a sacrament?**

The minister of a sacrament is a person who has received from Jesus the authority to act for Him in giving that particular sacrament.

**188. Does the effectiveness of a sacrament depend on the holiness of the minister?**

No. The only limiting factor to the measure of grace Jesus imparts through a sacrament is the disposition of the person receiving the sacrament.

**189. How should we be disposed when receiving the sacraments?**

We should receive the sacraments with an intensity of faith and love, but also with trust in God's mercy and sorrow for our sins.

**190. Is the state of grace necessary for the reception of the sacraments?**

The state of grace is absolutely necessary for four of the sacraments. They are Confirmation, Holy Eucharist, Holy Orders, and Matrimony. The state of grace is normally necessary for the Anointing of the Sick.

## Baptism

### *The First Sacrament*

### 191. What is Baptism?

"Holy Baptism is the basis of the whole Christian life, the gateway to life in the Spirit (*vitae spiritualis ianua*) [Cf. Council of Florence: DS 1314: *vitae spiritualis ianua*.], and the door which gives access to the other sacraments. Through Baptism we are freed from sin and reborn as sons of God; we become members of Christ, are incorporated into the Church and made sharers in her mission: 'Baptism is the sacrament of regeneration through water in the word.' [*Roman Catechism* II, 2, 5; cf. Council of Florence: DS 1314; Code of Canon Law, canon 204§1; 849; Corpus Canonum Ecclesiarum Orientalium, can 675§1.]"[21]

### 192. Did Jesus make Baptism obligatory?

Yes. Jesus told His Apostles to "go into all the world and preach the gospel to the whole creation ... *he who believes and is baptized will be saved*, but he who does not believe will be condemned" (Mark 16:15-16). It is with these words that Jesus made baptism obligatory (cf. John 3:5).

### 193. Does Baptism remove all sin?

Yes. Baptism removes the stain of original sin and all actual sins we have committed. It also removes all of the eternal punishment due to our sins.

---

[21] *Catechism of the Catholic Church*, 1213.

**194. What does the character of Baptism do for us?**
    The character or seal of baptism confers on us a permanent relationship with Christ which will identify us as Christians in this life and into eternity.

**195. Who usually baptizes?**
    The ordinary minister of Baptism is a priest or deacon.

*Emergency Baptism*

**196. In case of emergency, who can baptize?**
    In case of emergency (i.e., imminent death), anyone, even an atheist, can baptize.

**197. How is emergency Baptism given?**
    For emergency Baptism to be validly given, the following conditions must be met:
    1.  The person baptizing must have the Church's intention; that is, that the Baptism take away sin;
    2.  The person baptizing must pour water on the head three times in such a manner that it flows over the skin;
    3.  At the same time the water is being poured, the person baptizing must say: "I baptize you in the name of the Father, and of the Son, and of the Holy Spirit."

**198. If the person survives, should the baptism be repeated?**
    No. A re-baptism is not necessary, nor is it possible, since Baptism can be administered only once. Should the baptized survive, the ceremonies surrounding Baptism should be performed in church by a priest or deacon.

## Importance of Baptism

### 199. Is Baptism necessary for salvation?

Yes. Jesus made Baptism absolutely necessary for salvation. He indicated this to Nicodemus (John 3:5) and to His Apostles (Mark 16:15-16).

### 200. Should infants be baptized?

The early Christian Fathers are unanimous in insisting upon infant Baptism, basing it on the universal command of Christ to baptize all (Matthew 28:19, Mark 16:15-16; John 3:5), and on its divine power to cleanse original sin from the soul. Irenaeus (130-205) writes: "He came to save all who through Him are born again unto God; infants, and children, boys and youths, and elders" (*Adversus Haereses*). Origen (185-254) declared infant Baptism an apostolic institution (*Commentarii in Romanos*). St. Cyprian and the bishops of the Third Council of Carthage (253) taught that children should be baptized as soon as possible after birth. Yes, infants should be baptized, as the Church has taught for 2000 years.

### 201. What happens if an infant dies without Baptism?

There are two major schools of reputable thought on this subject. The first comes from those who hold that an infant who dies without Baptism goes to limbo. This school, espoused by St. Thomas Aquinas, teaches that limbo is a place of perfect natural happiness, but minus the vision of God. This is reasonable, since an unbaptized infant still possesses the stain of original sin.

The second school of thought is much more modern. It holds that the Holy Spirit enlightens the soul — which is capable of instantaneous enlightenment under divine direction (cf. Acts 1:1-16; 2:1-47) — at the moment of death to the totality of Catholic truth. Then the free-will of the soul, which is not influenced by the commission of actual sin, makes the decision to accept that truth, and passes into the next life with perfect contrition; therefore, being saved and made worthy of heaven, but without the seal of Baptism. In either case, the child is left to the infinite mercy of God.

**202. Can an adult who has died without Baptism be saved?**

An adult who dies unbaptized because he does not know about Baptism nor its importance can be saved if he lived his life trying to do good and avoiding evil. This is called *baptism of desire*. Indeed, the Church embraces as her own those who are studying the Faith with the intention of being received into the Church, so that they receive baptism of desire should they die prior to reception into the Church.

There are also those who may suffer martyrdom for the Faith, although they are not Catholic. Such a person would be the recipient of *baptism of blood*.

*Godparents or Sponsors*

**203. What are the responsibilities of godparents?**

Although it is a great honor to become the godparent of one who is to be baptized, it should not be viewed as a position or office of honor. It should instead be viewed as an active position in the life of a soul for the purpose of helping the soul to attain spiritual perfection and perfect unity with God. Being a godparent is an awesome responsibility, and God will judge the godparent on the basis of how seriously he undertook this responsibility.

As the godparent of an infant, it is the godparent's responsibility to see to it that the godchild is raised as a good Catholic if the natural parents become lax in their

God-given responsibilities. However, it is important to remember that the parents have a far greater role in the life of the child than the godparent.

In the case of an adult convert, the godparent should see to it that the godchild has all he or she needs to grow in the spiritual life and a deeper understanding of what the Church teaches. The important thing to remember in this case is that the godchild's free-will must be respected.

**204. Whom should be chosen as godparents?**

The parents of an infant should choose as godparents only those who *know and live* their Catholic Faith. Candidates for godparents must be at least sixteen years old. The same criteria should be considered by adult converts when selecting godparents.

**205. What promises do we make in Baptism?**

The promises we make in Baptism (done for a child by his parents) are that we will reject Satan and everything contrary to the law of God, and to live according to the teachings and example of Jesus Christ. These promises are important because they are our guide on the road to salvation.

## Confirmation

*Sacrament of Witness*

### 206. What is Confirmation?

Confirmation is the sacrament instituted by Christ that makes baptized persons "more perfectly bound to the Church and ... enriched with a special strength of the Holy Spirit. Hence [baptized persons] are, as true witnesses of Christ, more strictly obliged to spread and defend the faith by word and deed."[22]

### 207. What else does Confirmation do for us?

Confirmation increases sanctifying grace in our soul, increases the supernatural virtues, and gives an increase of the gifts of the Holy Spirit (cf. Question 166). It imprints on the soul an indelible spiritual mark and for this reason cannot be repeated. It enables us to courageously profess our faith, even under the threat of death. Indeed, without the Sacrament of Confirmation there would be far fewer martyrs in the Church's glorious history.

### 208. How do we know that Jesus instituted the Sacrament of Confirmation?

Although it is not called by the name Confirmation, we see it clearly in use by the Apostles in the historical books of the New Testament (cf. Acts 8:14-17; 19:6). Since the Apostles did and taught all and only that which Christ commanded, we are assured by their actions that Jesus instituted this sacrament.

---

[22] *Lumen Gentium*, 11.

## Rite of Confirmation

### 209. Who is the minister of Confirmation?

The ordinary minister of Confirmation is the local bishop, but priests may also confirm under certain conditions. For example, in a case of emergency (impending death) or with the bishop's prior permission (institutional situations, such as prisons) a priest may confirm.

### 210. How is Confirmation given?

Confirmation is given by tracing a cross on the person's forehead with a blessed oil, called holy chrism (a mixture of olive oil and an aromatic substance, blessed by the bishop), while reciting the form: "Be sealed with the gift of the Holy Spirit."

A cross is traced on the person's forehead as a symbol of the Faith that the confirmed must live and profess, even under the direst of circumstances.

## Importance of Confirmation

### 211. Who can receive Confirmation?

Confirmation may be received by any baptized person who has never been confirmed, after having been properly instructed in the duties and responsibilities of the Christian life.

### 212. How should one prepare for Confirmation?

One prepares for Confirmation by being in a state of grace and *knowing* the main truths and duties of the Catholic Faith.

**213. Is Confirmation valid if received by one in a state of mortal sin?**

Yes, Confirmation would be valid, but illicitly received. God will withhold the special graces of Confirmation until the confirmed is reconciled to God by way of a good confession. Furthermore, if Confirmation is received in a state of mortal sin, the confirmed commits the additional mortal sin of sacrilege. This, too, must be confessed.

**214. Who should be confirmed?**

All Catholics have an obligation to be confirmed at the appropriate time. In the case of children, parents have the grave obligation to see to it the children are properly instructed before receiving Confirmation. In the case of adult converts, both the convert and his godparent (sponsor) have a grave obligation to ensure complete and proper instruction.

**215. Are we obliged to continue to study our Catholic Faith after Confirmation?**

Absolutely! Every Catholic has an obligation to study the Faith for the entirety of his life. This is how we prepare ourselves to share the Faith with others, thus responding positively to the sacramental graces of Confirmation. Failure to study is a rejection of the graces God gives through Confirmation.

**216. Who should be chosen as the sponsor (godparent) for Confirmation?**

Certainly a practicing and knowledgeable Catholic should be chosen as the Confirmation sponsor (godparent). It is desirable for the Confirmation sponsor to be the same as that of Baptism (see Questions 203-204).

# Holy Eucharist

**Special Author's Note:** *The Holy Eucharist is the very heart of our holy and ancient Faith. Christianity makes absolutely no sense without this most precious of the divinely instituted sacraments. Indeed, it is beyond the imagination of this writer, who is a convert from agnosticism, what attraction exists in non-Catholic Christianity for those who do not accept the fullness of Christ's teaching on the Holy Eucharist. It is the singular truth of the Holy Eucharist that has made this convert (and countless others) fall helplessly, hopelessly, passionately in love with our Lord and Savior Jesus Christ. The Author's most sincere prayer is that the Holy Spirit will reach into the depths of your heart with these Eucharistic truths, and that you will respond with a life-long embrace of the One who gives you perfect love through this most adorable sacrament.*

## *Real Presence*

### 217. What is the Holy Eucharist?

In the Holy Eucharist Jesus gives us Himself, under the appearances of bread and wine, fully and completely; He is truly present in His Body, Blood, Soul, and Divinity, in order to give Himself to the Father for our salvation, and to give Himself to us as divine nourishment for our souls.

### 218. When did Jesus institute the Holy Eucharist?

Jesus instituted the Holy Eucharist on Holy Thursday night at the Last Supper, the night before He was crucified. The Last Supper was the very first Mass.

At the first Mass during the Last Supper, He took bread in His sacred hands, gave the Father thanks and praise, broke the bread and said: "Take, eat; this is my body." Then He took the cup of wine, gave thanks and said: "Drink of it, all of you; for this is my blood of the covenant, which is poured out for many for the forgiveness of sins" (cf. Matthew 26:26-29; Mark 14:22-25; Luke 22:17-20).

**219. When Jesus said, "This is my body" and "This is my blood," what happened to the bread and wine?**

When Jesus said "This is my Body," the substance of the bread was changed into the true Body of Jesus Christ. Only the appearances (called accidentals) of the bread remained; that is, all that remained of the bread are those things which effect the five senses: in this case, taste, appearance, touch, and smell.

The same is true of the wine. When Jesus said "This is my blood," the entire substance of the wine was changed into His real Blood. Therefore, Jesus' Body and Blood are really present in the Holy Eucharist.

We speak of "The Body of Christ" and "The Blood of Christ" to distinguish the two appearances. In fact, both are the same identical substance: Christ's Body, Blood, Soul and Divinity, which is Christ whole and entire.

**220. Why do Catholics believe that they receive the living Christ in Communion?**

We believe in the Real Presence of Jesus Christ in the Holy Eucharist because He promised to give us His Flesh as food and His Blood as drink. In order to see this we must turn to the sixth chapter of St. John's Gospel.

The sixth chapter of John begins with Jesus working a miracle in preparation for the Eucharistic promise He will make the next day. In verses one through fourteen we see that a multitude of people had followed Jesus into the hills, and that they became hungry. Jesus fed to their fill five thousand men with five loaves of bread and two fish. There was so much left over that the remnants filled twelve baskets.

That evening Jesus worked yet another preparatory miracle. Jesus told His Apostles to get in their boat at Tiberius and sail to Capernaum without Him. In the night (verses 16-22) the sea became rough because of a high wind. Suddenly, the Apostles saw Jesus walking on the water toward the boat. Then, once Jesus was in the boat, it miraculously landed at the shore of Capernaum.

The next morning (verses 22-24), the people who had eaten the loaves at Tiberias could not find Jesus. They had seen the Apostles sail away without Him, and they could not understand why they could not find Him. So the people went to Capernaum to find Him. When the people found Jesus at Capernaum, they asked Him how He got there. Jesus cut to the heart of the matter when He said, "Truly, truly, I say to you, you seek me, not because you saw signs, but because you ate your fill of the loaves" (verse 26). Jesus went on to tell them to work for the spiritual food that would get them to heaven, instead of the temporal food that spoils. He told them to do this by believing in Him (verse 29).

These disciples who ate the miraculous bread the day before now wanted a sign from Him to prove He was worthy of their belief. They told Jesus that Moses had given their fathers manna from heaven to eat. They wanted to know if He could top that!

"Jesus said to them, 'I am the bread of life; he who comes to me shall not hunger, and he who believes in me shall never thirst' " (John 6:35). He went on to explain through verse forty that He was the bread sent from heaven by the Father.

Up to that point Jesus' followers understood Him to be speaking symbolically. Jesus took this misconception away from them. He went on to tell them that He was the bread that they would have to eat to inherit eternal life.

"The Jews then disputed among themselves, saying, 'How can this man give us his flesh to eat?' So Jesus said to them, 'Truly, truly, I say to you, unless you eat the flesh of the Son of man and drink his blood, you have no life in you; he who eats my flesh and drinks my blood has eternal life, and I will raise him up on the last day. For my flesh is food indeed, and my blood is drink indeed. He who eats my flesh and drinks my blood abides in me, and I am him. As the living Father sent me, and I live because of the Father, so he who eats me will live because of me' " (John 6:52-57).

No longer did Jesus' followers believe He was being symbolic. They now understood Him to be speaking literally. He said "my flesh is food indeed, and my blood is drink indeed" (verse 55); the word "indeed" made His statement imperative. He prefaced His entire statement with the phrase "truly, truly"; which He always used to emphasize the importance of what He was about to teach.

The followers' literal understanding of what Jesus said repulsed them, "After this many of his disciples drew back and no longer went about with him" (John 6:66). If they misunderstood by taking Jesus' words literally, why didn't He stop them and explain what He meant? Any other time they misunderstood He would explain, so why not now? He did not go after them because He intended for them to take Him literally.

"Jesus said to the twelve, 'Will you also go away?' Simon Peter answered him, 'Lord, to whom shall we go? You have the words of eternal life; and we have believed, and have come to know, that you are the Holy One of God' " (John 6:67-69). The Apostles had been with Him from the beginning. They also understood what He said to be literal. They did not know *how* He would do what He said, but they believed that He would eventually show them.

Jesus finally explained the *how* to them at the Last Supper. In Luke 22:15 Jesus said, "I have earnestly desired to eat this Passover with you before I suffer." He had *earnestly desired* to give them His Flesh and Blood since He first made the promise. In verses sixteen through twenty Jesus proceeded to give what He had promised.

These passages, as well as others, explain why Catholics believe in the Real Presence of Jesus Christ in the Holy Eucharist. The short of it is that we believe in the Real Presence because Jesus said so!

### *Effecting Christ's Real Presence*

**221. How does Jesus become present in the Holy Eucharist?**

Jesus becomes present in the Holy Eucharist by a change called transubstantiation.

**222. What is transubstantiation?**

Transubstantiation is the change of the entire substance of the bread and the entire substance of the wine into the real Body and Blood of Jesus Christ. The word breaks down thusly: trans = to move or change; substanti = from the word substance; ation = a suffix denoting the taking place of an action. Resultantly, transubstantiation is the changing of the substance.

## 223. Didn't you Catholics invent transubstatiation in the 13th Century?

This is a false charge levied against the Church that usually finds its origin in a book by Loraine Boettner called *Roman Catholicism*.[23] This book is often referred to as the "anti-Catholic bible."

Boettner charges that transubstantiation was an invention by the Pope in the year 1215. "The implication is that transubstantiation was not believed until 1215 — that it was, indeed, an 'invention'. The facts are otherwise. Transubstantiation is just the technical term used to describe what happens when the bread and wine used at Mass are turned into the actual Body and Blood of Christ. The belief that this occurs has been held from the earliest times. It stems from the sixth chapter of John's Gospel, the eleventh chapter of First Corinthians, and the several accounts of the Last Supper. As centuries passed, theologians exercised their reason on the belief to understand more completely how such a thing could happen and what its happening would imply. Because some of them, in trying to explain the Real Presence, developed unsound theories, it became evident that more precise terminology was needed to ensure the integrity of the belief. The word *transubstantiation* was finally chosen because it eliminated certain unorthodox interpretations of the doctrine, and the term was formally imposed at the Fourth Lateran Council in 1215. So the use of the technical term was new, but not the doctrine."[24]

[23] *Roman Catholicism* (Philadelphia: Presbyterian and Reformed, 1962).
[24] Karl Keating, *Catholicism and Fundamentalism*, 42-43.

*Total Presence*

**224. Is the whole Christ truly present in the Holy Eucharist after the transubstantiation?**

Yes, the whole Christ in His Body, Blood, Soul, and Divinity — true God and true man — is truly present after the transubstantiation. Indeed, the whole Christ is present in each particle of the consecrated host and each drop of the consecrated wine.

**225. Is the Real Presence of Christ in the Holy Eucharist a mystery of faith?**

Yes, the Eucharistic Presence of Christ is a mystery of faith (see Question 16).

**226. How is Jesus able to change bread and wine into His Body and Blood?**

Jesus is able to change bread and wine into His Body and Blood because He is God and can do all things.

*The Mass*

**227. What is the Holy Sacrifice of the Mass?**

The Holy Sacrifice of the Mass (also called Eucharistic Celebration) is at one and the same time: the sacrifice of the cross made present on our altars; a memorial of Jesus' death, resurrection and ascension; and a sacred banquet at which we receive Him in Holy Communion.

**228. Who can celebrate The Holy Sacrifice of the Mass?**

Only a validly ordained priest can celebrate the Holy Sacrifice of the Mass, because he alone has been given the power of Christ to perform the consecration. In other words, only a validly ordained priest can change the bread and wine into the Body and Blood of Jesus.

**229. When did Jesus give priests the power to celebrate the Holy Sacrifice of the Mass?**

Jesus gave his priesthood the power to celebrate the Holy Sacrifice of the Mass in the upper room on Holy Thursday night at the Last Supper when He said to His Apostles: "Do this in remembrance of me" (Luke 22:19; cf. I Corinthians 11:24).

**230. When does the change of the bread and wine into the Body and Blood of Christ take place?**

This change of the substance of the bread and wine (transubstantiation) into the Body and Blood of Christ takes place at the consecration when the priest repeats Christ's words of institution: "This is my body," and "This is my blood."

*The Mass As Sacrifice*

**231. What is a sacrifice?**

A sacrifice is the offering of a victim by a priest to God. Throughout the Old Testament we find sacrifices of flesh, cereal (various grains and bread), and wine.

**232. Is the Mass a true sacrifice?**

Yes, because Jesus Christ offers Himself to the Father through the priest as a victim under the appearances of bread and wine.

### 233. Is the Mass the same sacrifice as that of the cross?

Absolutely! The Mass and Jesus' sacrifice on Calvary are one and the same; because in the Mass Jesus makes Himself present on the altar so that we can celebrate the memory of the cross, as well as apply its saving power for the forgiveness of our sins. According to the *Catechism of the Catholic Church*: "The sacrificial character of the Eucharist is manifested in the very words of institution: 'This is my body which is given for you' and 'This cup which is poured out for you is the New Covenant in my blood.' [*Lk* 22:19-20] In the Eucharist Christ gives us the very body he gave up for us on the cross, the very blood which he 'poured out for many for the forgiveness of sins.' [*Mt* 26:28]"[25]

### 234. In which ways are the sacrifice of the cross and the Sacrifice of the Mass the same?

In both the Sacrifice of the Mass and the sacrifice of the cross the victim is Jesus Christ. He acted as the High Priest who offered Himself to the Father from the cross; He continues to act as high priest of the same sacrifice in the Mass, but does so now through the ministry of His priests.

### 235. How do the Mass and sacrifice of the cross differ?

The difference is in the manner of presentation. Christ "who offered himself once in a bloody manner on the altar of the cross is contained and is offered in an unbloody manner"[26] on the altar of the Mass.

---

[25] *Catechism of the Catholic Church*, 1365.
[26] Council of Trent, 1743.

**236. At what point in the Mass does Jesus offer Himself to His heavenly Father as a victim for our salvation?**

Jesus offers Himself as a victim to the Father in the consecration of the Mass. The double consecration of the bread and wine represents the mystical separation of His body and blood. When body and blood are separated, death results. Reception of the Holy Eucharist is our participation in Christ's redemptive sacrifice on the cross.

*Purpose and Effects of the Mass*

**237. What is the purpose of the Sacrifice of the Mass?**

The purpose of the Sacrifice of the Mass and the sacrifice of the cross are one and the same. They both give glory, praise, and worship to the Father; they both provide expiation and reparation for our sins and the sins of all mankind; they both appeal to God for the natural and supernatural favors we need, particularly those which help us to become holy.

**238. Is the Mass offered to God alone?**

Yes, the Mass is offered to God alone. People are often confused by "Masses for saints," believing the Masses are offered to the saints. Masses are sometimes offered *in honor of*, and *not to*, saints. Saints are honored because of their holiness in the way they lived in imitation of Christ, and priests offer Masses in their honor to thank God for them, and hold them up for an example to all people. The Mass is the highest form of divine worship, so it is offered to God alone.

### 239. Can the Mass be offered for the poor souls in purgatory?

Not only can the Mass be offered for the poor souls in purgatory, but it should be offered for them on a frequent basis. The Mass both forgives sin and the punishment due for sin. The poor souls in purgatory have had their sins forgiven, which is why they are there; however, they are repaying God's justice for their sins with punishment in purgatory. To have Masses celebrated for them can get them liberated from purgatory so they can join God in heaven.

Too many people fool themselves by believing their departed loved ones go straight to heaven, which is seldom the case. A genuine act of love is to have Masses celebrated often for our departed friends and loved ones. Those Masses are not wasted, even if the person for whom they are offered are already in heaven, as God applies the merits of these Masses to other poor souls in purgatory. A good practice would be to have Masses celebrated each November (the month traditionally set aside for that purpose), the anniversary of the person's birth, and the anniversary of the person's death.

### 240. What are the personal effects of the Sacrifice of the Mass?

The Mass remits all venial sins and the punishment due to forgiven sin (mortal and venial), provided we participate in the Mass with the proper dispositions. It also increases sanctifying grace, the infused virtues of faith, hope, and charity, and the gifts of the Holy Spirit. Again, we receive these benefits according to our own dispositions.

**241. How should our participation and dispositions be in Mass?**

We should participate in the Mass by being attentive and joining our prayers with those of the priest. We should maintain the same dispositions we would have had at the foot of the cross on Calvary, of which the Mass is a perpetuation.

### Which Bread and Wine?

**242. In order for the Mass to be valid, what kind of bread and wine must be used?**

The bread for a valid Mass must be made of pure wheat flour and water. It cannot have other ingredients such as milk, honey, sugar, or eggs. In the Latin (Roman) Rite, the bread cannot be leavened.

The wine for a valid Mass must be natural grape wine of high quality.

### Parts of the Mass

**243. How is the Mass divided?**

The Mass is divided into two parts: the *Liturgy of the Word* (also called the *Liturgy of the Catechumens*), and the *Liturgy of the Eucharist*. In the first part, Jesus speaks to us through the Bible. In the second part, Jesus offers Himself to the Father for our salvation.

The *Liturgy of the Catechumens* (*Liturgy of the Word*), and the two part division of the Mass, has its origin in the ancient Roman persecutions. When the Church was forced into the catacombs by the persecuting Roman emperors, the Church's leaders had to be cautious of infiltration by spies. Catechumens (those learning the Faith with the intention of joining the Church) were permitted to stay during the first part of the Mass, but were asked to leave during the second part. This was done as a safe-guard to prevent Roman spies from desecrating Our Lord in the Eucharist. Hence the reason the first part of the Mass was called the *Liturgy of the Catechumens.*

## Holy Communion

### 244. What is Holy Communion?

Holy Communion is the nourishment of our souls by receiving the Body, Blood, Soul, and Divinity of Jesus Christ in the Holy Eucharist (John 6:53). Christ man-dated that we receive Him in the Eucharist for the life of our soul.

There are numerous fruits of Holy Communion. The chief fruit, of course, is an intimate, interior union with Christ. Just as Matrimony is the Sacrament that weds a man and woman, the Eucharist is the Sacrament that weds us to Christ.

Every person who has ever been in love has felt an attachment so strongly that he or she has wanted to be-come one physically with the object of that love, for one to crawl inside of the other person, as it were. Because He is truly human, Jesus feels this same attachment with us. Because He is God, He can make it actually happen through Communion.

When a man and woman are in love, they express that love in the bonds of Matrimony with a union of their bodies. God built us that way. He did so in order that we may fulfill that need to feel we have become one with our spouse. The need is not filled perfectly, but it is none-theless met. And the fruit of the union is often a child whom we nurture and help to grow for God's greater glory.

Communion of the Holy Eucharist is very similar. The marital act meets the need of two people in love trying to become one, but imperfectly. Communion allows us and

Jesus to meet that same need, but perfectly. His entire self comes into our entire self. He abides in us and we in Him. The fruit of this union is always the growth of our soul for God's greater glory. Furthermore, Holy Communion produces a brotherly unity between Christ and all of the members of His Mystical Body. *(Jesus is God; therefore, He is infinite. It is not possible for finite beings to adequately analogize attributes of the Infinite. Consequently, my analogy is intended only to help clarify for the reader the beauty and depth of this divine mystery. It must be noted, however, that it is not my intention to portray Christ as "needing" us in the same way a husband needs his wife.)*

Holy Communion also produces other fruits. It produces an increase of sanctifying grace, and increases the theological virtues of faith, hope, and charity. It also remits venial sin. Holy Communion weakens concupiscence, the propensity to sin that comes from our broken human nature. It also adds strength to the force of our will, preserves us from falling into mortal sin, and helps us to joyfully accept the duties and sacrifices that our Catholic life demand.

Finally, Jesus pledged to us in John 6:54 that by receiving Holy Communion worthily we can be assured of the resurrection and heavenly bliss. Holy Communion is the single greatest love affair in the history of man, and that love affair is between God and man.

**245. What are the necessary conditions for receiving Holy Communion worthily?**

Two conditions are necessary for us to receive Holy Communion worthily. They are: to be in a state of grace, and to have the right intention.

**246. What does it mean to be in a state of grace?**

To be in a state of grace means that we are in a state of friendship with God. That means to be in a state that is free of mortal sin.

**247. If a person is in a state of mortal sin and receives Holy Communion, does he still receive Jesus?**

The state of a person's soul in no way affects the presence of Christ in the Eucharist, since His presence is the result of the words and actions of consecration by the priest during Mass. A person who knows he is in a state of mortal sin when receiving Communion commits the additional sin of sacrilege, and risks condemning his soul to hell for all eternity. In order to rectify this the communicant must make a good confession, including the sin of sacrilege.

**248. What if a person recalls that he has a mortal sin he *forgot* to confess, but only remembers while awaiting Communion or just after having received Communion?**

In a case such as this, the communicant should not feel guilty for receiving Communion, as no sin of sacrilege is committed; however, the communicant has a grave obligation to make a good confession as soon as possible.

**249. What does it mean to have the right intention?**

Having the right intention means receiving Communion to show God we love Him. We must be careful to avoid other intentions. We are not receiving Communion for the respect of others, nor to make ourselves feel holy. By the mere fact that we are all sinners, none of us is worthy to receive Communion, but Jesus deems us worthy if we are free of mortal sin; therefore, we receive with only the intention of showing God our love for Him.

### 250. Are there any other dispositions we should have before receiving Communion?

Yes. We should be free, as far as possible, from fully deliberate venial sins. We should also make acts of faith, hope, charity, sorrow (for our sins), and desire (to receive Communion).

### 251. Is there a fast to be observed before receiving Communion?

Yes, the Church requires a fast for one hour prior to receiving Communion. We may not eat or drink anything, except water and prescription medication. The elderly, those with serious illnesses, and those who care for them are exempt from this Eucharistic fast.

### 252. Should we receive Communion standing or kneeling?

Holy Communion may be received either standing or kneeling. If we receive standing, we should make a gesture of reverence before receiving. Examples would be to bow or make the Sign of the Cross.

It is important to remember who it is that we are receiving. Since the Eucharist is Jesus, we should receive the Creator of the universe with the greatest humility and reverence. Most people would agree that these are most expressed by kneeling, for those who are physically able.

If we believe that genuflecting, bowing, or making the Sign of the Cross might unduly slow the distribution of Holy Communion, we can do it while the person in front of us is receiving. All present would understand that we are genuflecting to Christ, and not to the person in front of us.

### 253. Should we receive the Eucharist on the tongue or in the hand?

Both methods are permitted in the Church, however, there are two considerations before deciding whether to receive in the hand or on the tongue.

The first consideration is found in the ordination of a priest. During the rite of ordination the priest's hands are blessed with an anointing by the bishop. This is done to remind him and us that it is he who will hold the Body of Christ, and that his hands are worthy only because of the ordination and anointing he has received. We who are not ordained priests do not enjoy this special priestly privilege.

The second consideration is the risk of accidental abuse to Jesus in the Eucharist. By receiving Him in the hand we risk the possibility of dropping Him on the floor. This would be a grave abuse if done because of carelessness. If done by sheer accident, any lover of Christ would feel very badly.

Pope John Paul II, while repeatedly recognizing the right of the faithful to receive in the hand (provided the priest permits it), has shown his constant preference of Communion on the tongue by refusing to allow communicants to receive in the hand at the Masses he celebrates. We should take our lead from the Holy Father.

### 254. What should we do after receiving Holy Communion?

We should always offer an act of thanksgiving. This means that we should adore Jesus present in us, thank Him for coming, express our love and the desire to do His will, and ask for His blessings.

**255. How can we gain the greatest spiritual benefits from Holy Communion?**

Because the graces we receive from Communion are in direct proportion to the dispositions we maintain, the greatest spiritual benefits are derived from a good preparation and thanksgiving.

**256. Is there anytime when we are obliged to receive Holy Communion?**

Yes, the Church commands that we must receive Holy Communion at least once a year, during the Easter time. The law in the United States, by special permission of the Holy See, is expanded from universal law to be inclusive of the time from the first Sunday of Lent until Trinity Sunday. This is called the Easter Duty.

For some grave — repeat, grave — reason this duty may be fulfilled at another time during the year. Failure to fulfill our Easter Duty is a mortal sin.

**257. Is it good to receive Communion frequently?**

Absolutely! Holy Mother Church recommends that we receive Communion weekly at Sunday Mass, but she is most pleased to allow the faithful daily Communion so we may grow in grace and holiness.

**258. When are we obliged to begin receiving Communion?**

The obligation to begin receiving Holy Communion begins at the age of reason; that is, approximately at the age of seven. It is vital that a proper preparation is made before the reception of First Holy Communion. This means a thorough instruction in the Church's teachings on the Eucharist, and preparation for a good confession prior to First Holy Communion.

## Eucharistic Devotion

### 259. Does the Real Presence of Christ continue in the consecrated Host after Mass?

Yes, the Real Presence of Christ remains in the Host after Mass. That is why extra Hosts are consecrated at the Mass for deposit into the Tabernacle, so we may spend time in Adoration of Him.

The Tabernacle is a box-like structure that is centrally located some place in the parish church. Nearby is a candle or oil lamp that is lit, usually in a red glass, to let the faithful know that Jesus is present in the Tabernacle.

We should show our Eucharistic Lord how much we appreciate His presence by participating in various devotions. Such parish devotions are the Benediction of the Most Blessed Sacrament and the Forty Hours Devotion.

The greatest individual devotion in which we may participate is called the Holy Hour or Hour of Adoration. This is simply going to the church to spend an hour before the Tabernacle, keeping Jesus company while we pray to and adore Him. There are 168 hours in a week. Certainly any lover of Christ can find one hour out of those 168 to keep Him company and tell Him He is loved and appreciated.

## Penance

### 260. What is the Sacrament of Penance?

The Sacrament of Penance, also called the Sacrament of Reconciliation or Confession, is the sacrament instituted by Christ through which He forgives sins committed after baptism when the penitent confesses them to the priest and the priest grants absolution.

### 261. Isn't the Sacrament of Penance just an invention of the Church?

No. That the Sacrament of Penance was instituted by Christ can be proven in Sacred Scripture. To Peter in Matthew 16:18, and to Peter and the other Apostles in Matthew 18:18, Jesus said, "Truly, I say to you, whatever you bind on earth shall be bound in heaven, and whatever you loose on earth shall be loosed in heaven." There are two applications for Jesus' promise to Peter and the Apostles. The first is that they would have the power to govern the Church in His name. The second is one fulfilled later with a special commission.

In John 20:21-23 we find Jesus addressing the Apostles in the upper room on the evening of the first Easter Sunday: " 'Peace be with you. As the Father has sent me, even so I send you.' And when he had said this, he breathed on them, and said to them, 'Receive the Holy Spirit. If you forgive the sins of any, they are forgiven; if you retain the sins of any, they are retained.' "

In this special commission to the Apostles we find several interesting elements. The first is that Christ makes Himself clear that what He is giving the Apostles is indeed a commission-mandate when He tells them that He is sending them as the Father sent Him.

The second important element is that He breathed on them. In all of human history, this is only the second time that God breathed on man. The first time God had breathed on man was when He gave life to Adam. God is giving a new type of life to man here, as He is telling the Apostles that they now have His power to forgive sins to those who are repentant, or to not forgive the sins of those who are not repentant.

Anti-Catholic writer Loraine Boettner, author of *Roman Catholicism*, a book that Catholic apologist Karl Keating calls the *anti-Catholic bible*, writes that "auricular confession to a priest instead of to God" was invented by Pope Innocent III and the bishops of the Fourth Lateran Council in the year 1215.[27] This is the most generally held position by those who claim the Church invented the Sacrament of Penance. Even if the Church's opponents were to completely discount the Scriptural references to Confession — which they do — we should expect to find no historical evidence of the sacrament's existence prior to 1215. This is not the case.

There are many, many writings of early Christians dating to hundreds of years before the Fourth Lateran Council. St. Gregory the Great (590-604) in his homily on John 20:23 writes: "The Apostles, therefore, have received the Holy Spirit in order to loose sinners from the bonds of their sins. God has made them partakers of His right of judgment; they are to judge in His name and in His place. The bishops are the successors of the Apostles, and, therefore, possess the same right."[28]

St. Caesarius of Arles (470-542) writes: "It is God's will that we confess our sins not only to Him but to men,

---

[27] Loraine Boettner, *Roman Catholicism*, 8.
[28] Gregory the Great, *Homily* 26.

and since it is impossible for us to be free from sin, we must never fail to have recourse to the remedy of Confession."[29] In a sermon on the Last Judgment the saint tells us "to escape damnation by making a sincere Confession from the bottom of [our] hearts, and to fulfill the penance given by the priest."[30]

St. Leo the Great (440-461) writes: "God in His abundant mercy has provided two remedies for the sins of men; that they may gain eternal life by the grace of Baptism, and also by the remedy of Penance. Those who have violated their vows of Baptism may obtain the remission of their sins by condemning themselves; the divine goodness has so decreed that the pardon of God can only be obtained by sinners through the prayer of the priests. Jesus Christ has Himself conferred upon the rulers of the Church the power of imposing canonical penance upon sinners who confess their sins, and of allowing them to receive the Sacraments of Christ, after they have purified their souls by a salutary satisfaction.... Every Christian, therefore, must examine his conscience, and cease deferring from day to day the hour of his conversion; he ought not to expect to satisfy God's justice on his deathbed. It is dangerous for a weak and ignorant man to defer his conversion to the last uncertain days of his life, when he may be unable to confess and obtain priestly absolution; he ought, when he can, to merit pardon by a full satisfaction for his sins."[31]

The great bishop St. Augustine (354-430) tells his flock "not to listen to those who deny that the Church has the power to forgive all sins."[32]

---

[29] Caesarius, *Sermon* 253:1.

[30] Caesarius, *Sermon* 211.

[31] Leo the Great, *Epis.* 108.

[32] Augustine, *De Agon. Christ.* 3; Ser. 295. 2.

St. Ambrose (340-397) declares that priests pardon all sins, not in their own name, but as "ministers and instruments of God."[33]

Paulinus of Milan (395), a biographer of St. Ambrose, explicitly mentions the fact that the saint heard confessions. He writes: "As often as anyone, in order to receive penitence, confessed his faults to him, he wept so as to compel him to weep.... But he spoke of the causes of the crimes which they confessed to none but the Lord alone."[34]

Origen (185-254) in his commentary of Psalm 28 writes: "When you have eaten some indigestible food, and your stomach is filled with an excessive quantity of humor, you will suffer until you have gotten rid of it. So in like manner sinners, who hide and retain their sins within their breasts, become sick therefrom almost to death. If, however, they accuse themselves, confess their sins, and vomit forth their iniquity, they will completely drive from their souls the principle of evil. Consider carefully whom you choose to hearken to your sins. Know well the character of the physician to whom you intend to relate the nature of your sickness.... If he gives you advice, follow it; if he judges that your sickness is of such a nature that it should be revealed publicly in church for the edification of the brethren and your own more effective cure, do not hesitate to do what he tells you."

The great preponderance of evidence shows that Confession was not a thirteenth century invention of the Church, but that it had already been in place for centuries before the Fourth Lateran Council was convoked. Still, opponents of the Church on this issue, although they cannot explain these early writings, continue to have a prob-

---

[33] Ambrose, *De Poen.*, 1:2.
[34] Paulinus of Milan, *Vita Ambrosii*, 39.

lem reconciling John 20:23 to anything other than Confession.

Many claim that Jesus is merely repeating His precept that we must forgive one another. But this presents a problem. It is true that Jesus taught throughout the Gospels that we are to forgive others who sin against *us*, but that is not what John 20:23 says. In this passage Jesus speaks only to His Apostles. He gave them the power to *choose* whether to forgive sins. Either He was contradicting Himself in this passage from previous admonishments to forgive "seven times seventy", or He was giving the Apostles a power never given man before. Since He would soon be ascending to heaven and no longer be personally present to forgive sins as He had during His ministry, He gave this power to His priesthood by way of the Apostles. As Karl Keating writes: "If there is an 'invention' here, it is not the sacrament of penance, but the notion that the priestly forgiveness of sins is not to be found in the Bible or in early Christian history."[35]

### 262. Does the priest actually forgive our sins?

Yes. The *Catechism of the Catholic Church* says that "[s]ince Christ entrusted to his apostles the ministry of reconciliation, [Cf. *Jn* 20:23; *2 Cor* 5:18] bishops who are their successors, and priests, the bishops' collaborators, continue to exercise this ministry. Indeed *bishops and priests*, by virtue of the sacrament of Holy Orders, *have the power to forgive all sins* 'in the name of the Father, and of the Son, and of the Holy Spirit.' "[36]

In any sacrament in which a priest or bishop is the minister he acts *in persona Christi*; that is, in the person of Christ. To put it in purely secular terms for a better

---

[35] Karl Keating, *Catholicism and Fundamentalism*, 189.
[36] *Catechism of the Catholic Church*, 1461 (emphasis added).

understanding, bishops and priests hold a sort of special ambassadorship.

If the U.S. Ambassador to Japan works out a certain agreement with the Japanese and signs that agreement, it is the ambassador's negotiations and signature which make that agreement binding. However, the ambassador has acted in the person of the President of the United States.

So, too, does a priest or bishop act in the Sacrament of Penance. He hears the penitent's sins and makes a judgment call regarding those sins — a power granted by Christ in John 20:23 (cf. Matthew 16:18; 18:18) — then he grants absolution of these sins.

### 263. Why do we have to confess our sins to the priest in order to obtain forgiveness?

As previously stated, Jesus gave His priesthood the power to forgive or retain sins in John 20:23. In order for the priest to be able to exercise the power of absolution, he must first hear the sins to determine if the penitent is contrite and intends to avoid those sins and their near occasions in the future.

### 264. What are the matter and form of the Sacrament of Penance?

The matter consists of the penitent's sins and the acts required of the penitent. There are three such acts: contrition (sorrow), confession of sins, and acceptance of the penance.

"The formula of absolution used in the Latin Church expresses the essential elements of this sacrament: the Father of mercies is the source of all forgiveness. He effects the reconciliation of sinners through the Passover of his Son and the gift of his Spirit, through the prayer and ministry of the Church:

God, the Father of mercies, through the death and resurrection of his Son, has reconciled the world to himself and sent the Holy Spirit among us for the forgiveness of sins; through the ministry of the Church may God give you pardon and peace, and I absolve you from your sins in the name of the Father, and of the Son, and of the Holy Spirit [*Ordo Paenitentiae* 46: formula of absolution]."[37]

### 265. Who must receive the Sacrament of Penance?

Anyone who has committed a mortal sin since the last time he has received the Sacrament of Penance.

### 266. What does the Sacrament of Penance do for us?

If well received, the Sacrament of Penance "brings about a true 'spiritual resurrection', restoration of the dignity and blessings of the life of the children of God, of which the most precious is friendship with God [Cf. *Lk* 15:32]."[38]

The Sacrament of Penance:
- restores or increases sanctifying grace;
- forgives our sins;
- obliterates eternal punishment due for mortal sins;
- helps us with additional strength to avoid future sins;
- and restores all the merits that have been lost by the commission of mortal sins.

### 267. What is required to make a good confession?

There are five elements necessary for us to make a good confession:
- we must make a good examination of conscience;
- be truly sorry for our sins;

[37] *Catechism of the Catholic Church*, 1449.
[38] *Catechism of the Catholic Church*, 1468.

- resolve not to sin again (called a firm purpose of amendment);
- confess our sins to a priest;
- and accept the penance the priest assigns us.

**268. What does it mean to make a good examination of conscience?**

In order to make a good examination of conscience we must make a deliberate recalling of all the sins we have committed since our last good confession. This is done by going over in our minds all that is required of us by God's commandments and the Church's laws. The Church recommends that we do a brief examination of conscience each night before bedtime, which makes it much easier to do before confession.

There are a number of prayer books and leaflets available that have a *printed* examination of conscience. They merely list God's commandments and the Church's laws in order. Under each commandment or law are questions we should ask ourselves, as they pertain to each commandment and law. The two best printed forms of an examination of conscience we have seen are found in the *Queen of Apostles Prayerbook*,[39] and the *Handbook of Prayers*.[40]

**269. What is contrition?**

No better answer is found anywhere than in the *Catechism of the Catholic Church*, which echoes the Council of Trent: "Among the penitent's acts, contrition occupies first place. Contrition is 'sorrow of the soul and de-

---

[39] Daughters of St. Paul, *Queen of Apostles Prayerbook* (50 St. Paul's Ave., Boston, MA 02130, 1989 ed.).

[40] Fathers Belmonte and Socias, *Handbook of Prayers* (Scepter Publishers, Inc., 20 Nassau St., Princeton, NJ 08542, 1992 ed.).

testation for the sin committed, together with the resolution not to sin again.' [Council of Trent (1551): DS 1676]"[41] Contrition is absolutely necessary in order to receive absolution in the Sacrament of Penance.

**270. How many kinds of contrition are there?**

There are two kinds of contrition: perfect and imperfect.

**271. What is perfect contrition?**

Perfect contrition — more formally called *contrition of charity* — is sorrow for our sins with the purest of motives. Perfect contrition is hatred for our sins solely for the love we have for God and the offense our sins cause Him. "Such contrition remits venial sins; it also obtains forgiveness of mortal sins *if it includes the firm resolution to have recourse to sacramental confession as soon as possible* [Cf. Council of Trent (1551): DS 1677]."[42]

**272. What is imperfect contrition?**

Imperfect contrition — more formally called attrition — is sorrow for our sin for less pure motives. Like perfect contrition, imperfect contrition is still a gift of God, a prompting of the Holy Spirit. We experience imperfect contrition when we are sorry for our sins because we fear hell, or because of the inherent evil of sin.

---

[41] *Catechism of the Catholic Church*, 1451.

[42] *Catechism of the Catholic Church*, 1452 (emphasis added).

### 273. Which kind of contrition must we have to receive the Sacrament of Penance well?

Although perfect contrition is the better of the two, and certainly most pleasing to God, we may receive the sacrament well if we at least have imperfect contrition.

### 274. Should we also be sorry for all our venial sins?

We should be sorry for all our venial sins primarily because all sins offend God, even venial sins. We should also be sorry for venial sins because they weaken our will to resist mortal sins, and they make us deserving of temporal punishment.

### 275. What does it mean to be firmly resolved to sin no more?

A firm resolution to sin no more (firm purpose of amendment) is simply a determination not to sin, and to avoid the near occasions of sin.

### 276. When should we express our contrition to God?

The rite of the Sacrament of Penance allows for recital of the prayer called the *act of contrition*, of which there are many, and we should be sincere in the recitation of this prayer. Of course, we are free — even encouraged — to make an impromptu act of contrition if we wish.

Furthermore, we should make an act of contrition prior to confession, particularly at the close of the examination of conscience. It is also a good practice to make an act of contrition immediately after we commit a sin, especially a mortal sin (*see Appendix Two*).

By *act* of contrition we mean an act of the will, causing our will to be sorry for the sins we commit. We should not confuse subjective emotion with an objective act. For example, we may *feel* anger without permitting our will to acquiesce.

**277. What is confession?**

Confession is the actual telling of our sins to the priest. This is the only way he can absolve our sins, as he has no way of knowing what to absolve without first hearing them.

"The confession (or disclosure) of sins, even from a simply human point of view, frees us and facilitates our reconciliation with others. Through such an admission man looks squarely at the sins he is guilty of, takes responsibility for them, and thereby opens himself again to God and to the communion of the Church in order to make a new future possible."[43]

**278. How should we go to confession?**

The following is the format for going to confession:
1. Greet the priest; make the Sign of the Cross.
2. Say "Amen" to the prayer of the priest, or a Bible reading, if any. Then say: "It has been (*one week, one month, etc.*) since my last confession: these are my sins:"
3. Tell your sins to the priest, at least *all mortal sins*, according to their kind (nature) and the number of times committed: and it is good to tell all your venial sins, even the smallest.
4. Ask any questions, if you have any.
5. Conclude with: "Father, for these and all the sins of my past life I am heartily sorry."
6. Listen to any counsel the priest may give, pondering it later.
7. The priest will next assign the penance. Remember what it is, as you are obliged to fulfill it.
8. The priest will say: "Now make a good act of contrition." Recite it aloud.

---

[43] *Catechism of the Catholic Church*, 1455.

9. The priest will next grant absolution. Your only response is "Amen", but you make the Sign of the Cross while he says: "I absolve you from your sins in the name of the Father, and of the Son, and of the Holy Spirit."

10. The priest will say: "Give thanks to the Lord for He is good."

11. You respond; "His mercy endures forever."

12. The priest will say: "God has freed you from your sins. Go in peace."

13. You respond: "Thank you, Father."

**279. Must we confess every sin?**

We must confess every mortal sin. "Without being strictly necessary, confession of everyday faults (venial sins) is nevertheless strongly recommended by the Church [Cf. Council of Trent: DS 1680; Code of Canon Law, can. 988§2]. Indeed the regular confession of our venial sins helps us form our conscience, fight against evil tendencies, let ourselves be healed by Christ and progress in the life of the Spirit."[44]

**280. Is there any sin God will not pardon?**

Absolutely speaking, no sin is unpardonable by either God or the Church. It is God's will that all men be saved (I Timothy 2:4), and His mercy is infinite. Provided we are truly sorrowful, and make a good confession, we will always be pardoned by God's unfathomable mercy and love.

Many people quote Christ in Matthew 12:32, where He says: "And whoever says a word against the Son of man will be forgiven; but whoever speaks against the Holy Spirit will not be forgiven, either in this age or in the age

---

[44] *Catechism of the Catholic Church*, 1458.

to come" (cf. Mark 3:30; Luke 12:10). They use these words of Our Lord to show that at least one sin is unpardonable, but the Church — who alone has the divine right to interpret Scripture — teaches quite the opposite.

This passage is a reference to the sinner who refuses to repent, despite the graces God offers him. Such a person doesn't actually receive God's pardon, because he fails to ask for it, or fulfill the necessary conditions to obtain it.

The sin mentioned by Christ in the above passage referred to the willful rejection by the Pharisees of the miracles He performed as proof of His divine mission, and their maliciousness in crediting them to the power of Satan.

### 281. Should fear or shame ever prevent us from confessing a mortal sin?

Speaking from a purely human psychological standpoint, it is easy to understand how a penitent would be tempted to withhold a mortal sin in confession from a sense of embarrassment or fear; however, from the standpoints of theology, logic and reason, such feelings are superfluous. The priest to whom we confess our sins is acting in the person of Christ. It is actually Christ to whom we are confessing.

Furthermore, the priest is bound by the *seal of confession*. That means that he can never tell a soul — including his own confessor — anyone's confession. In the 2000 year history of the Church, not once has this seal been broken; not even by renegade priests such as Martin Luther, the man responsible for the Protestant Revolt. Indeed, many priests have been jailed, tortured, and murdered rather than divulge the contents of a penitent's confession.

The seal of confession even extends to the point that a priest cannot even use the knowledge from a confession for any reason. Following is an example.

Let's say that Fr. Patrick has appointed Judas Avarice to oversee the parish finances. One day, Judas goes to Father in confession and tells him that he has embezzled $250,000 from the parish funds. Since Judas must replace the money to satisfy God's justice, Fr. Patrick tells him to repay the money. However, there are two things Father *cannot* do. He cannot tell the police and have Judas prosecuted, as that would break the seal of confession. Furthermore, Father cannot later replace Judas in his position, as this would be acting on knowledge obtained in confession. The seal of confession is that strict!

### 282. What if someone deliberately omits confessing a mortal sin?

If a penitent deliberately omits the confession of a mortal sin he commits the additional mortal sin of sacrilege, risking eternal punishment in hell; furthermore, he leaves the confessional without having any of his sins forgiven. In order to be forgiven and re-acquire God's sanctifying grace, the penitent must confess the sin of sacrilege, any Holy Communion he received since his sin of sacrilege (which is itself a sin of sacrilege to be confessed), all of the sins from his sacrilegious confession, and all of the mortal sins he has committed since. It is much easier — emotionally and spiritually — to make a good confession in the first place.

If you are ever tempted to withhold a mortal sin in confession, immediately tell the priest and ask his help. The temptation will flee.

**283. What should we do if we *forget* to confess a mortal sin?**

Should we *forget* to confess a mortal sin it is okay to receive Communion, as God forgave the sin, because we made a good confession and did not deliberately omit a mortal sin: however, we are obliged to confess the forgotten mortal sin the next time we go to confession.

**284. May a priest refuse to give absolution?**

Yes, he may; provided the penitent shows no sign of sorrow for the mortal sins he has confessed, or if he indicates that he will not break with the sin.

For example, a man confesses several acts of adultery because he has a mistress. The confessor tells the man he must break off the adulterous relationship. The man refuses. The priest would be right to refuse absolution.

*Satisfaction for Sin*

**285. Why do we receive a penance after confession?**

We receive a penance to make at least some satisfaction for our sins, thus decreasing the punishment we deserve for those sins.

**286. What should we do after confession?**

We should first take time to thank God for the graces to make a good confession. Then, as soon as possible, we should perform the penance assigned with thoughtfulness, love, and devotion.

**287. Does the Sacrament of Penance remove all punishment due to sin?**

The Sacrament of Penance always removes all the eternal punishment in hell that is deserved by mortal sin, but it does not necessarily remove all the temporal punishment.

### 288. Why is temporal punishment required by God?

If God is infinitely merciful He must also be infinitely just. He cannot be perfect — in other words, cannot be God — if He is more merciful than just, and vice versa. Therefore, He must demand justice for our offenses.

Let's try to understand God's perfectly balanced justice and mercy by way of analogy. Let's say a friend borrows your car. He has a minor accident that dents the fender. He returns the car and says, "I wrecked your car. I'm sorry. Will you forgive me?" You are a good Catholic, so you reply, "Sure, I forgive you. Now, pay for the damage."

God, from whom our own sense of justice flows, reacts the same way to our sins. He says, "Sure, I forgive you. Now, pay for the damage of your sins."

### 289. How can we satisfy the debt of temporal punishment we owe to God for our sins?

The debt of temporal punishment can only be satisfied either in purgatory or on earth. Since there is no merit in purgatory, and since purgatory is not a pleasant place, we are far and away better off to satisfy the debt in this life.

The means of satisfying this debt, which also contributes to our own sanctification, are voluntary acts of penance, devout participation in the Mass, prayer, fasting, almsgiving, earning indulgences, performing the spiritual and temporal works of mercy, and patiently accepting the trials and sufferings God chooses to permit in our lives.

*Communal Celebration*

### 290. What is a communal celebration of Penance?

A penitential communal celebration consists of three primary elements: a communal penitential service; private confession and absolution; and a communal act of thanksgiving. The Second Vatican Council stated that "[t]he sacrament of Penance can also take place in the framework of a *communal celebration* in which we prepare ourselves together for confession and give thanks together for the forgiveness received. Here, the personal confession of sins and individual absolution are inserted into a liturgy of the word of God with readings and a homily, an examination of conscience conducted in common, a communal request for forgiveness, the Our Father and a thanksgiving in common."[45]

*First Penance*

### 291. When should children begin to go to confession?

Children should begin the habit of frequent confession when they reach the use of reason, usually at about seven years of age.

### 292. Should first Penance precede First Holy Communion?

Absolutely! A first penance must be made prior to First Holy Communion, as so commanded by the Church. This practice helps to preserve a child's innocence, aids in spiritual growth, and strengthens the child's will against temptations.

---

[45] *Sacrosanctum concilium*, 26.

*Indulgences*

### 293. What are indulgences?

"An indulgence is a remission before God of the temporal punishment due to sins whose guilt has already been forgiven, which the faithful Christian who is duly disposed gains under certain prescribed conditions through the action of the Church which, as the minister of redemption, dispenses and applies with authority the treasury of the satisfactions of Christ and the saints."[46]

In simpler terms, an indulgence "is a remission of the whole or part of the temporal punishment due to forgiven sin, granted by the Pope and the Bishops out of the Church's spiritual treasury, which is made up of the infinite redemptive merits of Jesus Christ, and the superabundant merits of the saints. It is more than a mere remission of canonical words of penance, for it really remits the whole or part of the punishment due the sinner by God, either here or in Purgatory...,

"The divine power of the Church to grant indulgences may be better understood, if we compare it with the State's custom of pardoning the whole or part of the punishment inflicted by the civil law upon the criminal. The President has the right to grant a complete pardon to any criminal within the confines of the United States; the Governor to any criminal in his State. The State, moreover, remits part of a criminal's punishment for good behavior while in prison.

"The State officials may grant a criminal pardon, even if he is not sorry for his crime, out of deference to powerful friends; the Church, on the contrary, never remits the

---

[46] Pope Paul VI, apostolic constitution, *Indulgentiarum doctrina*, Norm 1, 1967.

punishment unless the sinner has manifested his sorrows."[47]

Indulgences are granted in two forms: plenary and partial. A plenary indulgence remits all of the punishment due to forgiven sins. A partial indulgence remits some portion of the punishment due to forgiven sin.

**294. For whom and how can we gain an indulgence?**

We may gain an indulgence for ourselves or the poor souls in purgatory. We must be in a state of grace, have the desire to gain the indulgence, and perform the good acts required by the Church.

[47] Bertrand Conway, C.S.P., *The Question Box*, 294-295.

## Anointing of the Sick

### 295. What is the Anointing of the Sick?

The Anointing of the Sick is the sacrament instituted by Christ which gives spiritual health, and sometimes — within the providential will of God — physical healing, to persons who are in danger of death due to a serious illness, injury, or old age.

### 296. How do we know that Jesus instituted the Anointing of the Sick?

All the proof we need for this is found in the biblical writings of the Apostle James: "Is any among you sick? Let him call the elders of the church, and let them pray over him, anointing him with oil in the name of the Lord; and the prayer of faith will save the sick man, and the Lord will raise him up; and if he has committed sins, he will be forgiven" (James 5:14-15). Of course, we also see in the Gospels where Christ sends his Apostles and other disciples to perform this act while preaching (cf. Mark 6:12-13).

### 297. What does the Anointing of the Sick do for us?

The Anointing of the Sick increases sanctifying grace; allows the sick person the grace of uniting himself more closely to Christ's Passion, giving suffering a new meaning; "strengthens against the temptations of the evil one, the temptation to discouragement and anguish in the face of death [Cf. *Heb* 2:15]", removes temporal punishment due to sin; removes venial sin; and "lead[s] the sick person to healing of the soul, but also of the body if such is God's will [Cf. Council of Florence (1439): DS 1325]."[48]

---

[48] *Catechism of the Catholic Church*, cf. 1520-1523.

**298. How is the Anointing of the Sick a sacrament of reconciliation?**

This sacrament reconciles sinners to God in that it remits venial sins. Also, if the sick person is unable to make a good confession prior to receiving the sacrament (e.g., coma, delirium, paralysis, etc.) it will remit mortal sins as well, provided the sick person has at least imperfect contrition. If the sick person regains his health he is obliged to make a good confession if he was not in a state of grace prior to receiving the Anointing of the Sick.

**299. Who can confer the Anointing of the Sick?**

Only a validly ordained priest may confer the Anointing of the Sick.

**300. Who may receive the Anointing of the Sick?**

Anyone may receive the Anointing of the Sick who is baptized, has reached the use of reason, and is in danger of death — but not necessarily at the point of death — from sickness, old age, or injury.

**301. How should one prepare to receive the Anointing of the Sick?**

In order to best receive this sacrament, and if possible, one should prepare by making a good confession, making acts of faith, hope and charity, and be completely resigned to God's holy will.

**302. What is the matter of this sacrament?**

The proximate matter is the actual anointing. The remote matter is plant oil (usually olive oil) which has been blessed by the bishop or an authorized priest. Any priest may bless the plant oil in the event of an emergency.

### 303. How is the Anointing of the Sick conferred?

"The celebration of the sacrament includes the following principal elements: the 'priests of the Church' [*Jas* 5:14] — in silence — lay hands on the sick; they pray over them in the faith of the Church [Cf. *Jas* 5:15]...; they then anoint them with oil blessed, if possible, by the bishop."[49]

### 304. May the anointing be administered to a person about to undergo surgery?

Yes, this sacrament may and should be administered to anyone about to undergo surgery, if the surgery is for a serious condition, or if general anesthetic is being used. (No matter how minor the surgery, general anesthetic can be a risk to life.)

### 305. May a person be anointed more than once?

Yes, a person may be anointed more than once, if his condition worsens, or if he gets better and then has a relapse. The elderly, whether sick or in good health, may receive this sacrament at regular intervals.

### 306. May an unconscious person receive this sacrament?

An unconscious person may and should receive the anointing, if he is in danger of death.

### 307. Should a priest be called even if someone is apparently dead?

If any doubt at all exits that the person is already dead, resolve the doubt by calling a priest. Just because there

---

[49] *Catechism of the Catholic Church*, 1519.

are no brain waves, no heart beat, and no respiration does not necessarily mean the person is dead.

A certain man was lying in a bed in a large hospital of a major city. He was comatose when doctors made their final examination. He had no vital signs, so the physicians pronounced him dead. The poor man could hear all of this, but was incapable of alerting the doctors!

At that moment, a priest, responding to an earlier call, came into the room. The doctors told the priest he was wasting his time, that the patient was already dead. But the good priest, obedient to the teachings of the Church, ignored the doctors and began to administer the anointing.

Suddenly, the man regained consciousness and sat up in bed. He thanked the priest for his faithfulness, and explained all he had experienced.

This anecdote teaches us that the Anointing of the Sick not only cures the sick — when God so wills — but that apparent death is not necessarily real death. Be sure to call a priest to administer the anointing, even if the person has appeared to be dead for several hours.

## Holy Orders

### 308. What is Holy Orders?

"Holy Orders is the sacrament through which the mission entrusted by Christ to his apostles continues to be exercised in the Church until the end of time: thus it is the sacrament of apostolic ministry. It includes three degrees: episcopate [bishop], presbyterate [priest], and diaconate [deacon]."[50]

### 309. Who can administer Holy Orders?

Only a validly consecrated bishop can administer Holy Orders, and only with papal permission for each administration.

Note: *For a discussion of the hierarchy of Holy Orders, and the responsibility of those in the hierarchy, please refer to Questions 84-95.*

### 310. Who may receive Holy Orders?

" 'Only a baptized man (*vir*) validly receives sacred ordination.' [1983 Code of Canon Law, can. 1024.] The Lord Jesus chose men (*viri*) to form the college of the twelve apostles, and the apostles did the same when they chose collaborators to succeed them in their ministry [Cf, *Mk* 3:14-19; *Lk* 6:12-16; 1 *Tim* 3:1-13; 2 *Tim* 1:6; *Titus* 1:5-9; St. Clement of Rome, *Ad Cor.* 42, 4; 44, 3: Patrologia Graeca 1, 292-293; 300].... The Church recognizes herself to be bound by this choice made by the Lord himself. For this reason the ordination of women is not possible [Cf. John Paul II, *Mulieris Dignitatem* 26-27; Congregation for the Doctrine of the Faith, Decl. *In-*

[50] *Catechism of the Catholic Church*, 1536.

*ter insigniores*: Acta Apostolicae Sedis 69 (1977) 98-116].
No one has a *right* to receive the sacrament of Holy Orders ... he is called to it by God [Cf. *Heb* 5:4]."[51]
    The male candidate for the priesthood must be a good
Catholic, prepare himself by the necessary studies, have
the intention of giving his life to God's service, and be
accepted by his bishop or a religious superior for ordination.

### 311. What are the effects of Holy Orders?
    The effects of this sacrament are many. As with all of
the sacraments after baptism, Holy Orders increases sanctifying grace, gives a sacramental grace, and imprints an
indelible character on the soul.
    The increase in sanctifying grace is necessary for all
people, as this is how we strive to fulfill Christ's command that we are to "be perfect, as your heavenly Father
is perfect" (Matthew 5:48). This is important in a special
way to the recipient of Holy Orders, as this man must be
a Christ-like example to the souls he shepherds, as well
as save his own soul.
    The sacramental grace of Holy Orders benefits not
only the ordained, but also the lay faithful. This is so
because the sacramental grace of this sacrament allows
the priest[52] or deacon to truthfully proclaim the Gospel,
fulfill the ministry of the word of truth, and renew the
people by the "bath of rebirth" (baptism). The priest also
offers the Holy Sacrifice of the Mass, and reconciles sinners to God by way of the Sacrament of Penance.
    The sacramental grace of Holy Orders is especially
evident in the confessional. When a penitent goes to the

---

[51] *Catechism of the Catholic Church*, 1577-1578.
[52] Unless otherwise noted, we use the word priest here as a term that
is inclusive of the office of bishop.

same confessor with regularity and frequency, the priest comes to know the penitent's soul intimately. The sacramental grace he received in Holy Orders helps the priest to lead that soul on a journey to perfection in God.

There are also special benefits for a bishop from the sacramental grace of Holy Orders. Thanks to this grace, bishops have the ability to govern their dioceses (territories assigned to bishops by the Pope), as well as to present Church teachings in a manner that best benefits the souls of his flock.

Finally, the priest, by virtue of the sacrament of Holy Orders, acts *in persona Christi*. St. Thomas Aquinas says that "Christ is the source of all priesthood: the priest of the old law was a figure of Christ, and the priest of the new law acts in the person of Christ"[53] in the fulfillment of his liturgical-sacramental duties.

### 312. What are the chief supernatural powers of the priest?

Of these chief supernatural powers there are two: the power to change ordinary bread and wine into the Body and Blood of Jesus Christ in the Holy Sacrifice of the Mass; and to forgive sins in the Sacrament of Penance.

### 313. Why is it that priests do not marry?

"All the ordained ministers of the Latin Church ... are normally chosen from among men of faith who live a celibate life and who intend to remain *celibate* 'for the sake of the kingdom of heaven.' [*Mt* 19:12] Called to consecrate themselves with undivided heart to the Lord and to 'the affairs of the Lord,' [1 *Cor* 7:32] they give themselves entirely to God and to men. Celibacy is a

---

[53] St. Thomas Aquinas, *Summa Theologiae*, III, 22, 4c.

sign of this new life to the service of which the Church's minister is consecrated; accepted with a joyous heart celibacy radiantly proclaims the Reign of God [Cf. *Presbyterorum Ordinis* 16]."[54]

### 314. Do some Catholic priests marry?

In accord with their ancient traditions, and with approval from the Holy See, some priests of the various Eastern Rite Catholic Churches do marry. However, if they plan to marry, they must do so before ordination.

### 315. What is the role of the deacon?

Deacons are helpers of bishops and priests, and are subject to their authority. Deacons may officiate at weddings, perform baptisms, carry Communion to the sick, infirm, or confined, preside at graveside services at funerals, and serve in various other non-liturgical capacities.

### 316. May deacons marry?

A man who is already married may become a deacon, but he cannot remarry if his wife dies, nor can a married deacon become a priest.

### 317. How should we regard bishops and priests?

In this age of rudeness, disrespect, and crass familiarity, bishops and priests are often treated with grave disrespect and irreverence. Catholics who are guilty of this should be ashamed, and all others should be scandalized. The humility of priests and bishops often prevents them from chastising people for acts of disrespect, so lay people should work to correct the situation. After all, each of these men of Holy Orders daily perform miracles that the

---

[54] *Catechism of the Catholic Church*, 1579.

laity cannot. By their hands and words alone the Creator of the universe comes down from heaven to the altar. By their words and intentions alone are your sins forever obliterated from God's holy record.

A priest should be addressed as Father, because he is our spiritual father. A bishop should be addressed as Your Excellency, in keeping with old European court manner, as the highest form of respect. It is not wrong to kiss a priest's hand, because his alone holds the Body of Christ. It is not wrong to bow and kiss a bishop's ring in greeting, as this is a gesture of our fidelity and respect to his apostolic office. In this era of evil and uncertainty, we should return to the concreteness of reality that is the holy priesthood.

**318. Why do Catholics call the priest "Father" when Jesus commanded us not to call anyone Father, except God in heaven?**

The implied objection in this question refers to Christ's words in Matthew 23:9 when Jesus said: "And call no man your father on earth, for you have one Father, who is in heaven." People who make an objection to Catholics calling their priests "Father" do not consider Our Lord's words in context, nor do they consider the totality of Sacred Scripture.

Christ tells us in Matthew to call no man father, yet God gives us the fourth commandment: "Honor your father and your mother" (Exodus 20:12). Either there exists a contradiction between God the Father and God the Son, which is impossible, or those who say Catholics are wrong to call priests Father wrongly interpret Jesus' words in Matthew.

Christ was not finding fault with either the word rabbi (teacher) or father, but rather was teaching us that God alone is the source of all authority. The rebuke Jesus gave was not of the use of the word father, but of the pride of the Pharisees (cf. Matthew 23:2-10). If the rebuke was of the words father and teacher, no one would be right to call his male parent father; nor would he be right to call his old high school instructor teacher. No, it's absurd to believe Jesus was condemning the use of these words.

The early Christians never interpreted these words literally. St. Paul refers to himself as Timothy's father in Philippians 2:22 and I Timothy 1:2. He also refers to himself as the spiritual father of his converts: "For though you have countless guides in Christ, you do not have many fathers. For I became your *father* in Christ Jesus through the gospel" (I Corinthians 4:15). In writing to other Christian leaders, the Apostle John called them fathers: "I am writing to you, *fathers*, because you know him who is from the beginning" (I John 2:13). Are we to believe these two great Apostles, who were promised to remember all Christ had taught them with the assistance of the Holy Spirit, would directly and blatantly disobey Christ? The objection made against Catholics from Matthew 23:9 is without foundation.

## Matrimony

### Christian Marriage

**319. What is Matrimony?**

Matrimony is the sacrament instituted by Christ which unites for life a baptized man and a baptized woman for the purposes of fulfilling their lawful responsibilities to God, for which God gives them grace.

**320. What is the purpose of marriage?**

Unity and procreation is the two-fold purpose of marriage. By unity we mean that the bond of the Sacrament of Matrimony lasts until death, and that man and woman are to live together as one (Matthew 19:5-5). By procreation we mean the begetting and rearing of children in the fear and love of God. In short, the two-fold purpose of marriage is the giving of love and the giving of life.

**321. Is there another dimension to Christian marriage?**

As a natural extension of the giving of love, God gives the spouses all the graces necessary to help one another grow in holiness. Just as children produced in the matrimonial bond are a manifestation of marital love, so too is a positive response to God's graces by the parents to help their children become holy a manifestation of that love.

**322. When is marriage a sacrament?**

Marriage is a sacrament when both husband and wife are baptized. If one or both are not baptized at the time of marriage, the marriage is non-sacramental. The marriage becomes retroactively sacramental as soon as both husband and wife are baptized.

### 323. How do we know that Jesus instituted the Sacrament of Matrimony?

God instituted matrimony in the Garden of Eden, when He created Adam and Eve. Before the coming of Christ, matrimony was a *sacred contract*, but not a sacrament. Jesus raised matrimony to the level of a sacrament.

Jesus taught the indissolubility of marriage (cf. Matthew 19:6), and this requires supernatural help (grace). Paul compares Christian marriage to the permanent union between Christ and His Church (cf. Ephesians 5:22-23) and stresses its importance, reinforcing the sacramental character of matrimony. Also, early Christian writers refer to Christian marriage as something supernatural, which confers grace upon those who receive it. Finally, the Church has defined Matrimony as one of the seven sacraments instituted by Christ.

At the marriage feast at Cana, Christ worked His first miracle, thus manifesting the holiness of the married state. In the marriage contract, God has made a natural relation a means of grace for Christians.

### 324. How is the Sacrament of Matrimony conferred?

A baptized man and a baptized woman confer this sacrament upon each other by exchanging their marital vows of mutual consent before the Church.

### 325. What are the matter and form of Matrimony?

The matter is the mutual consent of the spouses to give themselves to each other. The form consists in the words or actions through which the spouses express their consent.

**326. Who is the minister of the Sacrament of Matrimony?**

The ministers are the bride and groom themselves. Each confers the sacrament on the other, in the presence of a witnessing priest or deacon.

**327. What is necessary for the worthy reception of Matrimony?**

Matrimony should be received by persons in the state of grace, who understand the responsibilities of married life and follow the marriage laws of the Church.

**328. What is the ordinary law regarding Matrimony?**

The ordinary law of the Church requires that a Catholic be married in the presence of a priest or a deacon and before two witnesses.

**329. Why does the Church make laws regarding the marriages of Catholics?**

The Church makes marriage laws because she has authority from Christ over all the sacraments and other spiritual matters that affect baptized persons.

**330. What is a Nuptial Mass?**

A Nuptial Mass is a Wedding Mass with special prayers to obtain God's blessings for the couple. Like the marriage feast at Cana, a Nuptial Mass makes Jesus truly present. A Nuptial Mass is not obligatory, but it is the most appropriate setting for the celebration of Matrimony.

**331. What are the effects of Matrimony?**

First, there is, as in all the sacraments after baptism, an increase in sanctifying grace.

Next, there is a *"marriage bond* [that] has been established by God himself in such a way that a marriage concluded and consummated between baptized persons can never be dissolved,"[55] except by death.

Finally, there is the sacramental grace of Matrimony. "This grace ... is intended to perfect the couple's love and to strengthen their indissoluble unity. By this grace they 'help one another to attain holiness in their married life and in welcoming and educating their children.' [*Lumen Gentium* 11§2; cf. *Lumen Gentium* 41]"[56]

**332. What would happen if one or both spouses were not in the state of grace at the time of their marriage?**

A mortal sin of sacrilege would be committed; however, the sacrament would have been performed, and the spouses would be truly married. Sanctifying grace would be restored, and the sacramental graces of matrimony received, as soon as the spouse or spouses made a good confession.

*Preparation for Matrimony*

**333. How should a Catholic prepare for marriage?**

"It is imperative to give suitable and timely instruction to young people, above all in the heart of their own families, about the dignity of married love, its role and its exercise, so that, having learned the value of chastity, they will be able at a suitable age to engage in honorable courtship and enter upon a marriage of their own."[57]

Once a Catholic has begun to date, he or she should pray for God's help in choosing a partner, consult his or her parents and confessor, live a virtuous and chaste life,

---

[55] *Catechism of the Catholic Church*, 1640.
[56] *Catechism of the Catholic Church*, 1641.
[57] *Gaudium et spes*, 49.3.

receive the Sacraments of Penance and Holy Eucharist often, and attend the premarital courses set up by the local bishop once a partner has been chosen.

The Church recommends that the bride and groom should prepare themselves for marriage by receiving the sacrament of penance. We would further recommend, for the sanctification of the bride and groom, and to give the marriage the proper focus, a spiritual retreat, guided by a good priest who is experienced with the affairs of the soul. After all, there are three being married: the bride, the groom, and God.

### 334. What qualities should one look for in a marriage partner?

The most important criterion for choosing a spouse is that he or she will help us walk toward the cross and salvation. We seek a spouse with reverence for God and the teachings of the Catholic Church, as well as a spirit of charity, industry and thrift.

### 335. What is meant by "impediments" to marriage?

Impediments are obstacles which can prevent a couple from marrying or can make a marriage unlawful. Some of these impediments are: lack of age, impotence, an existing valid marriage, a close blood relationship, or affinity.

### 336. If a couple marries without being aware of a serious impediment, is the marriage valid?

No, the marriage is invalid. A priest should be consulted, because in some cases a dispensation can be obtained from the bishop for the impediment. Then the marriage can be rectified, or blessed by the Church. In other cases, the marriage is simply void — non-existent.

**337. If a Marriage is found to be null, are the children illegitimate?**
No. The children produced in such a marriage are *legitimate* children of a *putative* marriage.

**338. What is a mixed marriage?**
Strictly speaking, a mixed marriage is a marriage between a Catholic and a baptized non-Catholic. A marriage between a Catholic and a non-baptized person is called "disparity of cult."

**339. Why does the Church discourage mixed marriages?**
Married people are called to perfect union of mind and communion of life, and this union can be broken or weakened when differences of opinion or disagreements touch on matters of religious truths and convictions.

**340. May a dispensation be obtained for a mixed marriage?**
Yes. It is normally sought from the bishop through a priest.

**341. What must the Catholic party express when asking for this dispensation?**
The Catholic spouse must declare that he or she is prepared to remove all dangers to his or her Faith. He or she also has the grave obligation to promise to have each of the children baptized and raised Catholic.

**342. What is the non-Catholic's role in this regard?**
Prior to the marriage, the non-Catholic party must be informed of the Catholic party's promises and obligations. He or she is to be well instructed in the duties, responsibilities, and character of Matrimony.

### 343. Is separation ever permitted by the Church?

The Church permits a couple to separate for serious reasons, with the bishop's permission, but without the right to remarry.

### 344. Is civil divorce ever permitted?

Civil divorce with the right to remarry is never permitted, because it is against God's law; however, a civil divorce for legal reasons is sometimes permitted by the bishop, but neither partner may remarry while the other partner is still living.

### *Children*

### 345. Can one validly enter into marriage with the intention of not having children?

One cannot validly enter into a marriage with the intention of not having children, because procreation is one of the primary purposes of marriage, as given by God.

### 346. Are Catholic couples obliged to have as many children as possible?

Catholic couples are not obliged to have as many children as possible, but rather to act in a responsible manner in bringing children into the world and rearing them well. Included in this responsibility is the recognition that the procreation of children is one of the fundamental purposes of marriage. This means that abortion and artificial birth control are forbidden by God and the Church.

### 347. Is marriage rendered invalid by childlessness?

No. If a couple married with the intention of accepting the children God would send them, childlessness does not render the marriage invalid.

## Duties of the Married

**348.  What are the chief duties of spouses to one another?**

These chief duties are fidelity, cohabitation, and mutual assistance. Fidelity is the obligation of each partner to refrain from any activity that is proper only to marriage with anyone other than the spouse. Cohabitation means that a husband and wife are to live together. Mutual assistance means friendship and mutual love, and all that they imply.

**349.  What are the special duties of a husband?**

A husband's special duties are to exercise his God-given authority with love, kindness, and respect toward his wife (Ephesians 5:25) and toward his children (Colossians 3:21).

**350.  What are the special duties of a wife?**

A wife's special duties are to agree with her husband in everything that is not sinful, and to be loving, devoted and generously dedicated to her children and the care of her home.

**351.  How can couples accomplish their duties and persevere in love until the end of their lives?**

By asking God daily for the assistance of His grace. This is absolutely necessary for couples to fulfill their roles as spouses and parents.

## Sacramentals

### 352. What is a sacramental?

Sacramentals "are sacred signs which bear a resemblance to the sacraments. They signify effects, particularly of a spiritual nature, which are obtained through the intercession of the Church [*Sacrosanctum Concilium* 60; cf. Code of Canon Law, can. 1166; Corpus Canonum Ecclesiarum Orientalium, can. 867]."[58]

### 353. How does a sacramental obtain blessings from God?

These blessings are obtained from the prayers that the Church offers for those using the sacramental, and because of the devotion that the object, action or word inspires.

### 354. What blessings are obtained through sacramentals?

Some of the blessings obtained through sacramentals are actual graces, the forgiveness of venial sins, the removal of temporal punishment deserved by our sins, health and other material blessings, and defense against the devil.

### 355. How do sacramentals differ from the sacraments?

Sacramentals are instituted by the Church, but the sacraments were instituted by Jesus Himself. Sacramentals obtain grace by the prayers of the Church, but the sacraments operate by the direct action of Christ. Finally, sacramentals are partly dependent upon the faith and dis-

---

[58] *Catechism of the Catholic Church*, 1667.

positions of the person using them, while the sacraments depend solely on the direct power of Christ.

### 356. Why did the Church institute sacramentals?

Sacramentals were instituted by the Church to add more dignity to the ritual of the sacraments, to help us receive the sacraments with better dispositions, and to inspire us to strive for holiness.

### 357. What are two principal sacramentals?

Two principal sacramentals are the liturgical year and the Liturgy of the Hours, called the breviary. However, among all sacramentals, blessings come first.

### 358. What is the liturgical year?

The liturgical year is a sacred time embracing the entire year, from the first Sunday of Advent to the last Sunday of Ordinary Time. It is a sacramental because it has been established by the Church to help us reflect on the mystery of our salvation and thus be inspired to live our life in conformity with the life of our Redeemer.

### 359. How is the liturgical year divided?

The liturgical year is divided into five seasons:
1. Advent: we prepare for the coming of Christ at Christmas and at the end of the world;[59]
2. Christmas Season: we adore Christ in His birth, infancy and hidden life;[60]
3. Lent: we commemorate Jesus' passion and death for our sins;

---

[59] Advent and Lent are seasons of penance.

[60] Christmas and Easter are festive seasons.

4. Easter Season: we celebrate the greatest event in human history, the resurrection of Jesus from the dead, His ascension into heaven, and Pentecost;
5. Ordinary Time: we reflect on the teachings of Christ during the thirty-three to thirty-four weeks of this season.

### 360. What is the Liturgy of the Hours?

The Liturgy of the Hours is the public prayer of the Church, and it is obligatory for men of Holy Orders and most men and women religious, according to the rule of their communities. It is highly recommended for the laity. Its "celebration, faithful to the apostolic exhortations to 'pray constantly,' is 'so devised that the whole course of the day and night is made holy by the praise of God.' [*Sacrosanctum Concilium* 84; *1 Th* 5:17; *Eph* 6:18.]"[61]

The liturgy of the Hours consists of seven prayers spaced throughout the waking hours: morning prayer, three daytime prayers, office of the readings, evening prayer, and night prayer. Not at all inconvenient, the Liturgy of the Hours, if properly prayed, takes less than a total of one and a half hours — the longest office takes twenty minutes, the shortest requires five minutes — so it is ideal for the laity, especially for those who cannot attend daily Mass.

### 361. What are the sacramentals most used by Catholics?

The sacramentals most used by Catholics are holy water, crucifixes, rosaries, medals, statues, scapulars, candles, blessed ashes, and blessed palms.

---

[61] *Catechism of the Catholic Church*, 1174.

*The Rosary*

## 362. What is the Rosary?

The Rosary is a prayer in honor of the Blessed Virgin, consisting of one hundred fifty *Hail Marys* and fifteen *Our Fathers* accompanied by meditation on the life, passion, and glory of Christ.

## 363. How did the Rosary originate?

In the first centuries of Christianity there were many hermits who could not read the one hundred fifty psalms, their daily prayer devotion. So they would substitute one Our Father and one Hail Mary for each psalm, and they would use stones or seeds strung on a cord to keep track of the number.

St. Dominic was the first to make generally accepted the practice of substituting one hundred fifty Hail Marys for the psalms. In the thirteenth century, heresy ravaged southern France and northern Italy, and the Pope appointed St. Dominic to preach against the heretical doctrines. Dominic had little success, so he prayed to the Blessed Virgin for the conversion of the heretics through the Rosary that she herself gave him. God blessed Dominic's devotion, and he was then successful in converting the heretics.

## 364. Has God given His approval to the Rosary through miracles?

The greatest miracle is always the conversion of a sinner to repentance through Christ's Church. The Rosary is a powerful prayer to obtain grace from God through the intercession of the Blessed Virgin. Quite literally innumerable are the conversions that had their beginning in the devotion of the Rosary! Hundreds of millions of Catholics make a practice of praying the Rosary daily.

The Rosary has also been responsible for miracles in times of danger and calamity. Such was the case with the Turks in the battle of Lepanto (1571), and the deliverance of Vienna (1683). It was in thanksgiving for these victories over the Moslems, who were trying to wipe Christianity from the face of the earth, that the Pope instituted the feast of the Holy Rosary on October 7.

### 365. Is the Rosary simple to pray?

The very simplicity of the Rosary makes it an ideal prayer for children, as it is easily memorized and begins children in the good habit of daily meditation; however, the contemplative aspects of the Rosary also make it satisfying to the soul and intellect of adults.

### 366. How is the Rosary prayed?

One third of the Rosary is ordinarily prayed: fifty Hail Marys and five Our Fathers prayed on a string of beads slipped through the fingers. The Rosary combines vocal and mental prayer. It is a summary of the most important parts of the Gospels. Catholics should not fail to pray at least five decades of the Rosary every day.

Ordinarily, we begin the Rosary with the Sign of the Cross and by reciting the Apostles' Creed. Then we pray one Our Father, three Hail Marys, and one Glory be to the Father for an increase in the virtues of faith, hope, and charity.

We pray the Our Father on the beads between each decade, and the Hail Mary on each of the ten consecutive beads. One Our Father and ten Hail Marys are referred to as a decade. It is customary to close each decade with a Glory be to the Father.

While we pray each decade, we should meditate upon one mystery of our Faith.[62] The Rosary is divided into three sets of five mysteries: the joyful, the sorrowful, and the glorious, each honoring respectively the life, passion and death, and glorification of Jesus Christ.

The rosary is typically ended by praying the *Hail Holy Queen* and the Sign of the Cross.

### The Brown Scapular

**367. What is the Brown Scapular?**

The full name of the Scapular is the Brown Scapular of Our Lady of Mt. Carmel. It is two small pieces of brown cloth, usually wool, attached by two cords. It is worn by placing it over the shoulders so that one piece of the cloth rests on the wearer's chest, the other on the back between the shoulder blades. The Scapular is usually worn beneath the person's clothing.

**368. What is the origin of the Brown Scapular?[63]**

Devotion to Our Lady of Mt. Carmel goes all the way back to the 8th century BC. Elias the prophet had ascended Mt. Carmel in Palestine to begin a long tradition of contemplation and prayer. Based on God's promise in Genesis 3:15 that the Savior would enter the world through a woman, Elias began a devotion to the Mother of God 800 years before she was even born. Elias and his fol-

---

[62] See the appendix for a listing of the fifteen mysteries.

[63] For the complete history and theology on the Brown Scapular, we recommend that the reader obtain the most exhaustive book on the subject of which we are aware: *Sign of Her Heart*, by John Mathias Haffert. It may be ordered from the World Apostolate of Fatima, P.O. Box 976, Washington, NJ 07882.

lowers dedicated themselves to this most chosen woman among all women to become the Mother of the Savior.

On the Jewish feast of Pentecost, the day the Holy Spirit awakened the Church, the spiritual descendants of Elias and his followers came down from Mt. Carmel to attend the ancient feast at Jerusalem.

At Peter's preaching the good hermits realized the Lady to whom they were devoted had come and given birth to the Savior, and that He had completed the work of redemption. Consequently, they were baptized by the Apostles. When the hermits were presented to Our Lady they were overcome with a sense of majesty and sanctity which they never forgot. Upon their return to Mt. Carmel, they erected the first chapel ever built in honor of the Blessed Virgin Mary. From that time to present, devotion to the Mother of God has been handed down by the hermits of Mt. Carmel.

In 1241, the Baron de Grey of England returned from the Crusades, bringing with him a group of Carmelites from the holy mountain. He generously gave the hermits a manor house in Aylesford for their religious order to live in and grow.

Ten years later, at the donated manor house, St. Simon Stock was praying to Our Lady for help when she appeared to him. As Mary handed St. Simon the Brown Scapular she said, "This shall be the privilege for you and all Carmelites, that anyone dying in this habit shall be saved."

### 369. Why do we wear the Scapular?

When Our Lady gave the Brown Scapular to St. Simon Stock, she made the following promise: "Take this Scapular. Whosoever dies wearing it shall not suffer eternal fire. It shall be a sign of salvation, a protection in danger, and a pledge of peace." On the very day that Our Lady gave the Scapular to St. Simon, Lord Peter of Lenton urgently called the saint: "Come quickly, Father, my brother is dying in despair!" St. Simon went immediately to the dying man, asking Our Lady to keep her promise. When draped with Simon's Scapular, the man immediately repented, made a good confession, and died in the state of grace. That night the dead man appeared to his brother and said, "I have been saved through the most powerful Queen and the habit of that man as a shield."

**370. Has God given approval to the Scapular through other miracles?**

Yes! There are far too many miracles to mention, so we shall treat only one here.

In the late summer of 1845, the English ship, *King of the Ocean*, found itself in a terrible hurricane. A Protestant minister, together with his wife and children and other passengers, struggled to the deck to pray for mercy and forgiveness, as the ship was about to sink and all aboard perish.

Among the crew was a young Irishman, John McAuliffe. Realizing the situation was hopeless, the young man opened his shirt, took off his Scapular, made the Sign of the Cross with it over the angry waves, and tossed it into the ocean.

At that moment the sea became calm. Only one more wave washed over the deck, tossing young John's Scapular at his feet. He put it back on, and went about his business. Mr. Fisher, the minister, had observed all of McAuliffe's actions. Upon questioning the young man, the minister and his family were told about the Holy Virgin and her Scapular. The Fishers were so impressed that they became Catholics as soon as possible, thus enjoying the Virgin's patronage.

### 371. May a non-Catholic wear the Scapular?

Yes! In so doing, a non-Catholic will receive many graces and blessings with this special sign of devotion to the Mother of God.

## Christian Morality

### Conscience

**372. What is conscience?**

"Conscience is a judgment of reason whereby the human person recognizes the moral quality of a concrete act that he is going to perform, is in the process of performing, or has already completed."[64]

**373. Must we follow our conscience?**

After diligent reflection, when we are certain something is the right thing to do, we must follow our conscience.

**374. But isn't conscience merely a formation of thought from a person's culture or religious belief system?**

No, conscience is not of human origin. Each human person "has in his heart a law inscribed by God."[65] The conscience is the most secret inner core of man, and it is a part of the soul's faculty of intellect. We are not aware of our conscience from the brain, a mere human organ, but from the movement of the soul. No neurologist or scientist can tell us what part of the brain governs the conscience, because the brain is incapable, as an organ, to judge the difference between good and evil.

**375. Are we truly responsible for our actions?**

Yes, we are responsible for all our actions, because God gave us an intellect and free will. We must use them

---

[64] *Catechism of the Catholic Church*, 1778.

[65] *Gaudium et spes*, 16.

to fulfill the purpose for which we were created, which is to know, love, and serve God in this life so we can be forever happy with Him in the next. To use the intellect and free will for anything contrary to God's laws is an abuse of those gifts.

### 376. What is a right conscience?

A right conscience is one in conformity with the natural law, divine law, and the Church's moral teachings.

### 377. How can a right conscience be formed?

We form a right conscience by studying God's moral code, as authoritatively taught by the Church. By learning and understanding Christian morality, and with the aid we ask from the Holy Spirit, we can form a conscience that will lead us to sanctity and salvation.

### 378. What is a doubtful conscience?

A doubtful conscience is one that cannot decide for or against the morality of an act. One must either refrain from acting or resolve the doubt. We may never act upon a doubtful conscience, as it is a sin to do so.

### 379. What is a scrupulous conscience?

A scrupulous conscience is one that is constantly in doubt. It is in dread of sin when none exists, or in dread of mortal sin when the sin is only venial. The ordinary cure for a scrupulous conscience is obedience to a good and wise confessor. Absent of such obedience, a person with a scrupulous conscience may eventually have to seek medical help from a competent mental health professional.

### 380. What is a lax conscience?

A lax conscience is one that judges more by convenience than by God's law. "This is the case when a man 'takes little trouble to find out what is true and good, or when conscience is by degrees almost blinded through the habit of committing sin.' [*Gaudium et spes* 16.] In such cases, the person is culpable for the evil he commits."[66]

**381. Is everything that is legal morally right?**

Not necessarily. Until the middle of the twentieth century, the laws of our occidental society could almost always be counted on to follow the moral norms of the natural law. This is not so any longer, as the example of legalized abortion demonstrates. We are obliged only to obey laws that comport to God's law, and we are forbidden to obey laws contrary to God's, even under the threat of imprisonment or death (Acts 5:29).

**382. Does a good end ever justify the use of evil means?**

We may never commit evil that good may come from it. Indeed, we must be willing to make whatever sacrifices are necessary to keep God's law.

Let's say that a police officer is called to testify in a criminal trial. The defense attorney has cornered the officer on a technicality during cross examination. The defendant's guilt is not in dispute, but he could be freed on the basis of this minor legal technicality. All the officer has to do to avoid having the case dismissed and the felon released is to tell a small lie. Can the officer tell this untruth? Absolutely not! He must be willing to see the case dismissed, the felon freed, and himself disgraced rather than to lie.

---

[66] *Catechism of the Catholic Church*, 1791.

**383. If a person errs because of invincible ignorance, does the person sin?**

No, a person cannot sin because he is invincibly ignorant (unavoidably unknowledgeable) of a moral situation. However, invincible ignorance "remains no less an evil, a privation, a disorder. One must therefore work to correct the errors of moral conscience."[67]

[67] *Catechism of the Catholic Church*, 1793.

## The Ten Commandments

### 384. What are the two great commandments?

The first is that " '[y]ou shall love the Lord your God with all your heart, and with all your soul, and with all your mind, and with all your strength.' The second is this, 'You shall love your neighbor as yourself.' There is no other commandment greater than these" (Mark 12:30-31).

### 385. How can we practice the two great commandments?

Simply by fulfilling the ten commandments, which are encompassed by the two great commandments. The first three of the ten commandments deal with man's relationship to God. The last seven deal with man's relationship to both God and man.

### 386. Where did the ten commandments come from?

"They were written 'with the finger of God' [*Ex* 31:18; *Dt* 5:22], unlike the other commandments written by Moses [Cf. *Dt* 31:9-24]."[68] They set forth the natural law.

### 387. What are the ten commandments?

The ten commandments are:
1. I, the Lord, am your God. You shall have no other gods besides me.
2. You shall not take the name of the Lord, your God, in vain.
3. Remember to keep holy the Lord's day.
4. Honor your father and your mother.

---

[68] *Catechism of the Catholic Church*, 2056.

5. You shall not commit murder.
6. You shall not commit adultery.
7. You shall not steal.
8. You shall not bear false witness against your neighbor.
9. You shall not covet your neighbor's wife.
10. You shall not covet anything that belongs to your neighbor.
   [Cf. *Ex* 20:1-17].

**388. Can we always keep the ten commandments?**

Yes. No matter how great the temptation, we can always keep God's commandments because He will always give us the necessary actual graces to do so (cf. Sirach 15:15).

**389. Is it enough merely to keep the ten commandments?**

No, keeping the ten commandments alone is not enough. We must always be willing to do the will of God in order to glorify God.

## The First Commandment

**"I, the Lord, am your God. You shall have no other gods besides me."**

*Divine Worship*

**390. What are we obliged to do by the first commandment?**

The first commandment obliges us to love God above all things, and to worship and adore only Him.

**391. How do we show God our love?**

We show God we love Him by believing in Him and His teachings, thanking Him, trusting Him, asking His forgiveness for failing Him in sin, asking for His help, doing penance for our sins, and obeying His laws.

**392. Are we to pray to God privately or with others?**

Since we are both individuals and social creatures, we should pray to God in private and with others.

**393. Is there any particularly important way to worship God?**

Participating well in the Holy Sacrifice of the Mass is the most important way to worship God.

**394. What does the first commandment forbid?**

The first commandment forbids superstition, idolatry, spiritism, sacrilege, atheism, and participating in certain acts of non-Catholic worship.

## 395. What is superstition?

Superstition is attributing to a creature a power that belongs only to God. Examples would be to use "lucky charms" or to be ruled by dreams.

## 396. What is idolatry?

"Idolatry consists in divinizing what is not God. Man commits idolatry when be honors and reveres a creature in place of God, whether this be gods or demons (for example, satanism), power, pleasure, race, ancestors, the state, money, etc."[69]

## 397. What is spiritism?

"*Spiritism* often implies divination [conjuring the dead or having recourse to demonic powers] or magical practices."[70]

## 398. What is sacrilege?

Sacrilege is an act of irreligion. It is the mistreatment of sacred persons, places, or things. An example would be to receive Communion if a state of mortal sin, since this would be an abuse of the Eucharist.

## 399. What is atheism?

Atheism is the denial of God's existence, or living a lifestyle that completely ignores God and His Laws.

## 400. Why is it wrong for Catholics to participate in certain acts of non-Catholic worship?

Although we should promote ecumenism as often as possible (ecumenism is the dialogue between Catholics and non-Catholics which leads to the reconcilliation of

[69] *Catechism of the Catholic Church*, 2113.
[70] *Catechism of the Catholic Church*, 2117.

all Christians in the unity of the one and only Church of Christ), there are still certain acts of non-Catholic worship that are wrong, because such activity would imply that a Catholic believes other religions that lack the fullness of truth are on an equal par with Catholicism. For example, Catholics may never participate in Protestant communion services, often called the "Lord's Supper" by them, because Christ is only truly present in the Holy Eucharist on Catholic altars; normally Catholics are not permitted to attend the wedding of a Catholic who is being married outside the Church, because this implies that the Sacrament of Matrimony, which is a form of worship because it is a sacrament, is not necessary to be married. When in doubt, consult your pastor.

### Honoring the Blessed Virgin and the Saints

### 401. Does the first commandment allow us to honor and pray to the Blessed Virgin and the saints?

Not only does the first commandment permit us to honor the Blessed Virgin and the saints, but Sacred Scripture encourages us to do so. In speaking of the just who have passed on from this mortal life, Sirach writes: "Their bodies were buried in peace, and their names live to all generations. Peoples will declare their wisdom, and the congregation proclaims their praise" (Sirach 44:14-15). In her *Magnificat*, Mary makes this prophetic statement: "For behold, henceforth all generations will call me blessed" (Luke 1:48).

### 402. What do we call the honor given to Mary and the saints?

There are three types of honor that can be given: latria, hyperdulia, and dulia. *Latria* is adoration and must be given to God alone. *Dulia* is the honor we give to the saints on all three planes: in the Church Suffering, in the Church Victorious, and in the Church Militant. In other words, this is the honor due to all Christians in this life and the next, but it is commonly thought of as the honor (also called veneration) given to the saints in heaven. Finally, there is *hyperdulia*, that veneration which is reserved to the Blessed Virgin alone.

Hyperdulia is reserved to Mary because she is the most special saint of human history. The Catholic Church has always paid special honor to the Blessed Virgin, because God honored her above all creatures by granting her the highest dignity He could confer — the divine maternity.

**403. How does the Church honor the Mother of God?**

The Church honors the Mother of God in the liturgy and various devotions. She encourages the faithful to know, imitate, love and pray to the Blessed Virgin in a special way. After all, from the beginning of her Son's public ministry until today she has been His chief evangelist, as she proved when she first spoke the words: "Do whatever he tells you" (John 2:5).

**404. Does the Blessed Virgin pray for us?**

Yes, the Blessed Virgin does pray for us, and her intercession is very powerful (cf. John 2:1-11).

**405. Why does the Church honor the angels?**

The Church honors the angels for several reasons. Firstly, in the order of nature the angels hold a superior position to all of creation. Secondly, they perpetually adore the Blessed Trinity. Finally, God has made them His special messengers to help us to attain our salvation.

**406. Why do we honor and pray to the saints?**

We honor and pray to the saints because they are His special friends who, through His grace, led holy lives and reflected His virtues to a heroic degree. By honoring the saints we honor God Himself.

This should not seem unusual to non-Catholics, as honoring people has always been a common practice. We call ministers *Reverend*, judges *Your Honor*, and refer to lawyers and politicians as *The Honorable*. Furthermore, God Himself commands us to *"honor* your father and mother" (Exodus 20:12); and in compliance with God's law, traditional wedding vows call upon the wife to "love, honor, and obey" her husband.

Karl Keating says that "if there can be nothing wrong with honoring the living, who still have an opportunity to ruin their lives through sin, or the uncanonized dead, about whose state of spiritual health we can only guess, certainly there can be no argument against giving honor to saints whose lives are done and who ended them in sanctity. If merit deserves to be honored wherever it is found, it surely should be honored among God's special friends."[71]

**407. How do we honor the saints?**

We honor the saints by learning about their lives so we can imitate their virtues, praying to them for their intercession, and respecting their relics and images.

**408. Why do we honor the bodies and relics of the saints?**

By honoring the bodies and relics of saints we are not only venerating their bodies and objects connected with

---

[71] Karl Keating, *Catholicism and Fundamentalism*, 260-261.

them (relics), but we are actually venerating the person whose relic it is. An excellent biblical example is found in Acts 19:11-12.

God Himself has given great honor to the bodies of many of His special friends by not permitting them to know decay after death. These bodies, none of which were embalmed or are mummified, have been left perfectly preserved as God's stamp of approval on the lives of these saints.[72]

## Images

### 409. Does the first commandment allow us to make use of statues and images?

Yes, provided they do not become objects of false worship. God forbade the Jews to make graven images because they lived among pagans, and that influence made them inclined to worship images.

Those who accuse Catholics of violating the first commandment because of our use of statues and holy cards do not properly interpret this commandment. We know that the Jews did not interpret this commandment as an absolute prohibition against images. There are many examples in Sacred Scripture to prove this. God forbade images in the first commandment, yet He ordered the brazen serpent (Numbers 21:8-9), and the golden cherubim atop the Ark of the Covenant (Exodus 25:18-20). Then there were also the carved garlands of flowers, fruit and

---

[72] For an excellent exposition on these saints whose bodies have been preserved by God from decay, we recommend *The Incorruptibles* by Joan Carroll Cruz (TAN Books, P. O. Box 424, Rockford, IL 61105). Over 100 saints are featured, and there are photographs of many of them in their incorrupt state.

trees (Numbers 8:4), and the carved lions that supported the king's throne (I Kings 7:27-37).

To criticize Catholics for the use of images is not honest. In order for these critics to be honest they would have to forbid themselves of the personal use of coinage, currency, photographs, sculptures, paintings, and even television.

**410. How should images and statues of Christ and the saints be treated?**

Such images and statues should be treated with the same respect we would treat pictures of our loved ones.

**411. Do Catholics pray to images, crucifixes and statues?**

Absolutely not! When Catholics pray before such images they are praying to the persons those images represent. Many of us carry photographs of our wife or children, but we never mistake the photograph for the wife herself.

## The Second Commandment

## "You shall not take the name of the Lord, your God, in vain."

### *Reverence in Speech*

**412. What are we obliged to do by the second commandment?**

The second commandment obliges us to always speak of God, the Blessed Virgin Mary, the saints and sacred persons, places and things with reverence. It also obliges us to take oaths truthfully, and to be faithful in fulfilling promissory oaths and vows.

**413. Why are we obliged to speak respectfully of sacred persons, places and things?**

We are so obliged because sacred persons, places and things are consecrated to God.

**414. What does the second commandment forbid?**

The second commandment forbids profanity, blasphemy, cursing, and carelessness or deceit in taking oaths and making vows.

**415. What is profanity?**

Profanity is *"the abuse of God's name*, i.e., every improper use of the names of God, Jesus Christ, but also of the Virgin Mary and all the saints."[73] We violate this — usually in a venial way — when, for example, we abuse these holy names when expressing anger or surprise.

---

[73] *Catechism of the Catholic Church*, 2146.

## Blasphemy and Cursing

### 416. What is blasphemy?

Blasphemy "consists in uttering against God — inwardly or outwardly — words of hatred, reproach, or defiance; in speaking ill of God, in failing in respect toward him in one's speech; in misusing God's name… The prohibition of blasphemy extends to language against Christ's Church, the saints, and sacred things… Blasphemy is contrary to the respect due God and his holy name. It is in itself a grave sin. [Cf. Code of Canon Law, can. 1369.]"[74]

### 417. What is cursing?

Many mistakenly believe that cursing is the use of vulgar language. This could not be further from the truth. While the use of vulgar language can be sinful if used in mixed company, or in the presence of children, in and of itself, vulgar language is not inherently evil. The equation of vulgar language with cursing is the result of a puritanistic morality that influences our occidental culture.

Cursing is actually what the term implies: the invoking of evil upon a person, place or thing. It is sinful to curse animals or things chiefly because of the uncontrolled anger or impatience involved. It is sinful to curse a human being because that person is made in the image and likeness of God.

[74] *Catechism of the Catholic Church*, 2148.

*Oaths and Vows*

### 418. What is an oath?

An oath is calling upon God to witness the truthfulness of what we say.

### 419. Under what conditions may we use an oath?

We may use an oath if:

- we have a good reason for taking it;
- we are sure we are speaking the truth;
- we do not have a sinful intention.

### 420. What constitutes a good reason for taking an oath?

The glory of God, the good of our neighbor, or our own personal good are valid reasons for taking an oath.

### 421. What is perjury?

Perjury is deliberately asking God to witness a lie. This abuse of an oath is a mortal sin.

### 422. Are we obliged to keep a promissory oath?

Such oaths are "[p]romises made to others in God's name [to] engage the divine honor, fidelity, truthfulness, and authority. They must be respected in justice. To be unfaithful to them is to misuse God's name and in some way to make God out to be a liar. [Cf. 1 *Jn* 1:10.]"[75]

### 423. What is a vow?

A vow is a free and deliberate promise made to God, by which a person binds himself under pain of sin to do

---

[75] *Catechism of the Catholic Church*, 2147.

something especially pleasing to God. The most common vows are those of poverty; chastity, and obedience, taken by members of religious orders. These and other vows may also be made by private individuals but they are cautioned to do so only after having consulted their confessor.

**424. What must one remember before making a vow?**
   One must remember that one is obliged to fulfill any vow made.

## The Third Commandment

## "Remember to keep holy the Lord's day."

### *Participation in the Mass*

**425. What are we obliged to do by the third commandment?**

"The precept of the Church specifies the law of the Lord more precisely: 'On Sundays and other holy days of obligation the faithful are bound to participate in the Mass.' 'The precept of participating in the Mass is satisfied by assistance at a Mass which is celebrated anywhere in a Catholic rite either on the holy day or on the evening of the preceding day.' "[76] This commandment also obligates us to avoid any activities which hinder the renewal of body and soul.

**426. Why are we obliged to participate in the Mass rather than simply worship God in our hearts?**

The Mass is the highest form of worship of God there is, as it is the perpetuation of Christ's redeeming sacrifice on the cross. As St. John Chrysostom wrote: "You cannot pray at home as at church, where there is a great multitude, where exclamations are cried out to God as from one great heart, and where there is something more: the union of minds, the accord of souls, the bond of charity, the prayers of the priests."[77]

---

[76] *Catechism of the Catholic Church*, 2180. (This paragraph excerpt from the C.C.C. quotes two of the canons from the Universal Code of Canon Law [1983]: can. 1247; can 1248.1.).

[77] St. John Chrysostom, *De incomprehensibili* 3, 6:PG 48, 725.

**427. Is it necessary to be physically present at Mass?**

Yes, we must be physically present at the Mass in order to fulfill our obligation. Televised Masses, although a consolation to the homebound who are unable to attend Mass, are not acceptable as a means of fulfilling our Sunday obligation. Furthermore, to miss a notable part of the Mass — that is, to arrive late or leave early — could be a sin and not meet the Sunday obligation.

**428. At what age does the obligation to participate in Mass begin?**

The obligation to participate in the Mass begins at the age of the use of reason; that is, at about seven years of age.

**429. How grave is the obligation to participate in the Mass on Sundays and holy days of obligation?**

Unless one is excused because of a very good reason, one commits a mortal sin to fail to participate in the Mass on Sundays and holy days.

**430. Why was Sunday set aside as the Lord's day in place of the Sabbath of the Old Testament?**

It obviously took some time for the Apostles to alter the Lord's day from the Sabbath to Sunday, as we see them continuing to attend the temple services on the Sabbath, followed by Mass on Sunday. From the Apostolic tradition of celebrating the Mass on Sunday we have come to know that as the Lord's day (Acts 20:7).

## A Day of Rest

### 431. What does the third commandment tell us to avoid?

We are to refrain from unnecessary servile works; that is, "work or activities that hinder the worship owed to God, the joy proper to the Lord's Day, the performance of the works of mercy, and the appropriate relaxation of mind and body. [Cf. Code of Canon Law, can. 1247.]"[78]

### 432. How else may we sanctify Sundays and the holy days?

"Christians will also sanctify Sunday by devoting time and care to their families and relatives, often difficult to do on other days of the week."[79]

---

[78] *Catechism of the Catholic Church*, 2185.

[79] *Catechism of the Catholic Church*, 2186.

## The Fourth Commandment

### "Honor your father and your mother."

*Children and Parents*

**433. What are we obliged to do by the fourth commandment?**

The fourth commandment obliges us to respect our parents, obey them in all that is not sinful, and help them in their needs.

**434. What is the source and basis of parental authority?**

"The divine fatherhood is the source of human fatherhood [Cf. *Eph* 3:14]; this is the foundation of the honor owed to parents. The respect of children, whether minors or adults, for their father and mother [Cf. *Prov* 1:8; *Tob* 4:3-4] is nourished by the natural affection born of the bond uniting them. It is required by God's commandment."[80]

**435. How do children show love and respect for parents?**

Children show their love and respect by speaking and acting with gratitude, trying to please their parents, readily accepting corrections, seeking parental advice in important decisions, and praying for their parents.

---

[80] *Catechism of the Catholic Church*, 2214.

**436. Do grown children still have obligations to their parents?**

Yes. Children are obliged to continue in the respect of their parents, and they are to give both material and moral support when their parents are in need.

**437. What are the duties of parents toward children?**

Parents are to provide for the spiritual and physical needs of their children.[81] *"The role of parents in education* is of such importance that it is almost impossible to provide an adequate substitute."*[82]

**438. What does the fourth commandment forbid?**

The fourth commandment forbids disobedience toward our parents and every form of disrespect, unkindness, stubbornness, spitefulness, wishing them evil, and violence.

### All Lawful Authority

**439. Does the fourth commandment also oblige us to obey all lawful authority?**

"God's fourth commandment also enjoins us to honor all who for our good have received authority in society from God. It clarifies the duties of those who exercise authority as well as those who benefit from it."[83]

**440. The term "lawful authority" includes whom?**

"Lawful authority" includes teachers, employers, public officials, and Church leaders.

---

[81] *Catechism of the Catholic Church*, 2221-2226.
[82] *Gravissimum educationis*, 3.
[83] *Catechism of the Catholic Church*, 2234.

*Workers and Employers*

### 441. What are the duties of workers toward their employer?

Workers are to respect their employer, and to serve him faithfully according to their agreement.

### 442. How should employers treat their workers?

Employers are to treat their workers with respect and fairness, bearing in mind that the authority God has given them is limited.

*Citizens and Public Officials*

### 443. What must a citizen do for his nation?

A citizen must love and be in the service of his country, obey just laws, respect the legitimate authority, pay his taxes, exercise his right to vote, and defend his country.[84]

### 444. Are we obliged to follow civil laws that contradict God's law?

No, we must never obey laws that are contrary to God's law. In fact, we are to work for the change of such laws.

### 445. Is it a sin to vote for an enemy of religion or of the common good?

If, after responsibly informing ourselves of the political issues and candidates, we discover that a candidate is an enemy of religion or of the common good, it could be a sin to vote for that candidate. Such a vote could equate to a voluntary participation in that candidate's evil. A

---

[84] *Catechism of the Catholic Church*, cf. 2238-2240.

common example in the modern political scene might be to vote for a candidate who favors legalized abortion over a candidate who is pro-life.

**446. What are the most important duties of public officials?**

"*Political authorities* are obliged to respect the fundamental rights of the human person... dispense justice humanely..."[85] and work for the common good.

[85] *Catechism of the Catholic Church*, 2237.

## The Fifth Commandment

## "You shall not commit murder."

*Sins Against Life*

### 447. What does the fifth commandment forbid?

The fifth commandment forbids intentional homicide, abortion, euthanasia, child abuse, sterilization, suicide, and all that can lead to physical or spiritual harm to oneself or others, such as anger, fighting, revenge, drunkenness, drug abuse, torments inflicted on body or mind, hatred, and bad example.

### 448. What is intentional homicide?

Intentional homicide is the unjust taking of a human life.

### 449. What is abortion?

Abortion is the intentional killing of a pre-born child at any time after conception. The God-given authority of a parent *does not* extend to the taking of the life of the pre-born child. Abortion, in any form, is always a mortal sin. The Church has taught from her inception that abortion is morally evil.[86]

### 450. Does rape or incest justify abortion?

Abortion is never justified, no matter what the cause of the child's conception. It is easy to understand how a mother would be inclined to not want a child conceived in the case of rape or incest, but the child still has as much

[86] *Catechism of the Catholic Church*, cf. 2270-2275.

right to life as the mother. The Church is very sympathetic to such involuntary mothers, and many organizations and agencies within the Church are set up to provide for counseling, temporal and medical assistance, and adoption as a moral alternative to abortion.

**451. Does the Church impose any penalty upon a person who procures an abortion?**

Yes, the Church does *automatically* impose the penalty of excommunication upon any person who procures an abortion.[87] This penalty extends to anyone who aids in its procurement or otherwise participates in any way with any abortion. This automatic excommunication, then, could extend, say, to Catholic politicians who are "pro-choice."

**452. What is excommunication?**

Excommunication is "[a] penalty or censure by which a baptized Roman Catholic is excluded from the communion of the faithful, for committing and remaining obstinate in certain serious offenses specified in canon law; e.g. heresy, schism, apostasy, abortion… by excommunication [the Catholic] is deprived of [Church membership and its spiritual goods] until he repents and receives absolution."[88]

**453. What is "indirect abortion"?**

Indirect abortion is not really abortion at all. Indirect abortion occurs when a surgical procedure is performed on a mother for a serious pathological condition in which the intention is to save the mother's life. In such a case,

---

[87] *Catechism of the Catholic Church*, cf. 2272.
[88] Felician A. Foy, ed., *1994 Catholic Almanac*, (Huntington, IN: Our Sunday Visitor, 1993), pg. 308.

the death of the fetus is an incidental and secondary result, which would have been avoided if possible. The fetus should still be baptized.

### 454. What is euthanasia?

Euthanasia, also called mercy killing, "consists in putting an end to the lives of handicapped, sick, or dying persons. It is morally unacceptable."[89]

### 455. Why is euthanasia immoral?

Euthanasia is immoral because life is taken with the excuse of avoiding pain, shortening suffering, or eliminating someone who is supposedly useless to society because of old age, defect, or illness. Only God can decide when life should end.

Christ sanctified suffering on the cross. For those who suffer and are not Catholic, the Holy Spirit can use that suffering in the process of the suffering person's conversion. The person who is already a Catholic can unite his suffering with the crucified Christ, thereby making his prayers very powerful and honorable in the sight of Christ.

### 456. Is it ever lawful to take the life of another?

It can be lawful to take the life of another person when there is no other means to defend one's own life or the life of another. "The act of self defense can have a double effect: the preservation of one's own life; and the killing of the aggressor... The one is intended, the other is not."[90] "Legitimate defense can be not only a right but a grave duty for one who is responsible for the lives of others.

---

[89] *Catechism of the Catholic Church*, 2277.

[90] St. Thomas Aquinas, *Summa Theologiae*, II-II, 64, 7, corp. art.

The defense of the common good requires that an unjust agressor be rendered unable to cause harm."[91] It can also be lawful to take the life of another person in a just war.

### 457. Does lawful public authority have the right to put a criminal to death?

Like abortion, capital punishment has come to be perceived more as a political question than a moral question. Few issues are more hotly debated than the death penalty, but the Roman Catholic Church has remained firmly resolved in the consistency of her moral teaching in this area.

If only the politicians, political pundits, and electorate would listen to Christ through His Church (Luke 10:16)! The Church tells us that she "does not exclude recourse to the death penalty, if this is the only possible way of effectively defending human lives against the unjust agressor."[92] However, she continues to say that "[i]f... non-lethal means are sufficient to defend and protect people's safety from the aggressor, authority will limit itself to such means...."[93] Due to the advanced state of modern penology, this essentially rules out the use of capital punishment in occidental society, but still does not make it immoral.

### 458. Why is direct or culpable suicide sinful?

Direct suicide is a mortal sin because God alone has the right over life and death. When a person commits suicide he attempts to displace God and His rightful authority. Of course, the victim of suicide who suffers from

---

[91] *Catechism of the Catholic Church*, 2265.

[92] *Catechism of the Catholic Church*, 2267.

[93] *Catechism of the Catholic Church*, 2267.

elements that restrict his free will may not be responsible for his act in God's sight.[94]

### 459. Is sterilization ever permitted?

When done with the intention of preventing conception, sterilization is always sinful. Direct sterilization removes for selfish reasons the procreative power given for the generation of human life. *Indirect* sterilization is not sinful, as it is done to correct a serious pathological condition.

### 460. Is abuse of alcohol and drugs sinful?

Any excess is sinful, and the abuse of drugs and alcohol is always excessive. Furthermore, the abuse of alcohol and drugs not only does harm to mind and body, but it places the abuser in a position where his own excesses can be harmful to others.

### 461. What is scandal?

Scandal is giving another person the occasion of committing sin through one's words, actions, or omissions.

*Preserving Life*

### 462. To what does the fifth commandment oblige us regarding physical life and health?

We are obliged to take the ordinary means to preserve our own life and health and that of our neighbor so far as we are able.

---

[94] *Catechism of the Catholic Church*, cf. 2280-2283.

**463. Are we obliged to take extraordinary means to preserve our life?**

We are not obliged to take extraordinary means which involve extreme difficulty in order to preserve our life. However, extraordinary means are to be taken when the person is very necessary to his family, the Church, or society.

**464. May a person ever risk his own life or health?**

A person may risk his life or health if there is a proportionately serious reason. A good example would be to sacrifice your own life to save another. This is, after all, what Jesus did for us all on the cross.

**465. Is the transplantation of vital organs ever permitted?**

The Church does permit the transplantation of vital organs, provided the donor is already truly dead, or if he can lead a normal life without the organ. Donating a kidney is an example.

## The Sixth And Ninth Commandments

**"You shall not commit adultery.
You shall not covet your neighbor's wife."**

### *The Commandments About Purity*

**466.  Why are the sixth and ninth commandments treated together?**

These two commandments are treated together because they both deal with sexual purity. The sixth commandment deals with external sexual purity, and the ninth commandment deals with interior purity.

### *The Sixth Commandment*

**467.  What is the sixth commandment?**

"You shall not commit adultery" (Exodus 20:14).

**468.  What are we obliged to do by the sixth commandment?**

The sixth commandment obliges us to be pure and modest in behavior when both alone and with others.

**469.  What does the sixth commandment forbid?**

The sixth commandment forbids impurity and immodest behavior, and everything that leads to impurity.

### 470. What are some of the sins committed against the sixth commandment?

Some of the sins committed against the sixth commandment are adultery, fornication, contraception, homosexual activity, prostitution, premarital sex, masturbation, and pornography.

*Fornication and Adultery*

### 471. What is fornication?

Fornication is sexual intercourse between an unmarried man and an unmarried woman.

### 472. What is adultery?

Adultery is sexual intercourse between two persons, at least one of whom is married. (cf. Matthew 5:27-28.)

*Contraception*

### 473. Why is contraception seriously sinful?

Contraception is seriously sinful because it rejects chaste married love and defies God by wanting to increase pleasure while avoiding the God-given responsibility of procreating children. Furthermore, the irresponsible use of sex via contraception leads to a lack of respect for both sex, the marriage partner as a person, and life.

### 474. What about the Pill?

The Pill is evil morally, ethically, and medically. It condemns women to a premature death, impedes the conception of children and destroys life in the womb. Furthermore, use of the Pill leads people into other immoral sexual activities that lead to eternal punishment in hell.[95]

### Overcoming Sterility and Natural Family Planning

**475. Are fertility drugs morally acceptable?**
Yes. In fact, the Church teaches that "[r]esearch aimed at reducing human sterility is to be encouraged...."[96]

**476. What about *in vitro* fertilization (test tube babies)?**
This is a moral evil because it "dissociate[s] the sexual act from the procreative act."[97]

**477. What about the use of sperm or an ovum from a third party?**
"Techniques that entail the dissociation of husband and wife, by the intrusion of a person other than the couple (donation of sperm or an ovum, surrogate uterus), are gravely immoral."[98]

**478. How should married persons who are sterile view their situation?**
"The Gospel shows that physical sterility is not an absolute evil. Spouses who still suffer from infertility after exhausting legitimate medical procedures should unite themselves with the Lord's Cross, the source of all

---

[95] It is suggested that married persons read the following two papal encyclicals: *Humanae Vitae*, written by Pope Paul VI in 1968; and *Evangelium Vitae*, from Pope John Paul II in 1995. Both are available from the Daughters of St. Paul (see appendix).
[96] *Catechism of the Catholic Church*, 2375.
[97] *Catechism of the Catholic Church*, 2377.
[98] *Catechism of the Catholic Church*, 2376.

spiritual fecundity. They can give expression to their generosity by adopting abandoned children or performing demanding services for others."[99]

### 479. Are there methods of birth control that do not offend God?

Yes, there are natural methods of birth control which do not offend God if used for right reasons.[100]

### 480. What is Natural Family Planning?

Natural Family Planning refers to several methods, which are in conformity to the biological harmonies God has impressed upon the human nature. These methods use no chemicals nor gadgets. They are based on sound scientific knowledge; and they are completely harmless, reliable, and healthy.

### 481. Is Natural Family Planing morally and religiously acceptable?

*Rightly used*, Natural Family Planning is morally and religiously acceptable.

### 482. What do we mean by "rightly used"?

By "rightly used" we mean that Natural Family Planning requires the use of intelligence and self-control, and that it should only be used when married people have serious motives for spacing out births.

---

[99] *Catechism of the Catholic Church*, 2379.
[100] The foremost promoter and teacher of these various forms of morally acceptable birth control is the *Couple to Couple League*, founded and operated by John and Sheila Kippley. The address is: P.O. Box 111184, Cincinnati, OH 45211. Phone: 513-471-2000.

**483. What might create serious reasons for spacing out births?**

Serious reasons for spacing out births may come from physical or psychological conditions of the husband or wife, or from external conditions. However, selfishness is a sinful motive.

### Homosexual Activity, Premarital Sex, Masturbation

**484. What is homosexual activity?**

Homosexual activity is sexual relations between people of the same sex. Homosexuality is a gravely disordered condition, and homosexual activity is always mortally sinful.

**485. Why is homosexual activity immoral?**

"Basing itself on Sacred Scripture, which presents homosexual acts as acts of grave depravity,[101] tradition has always declared that 'homosexual acts are intrinsically disordered.' [Congregation for the Doctrine of the Faith, *Persona humana* 8.] They are contrary to the natural law. They close the sexual act to the gift of life. They do not proceed from a genuine affective and sexual complementarity. Under no circumstances can they be approved."[102] We must remember, though, that it is homosexual *activity* that is immoral, not the homosexual person. Although being homosexual is disordered, as long as the homosexual lives a chaste life, it is no more immoral to be a homosexual than to be a heterosexual.

---

[101] Cf. Genesis 19:1-29; Romans 1:24-27; I Corinthians 6:10; I Timothy 1:10.
[102] *Catechism of the Catholic Church*, 2357.

### 486. What is premarital sex?

Premarital sex is sexual intercourse before marriage, founded on the error that in it consists the total commitment of the future spouses. Such sexual relations arc mortally sinful, because sex is reserved to the bond of matrimony.

### 487. What is masturbation?

Masturbation is "the deliberate stimulation of the genital organs in order to derive sexual pleasure. 'Both the Magisterium of the Church, in the course of a constant tradition and the moral sense of the faithful have been in no doubt and have firmly maintained that masturbation is an intrinsically and gravely disordered action.' [Congregation for the Doctrine of the Faith *Persona humana* 9.]"[103]

## *The Ninth Commandment*

### 488. What is the ninth commandment?

"You shall not covet your neighbor's wife" (Exodus 20:17).

### 489. What are we obliged to do by the ninth commandment?[104]

The ninth commandment obliges us to be pure in all our thoughts and desires.

### 490. What does the ninth commandment forbid?

The ninth commandment forbids all deliberate impure thoughts, intentions, imaginings, desires, and feelings deliberately aroused or indulged in.

---

[103] *Catechism of the Catholic Church*, 2352.
[104] *Catechism of the Catholic Church*, cf. 2514-2533.

**491. Are all impure temptations sinful?**

Impure temptations are not sinful in themselves, but become sinful if they are deliberately aroused, indulged in, or consented to. They must be rejected at once.

## The Preservation of Chastity

**492. What are the main dangers to chastity?**

The main dangers to chastity are laziness, unbridled curiosity, bad company, excessive drinking and drug abuse, immodest dress, pornography, suggestive music, and obscene talk.

**493. How can chastity be preserved?**

Chastity may be protected by avoiding the dangers to chastity whenever possible, praying for God's grace and help, going to confession and receiving Communion often, and cultivating a tender devotion to the Blessed Virgin Mary.[105]

While dating, it is extremely important to be on guard against dangers to chastity. Couples should avoid excessive petting, spending too much time in seclusion, and what is called "French kissing".

---

[105] The *Catechism of the Catholic Church* offers an entire section (cf. 2520-2527) that is most helpful on this question.

## The Seventh and Tenth Commandments

**"You shall not steal. You shall not covet your neighbor's goods."**

*Respect for Property*

**494. Why are the seventh and tenth commandments treated together?**

The seventh and tenth commandments are treated together because they both deal with respect for the property of others.

**495. What is the seventh commandment?**

"You shall not steal" (Exodus 20:15).

**496. Does everyone have a right to private ownership?**

Yes, God has given everyone the right to private ownership so that we can enjoy the fruit of our labors, live with the dignity due our humanity, and maintain a certain independence.

**497. To what does the seventh commandment oblige us?**

The seventh commandment obliges us to respect the property of others, to keep our business agreements, and to pay our debts.

**498. What does the seventh commandment forbid?**

The seventh commandment forbids stealing, robbery, cheating, contracting debts beyond our means, unjustly damaging the property of others, accepting bribes, and knowingly buying or receiving stolen goods.

### Stealing, Damaging, Cheating

**499.  How serious a sin is theft?**

Stealing is a serious sin if the thing stolen is of considerable value.  Stealing something of small value from a poor person can be mortally sinful.  Stealing in small amounts over a period of time could eventually become mortal sin if the accumulated total becomes sufficiently large.

Let's say that the cashier at the supermarket gives you a dollar too much in change, and you decide to keep it.  This would be a venial sin.  If that same dollar was stolen from, say, a blind beggar on a street corner, that could be mortally sinful.

If a bank teller manages to steal five dollars from his till, that is a venial sin.  If he were to do this every week for an extended period of time he would commit a mortal sin.

**500.  Must a thief return stolen goods?**

We are obliged to restore to the owner stolen goods, or their value, whenever we are able (Exodus 22:1).  If the rightful owner is dead, the property must be restored to his heirs.  If there are no heirs, it must be given to the poor or for some other charitable purpose.

If a thief cannot restore all he has stolen, he must restore all he can.  If he has used what has been stolen, he must repair the damage done by restoring the equivalent.  If he cannot restore anything, he must at least pray for the person he has wronged.

If poverty or some other circumstance prevents the thief from making restitution immediately, he must resolve to do so as soon as possible, and must make an effort to fulfill his resolution.

Restitution may be made secretly, without letting the owner know that restitution is being made. For instance, a money-order may be sent with an alias; or the priest, who is pledged to secrecy, may be entrusted with the property to be restored.

**501. If we know or find out we have purchased stolen goods, may we keep them?**

No. We must restore such goods to their rightful owner, unless we have no way of locating him. It is also wrong for us to ask the owner to reimburse us for our monetary loss. The only person from whom we can ask reimbursement is the person who sold us the goods.

**502. May we keep what we find?**

If we find an article of value, we must strive to discover the owner in order to restore the article. The more valuable it is, the greater our obligation to return the article. If, after all our earnest efforts, we are unable to find the owner, we may keep the article.

**503. Is it wrong to keep what we have borrowed?**

Yes, it is wrong to keep what we have borrowed beyond the length of time established or agreed upon with the owner. If no time has been established or agreed upon, we may not keep the borrowed item beyond what common sense and our conscience tell us is reasonable.

**504. Must one repair damage he has unjustly done to someone else's property?**

We are obliged to repair damage unjustly done to the property of others, or to pay the amount of the damage, as far as we are able (Exodus 22:4).

**505. What are some forms of cheating?**

Some forms of cheating are: negligence in working, tax evasion, false advertisement, fraudulent contracts, false insurance claims, and copying in an examination.

## Specific Obligations

**506. What are the duties of workers by the seventh commandment?**

Workers must conscientiously provide quantitative and qualitative work that they are being paid to perform, as well as guard against damage to their employer's property.

**507. May workers strike?**

Strikes are justifiable when: rights are violated or ignored; lawful contracts are broken; other difficulties of a serious nature exist. A striking worker may not use violence to achieve his objective.

**508. What are the duties of employers by the seventh commandment?**

Sacred Scripture tells us well the duties of employers. The prophet tells us that "[t]o take away a neighbor's living is to murder him; to deprive an employee of his wages is to shed blood' (Sirach 34:22). And the apostle states that "the wages of the laborers who mowed your fields, which you kept back by fraud, cry out; and the cries of the harvesters have reached the ears of the Lord of hosts" (James 5:4).

These passages tell us that employers must see to it that their workers are paid just wages, without undue delays. They must also see to it that working conditions are in accord with human dignity and are reasonably safe.

**509. What are the obligations of public officials?**

Public officials are not to accept bribes or advance themselves by other dishonest means. They have a serious obligation to discharge their positions with honor, justice, and diligence.

**510. What is usury?**

Usury is the charging of excessive interest on money. A usurer takes unjust advantage of the need of another in order to make excessive profits.

**511. Can one who has broken the seventh commandment receive absolution if he doesn't intend to make restitution?**

No, one may not receive absolution after breaking the seventh commandment if he does not intend to make restitution.

*Irresponsible Use of Money and Goods*

**512. In the name of justice, may the wealthy leave the poor destitute?**

Even if a wealthy person has a just claim on the possessions of a poor person, he may not exercise that claim if it would leave the poor destitute.

**513. Is it wrong to live beyond one's means?**

Yes, to contract debts beyond one's means is an injustice to both one's creditors and one's dependents.

**514. What is gambling?**

Gambling is the staking of money or valuables on a future event or game of chance, the results of which are unknown to the participants.

**515. Is gambling a sin?**

This is another issue which suffers from puritanistic influence. Opponents to gambling — particularly Protestant Fundamentalists — claim gambling is wrong because it is both irresponsible, wasteful, and the desire to gain something for nothing. As is typical of Puritanism, such reasoning is flawed and intellectually dishonest.

**Irresponsible and wasteful?** The stock market is nothing more than gambling, as is seen by the above definition. Our global economy would collapse without stock markets, yet none of the gambling opponents are crying out for its abolition. This is intellectually dishonest.

**Something for nothing?** Intellectual dishonesty reigns here, too. Ask a gambling opponent if he would turn down a prize awarded by a merchant because he patronized the merchant's business. Of course not! And what is this but getting something for nothing? Indeed, merchants regularly practice such marketing methods, simply to get customers to come back.

There is also another argument for the idea of gambling being wasteful. Gambling opponents suggest that gambling is wasteful because the gambler, if he loses, has nothing to show for his money. If a couple hires a baby-sitter to watch the kids, go out to dinner, then to a movie, what have they got to show for the usually hefty sum of money spent? Nothing, except a good time. Legitimate pleasure is what the couple paid for, and this is all gambling is — a legitimate pleasure.

Gambling is not sinful if done with moderation. It can become sinful — even a mortal sin — if it leads to dishonesty or risks the welfare of one's family. In other words, gambling should be fair and done only with money that has been budgeted for recreation.

## *Desiring Others' Goods* [106]

### 516. What is the tenth commandment?

"You shall not covet anything which belongs to your neighbor" (Exodus 20:17).

### 517. What does "covet" mean?

"Covet" means to unlawfully desire something that belongs to another.

### 518. What does the tenth commandment forbid?

The tenth commandment forbids the desire to take or keep what belongs to another. It also forbids envy of the good fortune or success of others.

### 519. Is it ever permissible to desire what belongs to another?

Certainly it is morally permissible to desire what belongs to another if he is willing to make the possession a gift or to sell it. The prohibition of the tenth commandment applies only to dishonest desires. If this were not so, one could never, say, purchase a car. The car belongs to a dealer, but he is certainly willing to sell it; therefore, it is morally acceptable for you to desire it, provided you are willing to pay for it.

---

[106] *Catechism of the Catholic Church, cf. 2534-2557.*

## The Eighth Commandment

### "You shall not bear false witness against your neighbor."

*Reputation*

**520. What does the eighth commandment oblige us to do?**

The eighth commandment obliges us to always be truthful, especially when it concerns someone's good name and reputation. We are also obliged to interpret the actions of our neighbor in the best way possible.

**521. What does the eighth commandment forbid?**

The eighth commandment forbids false witnessing, lying, rash judging, rash suspicions, flattery, tale bearing, detractions, calumny, contumely, libel, and the telling of secrets we are obliged to keep.

**522. What is a lie?**

A lie is anything which we know or suspect to be untrue, usually for the purpose of deceiving others.

**523. Can lying be excused if done for a good reason?**

"Man tends by nature toward the truth."[107] It is a perversion of man's nature to tell a lie, because God made man to know and tell the truth. Therefore, no excuse can make the telling of a lie good, since lying in itself is an evil.

---

[107] *Catechism of the Catholic Church*, 2467.

**524. What is a jocose lie?**

A jocose lie is a story made up in order to amuse or instruct others. It is sinful if the story-teller fails to make it clear in some way that the story is not to be taken literally.

**525. Are there lies in actions as well as in words?**

Yes. Lies in actions are called hypocrisy (Sirach 1:29-30).

**526. What is rash judging?**

Rash judging is believing something harmful about someone's character without a sufficient reason.

**527. Why is rash judging wrong?**

Rash judging is wrong because such disrespect for one's reputation equates to disrespect for the person being rashly judged, and everyone deserves our respect.

*Uncharitable Telling of the Truth*

**528. What is tale bearing?**

Tale bearing is telling the unkind things others have said about him or her. It is sinful because it provokes a person to anger, hatred, revenge, and other sins.

**529. What is detraction?**

Detraction is acting without an objectively valid reason to tell "another's faults and failings to persons who did not know them [Cf. *Sir* 21:28]."[108]  Detraction is wrong because our neighbor has a right to his good name and reputation, whether or not we subjectively believe he deserves it.

---

[108] *Catechism of the Catholic Church*, 2477.

### 530. Is anyone ever allowed to tell the faults of another?

We may tell the faults of another to the proper authority — teachers, parents, police, etc. — if we believe the wrongdoer can be helped or stopped from further wrongdoing, or to keep the wrongs from becoming worse. It is important to stress though, that we should be more concerned with seeing a sinner break with sin than to see the sinner punished.

## Calumny, Contumely, Libel

### 531. What is calumny?

Calumny is the making of "remarks contrary to the truth, [which harm] the reputation of others and give occasion [of] false judgment concerning them."[109]

### 532. What is contumely?

Contumely is showing contempt for a person by unjustly dishonoring him. It may be committed by ignoring the person, refusing to show the proper signs of respect, detraction, or ridicule.

### 533. What is libel?

Libel is any false or malicious written or printed statement or any sign, picture, or effigy tending to injure a person's reputation in any way.

## Secrets

### 534. Must we keep secrets?

We must keep secrets if we have promised to do so, if our office requires it, or if the good of others demands it.

---

[109] *Catechism of the Catholic Church*, 2477.

## 535. Does the seal of confession oblige anyone other than the priest?

"The *secret of the sacrament of reconciliation* is sacred, and cannot be violated under any pretext."[110] Therefore, one who somehow gains knowledge of matter from confession must never reveal that knowledge.

## 536. Is one ever permitted to read the letters or private writings of others?

We may never read the letters or private writings of others without their permission, unless the motive is to prevent grave harm to oneself, another, or society.

## *Reparation*

## 537. What must we do if we sin against the eighth commandment?

"Every offense committed against justice and truth entails the *duty of reparation*, even if its author has been forgiven. When it is impossible publicly to make reparation for a wrong, it must be made secretly. If someone who has suffered harm cannot be directly compensated, he must be given moral satisfaction in the name of charity. The duty of reparation also concerns offenses against another's reputation. This reparation, moral and sometimes material, must be evaluated in terms of the extent of the damage inflicted. It obliges in conscience."[111]

---

[110] *Catechism of the Catholic Church*, 2490.
[111] *Catechism of the Catholic Church*, 2487. (When in doubt, consult a priest.)

## The Precepts of the Church

*Specific Duties of Catholics*

### 538. Does the Catholic Church have the authority to make laws and precepts?

Yes, the Church does have the authority to make laws and precepts, an authority granted by Christ Himself. Jesus gave this authority when He told His Apostles: "He who hears you hears me, and he who rejects you rejects me, and he who rejects me rejects him who sent me" (Luke 10:16). To Peter, the Church's first Pope, Jesus said: "I will give you the keys of the kingdom of heaven, and whatever you bind on earth shall be bound in heaven, and whatever you loose on earth shall be loosed in heaven" (Matthew 16:19). This power was given to the Pope in a special way, as is evident by the presentation of the keys. Finally, the bishops, by way of their predecessors, the Apostles, were given this same power in a lesser way when Jesus said: "Truly, I say to you, whatever you bind on earth shall be bound in heaven, and whatever you loose on earth shall be loosed in heaven" (Matthew 18:18).

The reason the Church makes laws and precepts is "to guarantee to the faithful the very necessary minimum in the spirit of prayer and moral effort, [and] in the growth in love of God and neighbor...."[112]

### 539. Are we obliged to keep the Church's precepts?

All Catholics are obliged to keep the Church's precepts.

---

[112] *Catechism of the Catholic Church*, 2041.

**540. What are some of the chief duties of today's Catholics?**

Some of the chief duties of Catholics are (Those traditionally called the Precepts of the Church are in italics.):

1. *You shall attend Mass on Sundays and holy days of obligation.* This precept requires us to make holy the Lord's day, to observe special holy days that are meant to recall us to the gospel message, and to avoid those activities that hinder the renewal of soul and body.

2. *You shall confess your serious sins at least once a year.* This precept "ensures preparation for the Eucharist by the reception of the sacrament of reconciliation... [Cf. Code of Canon Law, can. 989; Corpus Canonum Ecclesiarum Orientalium, can. 719]."[113]

3. *You shall humbly receive your Creator in Holy Communion at least during the Easter season.* We must receive Holy Communion, under pain of mortal sin, between the First Sunday of Lent and Trinity Sunday in the United States. The universal Church ends the Easter season on Pentecost Sunday, but the Holy See granted permission to the U.S. Bishops to extend it the extra week to Trinity Sunday for the benefit of U.S. Catholics.

4. *You shall observe the days of fasting and abstinence established by the Church.* There are only two fast days in the United States: Ash Wednesday and Good Friday. All Fridays of the year are days of penance, but only the Fridays of Lent (beginning with the Friday after Ash Wednesday) are

---

[113] *Catechism of the Catholic Church*, 2042.

obligatory days of abstinence under pain of sin. On those Fridays outside of Lent we should perform some act of penance at least as sacrificial as abstinence, or abstain.

5. "'You shall help to provide for the needs of the Church' means that the faithful are obliged to assist with the material needs of the church, each according to his own ability. [Cf. Code of Canon Law, can. 222]."[114]

6. The faithful are to study Catholic teaching in preparation for the Sacrament of Confirmation, be confirmed, and then to continue study and advance the cause of Christ.

7. The faithful are to observe the marriage laws of the Church and to give religious training to their children.

8. The faithful are to join in the missionary spirit and apostolate of the Church. In other words, to evangelize all peoples, in so far as we are able.

### Sundays and Holy Days

**541. Is it a grave obligation to attend Mass on Sundays and holy days of obligation?**

Yes, this precept is binding under pain of mortal sin.

**542. Is there any other day on which this obligation can be fulfilled?**

Yes, this obligation may be fulfilled by participating at an anticipated Mass on the evening before.

---

[114] *Catechism of the Catholic Church*, 2043.

## Reconciliation and Eucharist

**543. What does it mean to confess our sins once a year?**

Making an annual confession means to prepare for reception of the Eucharist by making a good confession, usually prior to the Easter season. This is the bare minimum. The Church recommends confession at least once a month, but teaches that weekly confession is much better.

**544. Why does the Church require us to receive Holy Communion once a year, during the Easter time?**

The Church requires the annual Communion as a minimum because of what Christ taught us in John 6:51: "I am the living bread which came down from heaven; if anyone eats of this bread, he will live for ever; and the bread which I shall give for the life of the world is my flesh."

Although the Church only requires annual reception of the Eucharist, it is to be understood that this is the minimum. The Church recommends weekly Communion, but teaches daily reception is better.

## Penances

**545. What is a day of fast?**

A day of fast (Ash Wednesday and Good Friday) is a day on which we eat one full meal and two other meals that together do not equal one full meal. Eating between meals is forbidden; however, we are permitted liquids, including milk and fruit juice.

**546. Who are obliged to fast?**

All Catholics from the age of eighteen through the age of fifty-nine are obliged to fast.

**547. What is a day of abstinence?**

A day of abstinence (Ash Wednesday and all the Fridays of Lent) is a day on which we do not eat meat. (Seafood is permitted.)

**548. Who are obliged to abstain?**

All Catholics fourteen years of age and over are obliged to abstain.

## The Life of Virtue

### The Virtues

**549. What is a virtue?**
A virtue is the habit of doing good. "It allows the person not only to perform good acts, but to give the best of himself."[115]

**550. How many kinds of virtues are there?**
There are two kinds of virtues: supernatural virtues, which are infused into the soul by God; and natural virtues, acquired by repeating naturally good acts.

**551. What are the most important virtues?**
The most important virtues are those called the theological virtues.

### The Theological Virtues

**552. What does "theological virtues" mean?**
"[T]he theological virtues relate directly to God. They dispose Christians to live in a relationship with the Holy Trinity. They have the One and Triune God for their origin, motive, and object."[116]

**553. What are the theological virtues?**
The three theological virtues are faith, hope, and charity.

---

[115] *Catechism of the Catholic Church*, 1803.
[116] *Catechism of the Catholic Church*, 1812.

**554.  What is faith?**

"Faith is the theological virtue by which we believe in God and believe all that he has said and revealed to us, and that Holy Church proposes for our belief, because he is truth itself."[117]

**555.  Can we be saved by faith alone?**

No, we cannot be saved by faith alone. This is a heresy that was begun by Martin Luther in the year 1517. It was condemned by the Council of Trent (1545-1563) because it clearly contradicted Sacred Scripture. St. James tells us that "faith apart from works is dead" (James 2:26). Luther's idea of faith meant a man's confidence that his sins had been forgiven by God for Christ's sake, but Christ and His Apostles always taught that faith implied the acceptance of all God's revelation on His word. Without faith justification is impossible. But other dispositions are required, as faith necessarily leads to action. We must not only believe, but we must hope, repent, and love. "We are saved by hope" (Romans 8:24). "Repent, and be baptized every one of you in the name of Jesus Christ for the forgiveness of your sins ..." (Acts 2:38). "[I]f I have all faith, so as to remove mountains, but have not love, I am nothing" (I Corinthians 13:2).

**556.  How do we live by faith?**

We live by faith by studying the Church and her teachings, reading the Bible, believing God's revelation, and openly professing our Faith, even at the risk of death.

---

[117] *Catechism of the Catholic Church*, 1814.

### 557. How can a Catholic sin against faith?

A Catholic sins against faith by joining a non-Catholic church, denying a truth of faith, being indifferent toward the Catholic religion, and, in many cases, by taking an active part in non-Catholic worship. We must protect our faith by praying for an increase in faith, studying the truths of Catholicism, living by God's holy will, choosing friends and associates wisely, and avoiding all that is contrary to the teachings of the Church.

### 558. What is hope?

"Hope is the theological virtue by which we desire the kingdom of heaven and eternal life as our happiness, placing our trust in Christ's promises and relying not on our own strength, but on the help of the grace of the Holy Spirit."[118]

### 559. How do we live by hope?

We live by hope by trusting in God to give us the graces necessary for salvation.

### 560. How can we sin against hope?

We can sin against hope by presumption and despair.

### 561. What is presumption?

Presumption is thinking that God will save us without any effort on our part, or of thinking that we do not need God's help to reach heaven. Presumption is a mortal sin.

---

[118] *Catechism of the Catholic Church*, 1817.

### 562. What is despair?

A direct opposite of presumption, despair is deliberately refusing to believe that God will always give the necessary help for salvation to all who ask for it. This, too, is a mortal sin.

### 563. What is charity?

"Charity is the theological virtue by which we love God above all things for his own sake, and our neighbor as ourselves for the love of God."[119]

### 564. How do we live by charity?

We live by charity by obeying the two great commandments (cf. Questions 384-385). In practice this means obeying the commandments of God and His Church, and performing the works of mercy.

### 565. How can we sin against charity?

There are many ways to sin against charity: hating God, hating our neighbor, envy, sloth, scandal, etc.

### *The Moral Virtues*

### 566. What is meant by "moral virtues"?

A moral virtue is a virtue that disposes us to treat others and ourselves in a way that is morally right.

### 567. What are the most important moral virtues?

The most important moral virtues are religion, which helps us to worship God, and the cardinal virtues: prudence, justice, fortitude, and temperance.

---

[119] *Catechism of the Catholic Church*, 1822.

## 568. What is prudence?

"*Prudence* is the virtue that disposes practical reason to discern our true good in every circumstance and to choose the right means of achieving it … Prudence is 'right reason in action' [St. Thomas Aquinas, *Summa Theologiae* II-II, 47, 2.] … It is not to be confused with timidity or fear, nor with duplicity or dissimulation … it guides the other virtues by setting rule and measure. It is prudence that immediately guides the judgment of conscience … With the help of this virtue we apply moral principles to particular cases without error and overcome doubts about the good to achieve and the evil to avoid."[120]

## 569. What is justice?

"*Justice* is the moral virtue that consists in the constant and firm will to give their due to God and neighbor … The just man, often mentioned in the Sacred Scriptures, is distinguished by habitual right thinking and the uprightness of his conduct toward his neighbor."[121]

## 570. What is fortitude?

"*Fortitude* is the moral virtue that assures firmness in difficulties and constancy in the pursuit of the good. It strengthens the resolve to resist temptations and to overcome obstacles in the moral life. The virtue of fortitude enables one to conquer fear, even fear of death, and to face trials and persecutions. It disposes one even to renounce and sacrifice his life in defense of a just cause."[122]

---

[120] *Catechism of the Catholic Church*, 1806.
[121] *Catechism of the Catholic Church*, 1807.
[122] *Catechism of the Catholic Church*, 1808.

**571. What is temperance?**

*"Temperance* is the moral virtue that moderates the attraction of pleasures and provides balance in the use of created goods. It ensures the will's mastery over instincts and keeps desires within the limits of what is honorable. The temperate person directs the sensitive appetites toward what is good and maintains a healthy discretion.... Temperance is often praised in the Old Testament.... In the New Testament it is called 'moderation' or 'sobriety.' "[123]

**572. What are some other moral virtues?**

Some other moral virtues are:

- *Filial piety* and *patriotism*, which help us to love, honor, and respect our nation;
- *Obedience*, which helps us to obey any legitimate authority, which represents God;
- *Truthfulness*, which helps us to always tell the truth;
- *Liberality*, which helps us to use created things wisely;
- *Patience*, which helps us take the trials and difficulties God permits to help make us holy;
- *Humility*, which helps us to know ourselves and to recognize that whatever is good in us comes from God;
- *Chastity*, which helps us to be pure in mind, heart, and body.

There are many other virtues in addition to these.

---

[123] *Catechism of the Catholic Church*, 1809.

## The Beatitudes

### 573. What are beatitudes?

Beatitudes are qualities that Jesus asks His followers to live by that will pave their road to heaven.

### 574. What are the eight beatitudes?

The eight beatitudes are:

1. "Blessed are the poor in spirit, for theirs is the kingdom of heaven" (Matthew 5:3).
2. "Blessed are those who mourn, for they shall be comforted" (Matthew 5:4).
3. "Blessed are the meek, for they shall inherit the earth" (Matthew 5:5).
4. "Blessed are those who hunger and thirst for righteousness, for they shall be satisfied" (Matthew 5:6).
5. "Blessed are the merciful, for they shall obtain mercy" (Matthew 5:7).
6. "Blessed are the pure in heart, for they shall see God" (Matthew 5:8).
7. "Blessed are the peacemakers, for they shall be called sons of God" (Matthew 5:9).
8. "Blessed are those who are persecuted for righteousness sake, for theirs is the kingdom of heaven" (Matthew 5:10).

### 575. Why does Jesus apply the term "blessed" to those in the beatitudes?

Jesus calls such persons blessed because those who practice the beatitudes live with peace of mind and a clear conscience, and they will reap great rewards in heaven.

## The Works of Mercy

### 576. Are there any particular acts of virtue that Jesus recommended to everyone?

Jesus recommended to His followers, by way of word and example, the works of mercy. There are the corporal works of mercy, which allow us to serve God in our neighbor, and the spiritual works of mercy, which are directed toward perfection of soul.

### 577. What are the corporal works of mercy?

The corporal works of mercy are found in Matthew 25 by direct instruction from Jesus, and in Tobit 1:16 by example (burying the dead). "The corporal works of mercy consist especially in feeding the hungry, sheltering the homeless, clothing the naked, visiting the sick and the imprisoned, and burying the dead [Cf. *Mt* 25:31-46]."[124]

### 578. What are the spiritual works of mercy?

The spiritual works of mercy are to admonish the sinner, instruct the ignorant, counsel the doubtful, comfort the sorrowful, bear wrongs patiently, forgive all injuries, and pray for the living and the dead.[125]

### 579. Are we all to perform works of mercy?

All of us are obliged to perform the works of mercy, so far as we are able and in accord with our neighbor's need.

---

[124] *Catechism of the Catholic Church*, 2447.
[125] *Catechism of the Catholic Church*, 2447.

## Vices

**580. What is the opposite of virtue?**

The opposite of virtue is vice, which is the habit of doing evil.

**581. What are the principal vices?**

The principal vices are the capital sins, of which there are seven: pride, covetousness, lust, gluttony, anger, envy, and sloth.

**582. How can we overcome these principal vices?**

We can overcome these principal vices by prayer and by practicing their opposite virtues:

pride — humility

covetousness — justice and liberality

lust — chastity

gluttony — temperance

anger — meekness

envy — love of neighbor

sloth — love of God and diligence in His service.

## The Life of Prayer

*Prayer*

### 583. What is prayer?

Prayer is raising our hearts and minds to God in loving conversation with Him so we may ask for His good in our lives.

### 584. Why should we pray?

We should pray to God to adore Him, thank Him for His blessings, ask His forgiveness, and beg Him for the graces we need.

### 585. How should we pray?

As Jesus Himself taught us through word and example, we should pray with an awareness of God's presence, humility, confidence, and perseverance.

### 586. For whom should we pray?

We should pray for ourselves, our friends and loved ones, sinners, the poor souls in purgatory, all those in authority, religious, priests, bishops, the laity, and especially the Pope.

### 587. Does God always hear our prayers?

God always hears our prayers if we pray well (John 15:16).

### 588. Will God always give us what we pray for?

Just as a parent knows what is best for his child; so too, does God know what is best for us. We often ask for things that God knows are not for our benefit, so His answer is sometimes either "no" or "yes, but later."

**589. What is mental prayer?**
Mental prayer is made from within our mind, uniting our thoughts and heart to God.

**590. What is vocal prayer?**
Vocal prayer is praying with words, but we are to unite the words with our heart and mind.

**591. What is an aspiration?**
An aspiration, also called an ejaculatory prayer, is a short prayer. An example would be a prayer like: "My Jesus, mercy."

**592. Which prayers should Catholics memorize?**
The minimum prayers that every Catholic should memorize are the: Our Father, Hail Mary, Glory Be to the Father, Apostles' Creed, act of faith, act of hope, act of love, act of contrition, and the Rosary.[126]

**593. Are distractions in prayer sins?**
Distractions in prayer can be a venial sin if they are deliberate. If distractions are not deliberate, and if we refuse to dwell on them, our prayers become even more pleasing to God.

**594. Is it good to use our own words in prayer?**
Formulated prayers are good, because they are well thought out and cover all the bases, so to speak; however, prayers that are impromptu are especially pleasing to God, because such prayers are how we develop an intimate relationship with Him.

---

[126] All of these prayers, and more, are in the appendix of this text.

## The Our Father

**595. Why is the Our Father a perfect prayer?**

The Our Father is a perfect prayer because Jesus, who is Himself perfect, taught it to us. It is perfect because we ask first for God's glory and then for everything we need, both spiritually and materially, for ourselves and for all men. "'The Lord's Prayer is truly the summary of the whole gospel' [Tertullian, *De orat.* 1:Patrologia Latina (Paris: 1841-1855) 1, 1251-1255], the 'most perfect of prayers' [St. Thomas Aquinas, *Summa Theologiae* II-II, 83, 9]. It is at the center of the Scriptures."[127]

**596. When we say *"Our* Father" what do we mean?**

"When we say 'our' Father, we recognize first that all his promises of love announced by the prophets are fulfilled in the *new and eternal covenant* in his Christ: we have become 'his' people and he is henceforth 'our' God."[128]

**597. What does "Our Father who art in heaven" mean?**

"Our Father who art in heaven" means that God is truly our loving Father, who cares for us and made us His adopted children through sanctifying grace and who wants us with Him in heaven forever. "This biblical expression does not mean a place ('space'), but a way of being; it does not mean that God is distant, but majestic.... The symbol of the heavens refers us back to the mystery of the covenant we are living when we pray to our Father.

---

[127] *Catechism of the Catholic Church*, 2774.
[128] *Catechism of the Catholic Church*, 2787.

He is in heaven, his dwelling place; the Father's house is our homeland."[129]

**598. What does "hallowed be Thy name" mean?**

This phrase means that we pray that everyone may know, respect and love God's holy name.

**599. What does "Thy kingdom come" mean?**

When we pray "Thy kingdom come" we are praying that God's kingdom of love, mercy, and justice is spread all over the world so that we may all share His kingdom of heaven together.

**600. What does "Thy will be done on earth as it is in heaven" mean?**

This phrase means we are praying for ourselves and others to be as quickly obedient to the will of God as are His holy angels.

**601. What does "Give us this day our daily bread" mean?**

" '*Give us*': The trust of children who look to their Father for everything is beautiful.... Jesus teaches us this petition, because it glorifies our Father by acknowledging how good he is, beyond all goodness. '*Give us*' also expresses the covenant."[130]

" '*Our bread*': The Father who gives us life cannot but give us the nourishment life requires — all appropriate goods and blessings, both material and spiritual."[131]

---

[129] *Catechism of the Catholic Church*, 2794-2795.
[130] *Catechism of the Catholic Church*, 2828-2829.
[131] *Catechism of the Catholic Church*, 2830.

**602. What does "And forgive us our trespasses as we forgive those who trespass against us" mean?**

"This petition is astonishing. If it consisted only of the first phrase, 'And forgive us our trespasses,' it might have been included, implicitly, in the first three petitions of the Lord's Prayer, since Christ's sacrifice is 'that sins may be forgiven.' But, according to the second phrase, our petition will not be heard unless we have first met a strict requirement. Our petition looks to the future, but our response must come first, for the two parts are joined by the single word 'as'."[132]

**603. What does "lead us not into temptation" mean?**

"This petition goes to the root of the preceding one, for our sins result from our consenting to temptation; we therefore ask our Father not to 'lead' us into temptation.... We ask him not to allow us to take the way that leads to sin. We are engaged in the battle 'between flesh and spirit'; this petition implores the Spirit of discernment and strength."[133]

**604. What does "deliver us from evil" mean?**

"The last petition to our Father is also included in Jesus' prayer: 'I am not asking you to take them out of the world, but I ask you to protect them from the evil one.' [*Jn* 17:15] It touches each of us personally, but it is always 'we' who pray, in communion with the whole Church, for the deliverance of the whole human family."[134]

---

[132] *Catechism of the Catholic Church*, 2838.

[133] *Catechism of the Catholic Church*, 2846.

[134] *Catechism of the Catholic Church*, 2850.

## 605. What does "Amen" mean?

"Amen" means "so be it". By this closing statement we are expressing our agreement and belief of everything contained in the prayer.

### The Spiritual Life And The Bible

## 606. What are the main enemies of our spiritual life?

The main enemies of our spiritual life are the world, the flesh, and the devil.

## 607. How is the devil an enemy of our spiritual life?

"Scripture witnesses to the disastrous influence of the one Jesus calls 'a murderer from the beginning', who would even try to divert Jesus from the mission received from his Father [*Jn* 8:44; cf. *Mt* 4:1-11]."[135] "The power of Satan is, nonetheless, not infinite. He is only a creature, powerful from the fact that he is pure spirit, but still a creature.... It is a great mystery that providence should permit diabolical activity, but 'we know that in everything God works for good with those who love him' [*Rom* 8:28]."[136]

## 608. How is the world an enemy of our spiritual life?

The world, which is to say its man-made pleasures, entices us to embrace a love of wealth, pleasure, and power. When these things become more important than God in our lives, the spiritual life is destroyed by our new gods.

---

[135] *Catechism of the Catholic Church*, 394.
[136] *Catechism of the Catholic Church*, 395.

**609. How is the flesh an enemy of our spiritual life?**

The flesh is an enemy of our spiritual life because of our weak and fallen nature, which makes us inclined to follow our passions. Our Lady of Fatima told Jacinta that more souls go to hell because of sins of the flesh (i.e., impurity; see Questions 466-493) than for any other reason. That was in 1917. Imagine how much more dangerous this is for us today.

**610. How can we overcome these enemies?**

These main enemies can be overcome by reliance on God's grace, prayer, constant and careful vigilance, frequent reception of the sacraments, and penance.

**611. What does it mean to take up our daily cross?**

Taking up our daily cross means to unite all of our activities to the crucified Christ, especially our sufferings. Many people believe Jesus promised us a bed of roses, when He actually promised us only the thorns. Those thorns, or sufferings, are the consequence of our fallen, sinful nature. Suffering is evil in itself, but through His sacrifice on the cross, Jesus has made a way to sanctify those sufferings, making them holy by giving to our suffering a supernatural value.

Jesus told us that "he who does not take up his cross and follow me *is not worthy of me*."[137] Our Lord's words are very strong, but they were even stronger to the audience listening to Him for the first time. To the Jew, there was no more humiliating way to die than on the cross. To the Roman, the cross was the most excruciatingly painful mode of death imaginable. In effect, Jesus is telling us

---

[137] *Matthew* 10:38.

we must daily die for Him, to Him, and with Him; He tells us we must die to ourselves to follow Him, and to accept our sufferings so they can be offered back to the Father — through Jesus — in reparation for our sins and the sins of the whole world.

### 612. What is meditation?

"Meditation is above all a quest. The mind seeks to understand the why and how of the Christian life, in order to adhere and respond to what the Lord is asking. The required attentiveness is difficult to sustain. We are usually helped by books...."[138]

"To meditate on what we read helps us to make it our own by confronting it with ourselves. Here, another book is opened: the book of life. We pass from thoughts to reality. To the extent that we are humble and faithful, we discover in meditation the movements that stir the heart and we are able to discern them. It is a question in acting truthfully in order to come into the light: 'Lord, what do you want me to do?'"[139]

### 613. Should we meditate daily?

Absolutely! Meditation, like anything else worth doing on a regular basis, must become a habit by daily discipline and perseverance. We have always recommended to students that the best way to begin is by meditating on one of the events in the Passion and death of Christ.

The ideal period for daily meditation is an hour, but nobody starts at such length. We recommend beginning with just five minutes, and gradually building from there over a period of weeks or months.

---

[138] *Catechism of the Catholic Church*, 2705.
[139] *Catechism of the Catholic Church*, 2706.

The best time of day for meditation is early in the morning, before beginning the hustle and bustle of the day's work and activities. Ideally, the place for your daily meditation is before our Lord in His Tabernacle, but any quiet place will do. Many people who cannot go to meditate before the Tabernacle in their parish church find the appropriate setting to be in the outdoors, where nature helps them to commune with God.

Although it is difficult to build the habit of meditating, this is a simple form of prayer. Its benefits cannot be captured by mere words.

### 614. Is spiritual reading helpful in the spiritual life?

Yes, the reading of spiritual books is most helpful in the spiritual life. This reading helps inspire us to greater sanctity, and gives us material for daily meditation. It also helps us to be stronger in resisting temptation.

We recommend reading the Bible at least fifteen minutes a day. It is always good to begin with reading lives of the saints. As we grow in knowledge and piety, deeper theological works will become important. There is a list of recommended books in the appendix.

### 615. What is the Bible?

The Bible is the book which contains His inspired word. It was written by men inspired by the Holy Spirit so they would write only what He wanted written. God speaks to us through the Bible, and His Church, which alone has the authority to interpret Scripture, helps us to understand best what He is saying to us.

### 616. How is the Bible divided?

The Bible is divided into two parts: the Old Testament, with forty-six books; and the New Testament, with twenty-seven books.

### 617. What is the Old Testament?

The Old Testament was written before the birth of Christ. It tells us the history of God's people, and His first covenant with them. It shows us how God prepared His people for the coming of Christ.

### 618. What is the New Testament?

The New Testament was written after Jesus returned to the Father in heaven. It tells us about the birth, life, teachings, Passion, death, resurrection, and ascension of Jesus. It also tells us about life in the early Church. Finally, working with Sacred Tradition, the New Testament — indeed, the whole Bible! — tells us how to apply Christ's teachings to our own lives.

### 619. How should we read the Bible?

We should read the Bible prayerfully in order to get the greatest good God would have us gain, and humbly in order to avoid personal interpretation that leads to a false interpretation.

# Appendix One

## Some Common Objections to the Catholic Faith
## and
## *The Church's Answers*

The great and beloved Archbishop Fulton J. Sheen once stated that he genuinely believed there were not one hundred people in all of America who hate the Catholic Church, but that there were millions who hate what they believe the Catholic Church is. At no time in the history of the Church in the United States is this more true than today. Not only is the Church detracted by those from outside who do not truly know what she teaches, but she has detractors from within who have never been properly taught the Catholic Faith ... or who are so obstinate in their sins that they refuse to accept divine revelation as transmitted by Holy Mother Church. It is my prayerful hope that this catechism, used as an evangelistic tool, will help in some way to rectify this terrible situation. This also explains the reason for this added appendix.

The most vehement attacks from outside the Church come from Protestant Fundamentalists. There are several things that we must understand about these good people before we can help them to better understand Catholicism.

Despite the vehement, and often uncharitable and *objectively* sinful attacks Fundamentalists launch against the Church, we must recognize that they are acting in clear conscience. They believe they are bringing God's scourge on what they have been taught is the "Whore of Babylon." Because Fundamentalists try to live the limited divine truths they possess, believe it or not, God actually counts to their credit their attacks against His own Church, simply because they attack the Church out of love for Him! I realize this is a difficult concept, but it is worthy of the time spent in meditation.

The point to this is that Fundamentalists should not be treated with disdain or otherwise uncharitably. Indeed, they should be treated with love. But please do not misunderstand my exhortation. Fundamentalists should not be given pollyanna or milquetoast defenses of the Catholic Faith. They are taught a very conservative and aggressive form of Protestantism. We must be equally aggressive in defending the Catholic Faith, but do so with charity, or Fundamentalists will perceive us as weak and uncertain. Due to their own training and mind set, an aggressive but charitable defense is the only way we can get Fundamentalists to hear what we say.

Fundamentalism is itself a very narcissistic religion. Its adherents believe it is the only true form of Christianity. Of course, we make the same claim. The difference is that we can back our claim with truth — historically, scriputrally, theologically, and patristically — but they cannot. Historically speaking, Fundamentalism is a religion whose roots are found right here in America. They cannot be the true Christian religion if their history shows that it is barely one hundred years old, a drop in the bucket of time when compared with Catholicism's two thousand year history. Armed with this knowledge, the fledgling Catholic apologist should view the intimidation factor from Fundamentalists as greatly reduced.

The final thing to recognize about Fundamentalists is that, ultimately, they all get their anti-Catholic arguments from the same place. The primary anti-Catholc source is a book by Loraine Boettner called *Roman Catholicism*. Few anti-Catholics have ever read or heard of Boettner's book, but the arguments all come from it nonetheless. Like Apostolic Tradition (and God forgive me if the comparison is erroneous), Boettner's arguments have been passed down from readers of his book to millions of Fundamentalist adherents. Therefore, I suggest to the fledgling apologist that he eventually read *Roman Catholicism.* Indeed, a number of books are listed in another appendix as recommended reading.

This addendix is provided as an aid to the fledgling apologist, and to help the Catholic who rightly uses this catechism as a tool for evangelism. Many of the objections answered in this appendix will be raised by most inquirers and catechumens. In fact, if your student does not raise questions or objections, then you are either doing a poor job of teaching, or the student is not serious about learning. Regardless of your student's disposition, act and teach as though you are under God's direct gaze. Indeed, you are.

### 620. Isn't one Christian religion as good as another?

Such a notion is offensive to Scripture, history, and reason. This idea is a heresy, called *indifferentism* by the Church.

God is one, and He is perfect. Because He is perfect, He cannot contradict Himself. Since 1517 there have been over 28,000 Christian religions founded, all of whom claim to possess the totality of divinely revealed truth. If it were true that all 28,000 sects are right about their claims, and all do indeed dispute with one another on various doctrines, then they say in effect that God is not perfect because He contradicts Himself. If He is imperfect He cannot be God.

History proves beyond question, as non-Catholic Christian scholars and historians will agree, that no Christian religion except the Roman Catholic Church existed prior to 1517. In the light of history, all other Christian religions are mere johnny-come-latelies.

Scripture tells us that Jesus founded *one* Church (Matthew 16:18), that He gave it *one* visible head (Matthew 16:19), that we are to obey the Church and its visible head (Luke 10:16) or perish eternally in the alternative (Mark 16:16). It is crystal clear in Scripture that Jesus did not found many churches. And since He founded only one Church, and expects us to obey it (Luke 10:16), we are bound to belong to it and it alone. Scripture, history, patristics, and reason tell us that the one Church Jesus founded is the Catholic Church.

**621. Isn't the Bible the sole rule of faith?**

This is yet another heresy, called *sola scriptura* (scripture alone). It was condemned by the Council of Trent (1545-1563), the ecumenical council called to refute the errors of Martin Luther, *et alia*.

The Bible itself denies that it is the sole source of divine revelation. John tells us that everything Jesus taught *was not* committed to writing (John 21:25). The Apostle Paul tells the Bishop Timothy that what he has *heard* from Paul is to be passed on to others who will teach it faithfully (II Timothy 2:2). St. Paul also tells the Thessalonians to hold to what they have been taught "*by word of mouth* or by letter" (II Thessalonians 2:15).

St. Luke tells us that the first Christians "devoted themselves to the apostles' teaching" that they *heard* through preaching (Acts 2:42). And why was the truth transmitted by the Apostles orally? Because Jesus commanded them to *preach* the gospel (Mark 16:15). St. Paul clearly understood that he and the other apostles were to teach Jesus' divine revelation in this way, and that Christians were to accept it (Romans 10:17).

If the Bible is the sole rule of faith, what did the Christians do in the early centuries? Not a word of the New Testament was even written until at least twenty years after Jesus returned to the Father, and the New Testament only came into existence by decree of the Council of Carthage in 397. In essence, then, all of Christ's teachings were handed down by word of mouth until 397.

Handing down sacred truths by word of mouth is called Sacred Tradition. Tradition was nothing new to the Jews, who made up the totality of the Church's earliest body of believers. St. Matthew, who was a Jew before he answered Christ's call, demonstrates to us his own acceptance of Tradition.

In telling us about Jesus' infancy, Matthew writes: "And he went and dwelt in a city called Nazareth, that what was spoken by the prophets might be fulfilled. 'He shall be called a Nazarene' " (Matthew 2:23). There are two interesting points to be made from this passage, one building on the next.

The first is that an exhaustive search of the Old Testament will not yield a single prophet who tells that the Messiah would be called a Nazarene. It's simply not there.

The second is a key word in Matthew's phrase concerning the prophet. He said it was *spoken* by the prophet, not written. Every time the Gospels speak of prophecies regarding Christ, the writers tell us it is written by a prophet. This lone passage in Matthew is the only exception. He obviously believed in Tradition.

No, *sola scriptura* doesn't cut it. Divine revelation is not from a single legged balancing beam, but rather from a three legged stool: Sacred Scripture, Sacred Tradition, and the Church's Magisterium.

**622. The Catholic Church forbids Catholics to read the Bible.**

This is one of the more absurd charges made against the Church. Rather than forbidden, Catholics are strongly encouraged to read the Bible. Such has always been the Church's stand.

This charge against the Church has as its basis a misunderstanding of history. The Catholic Church, as the guardian and interpreter of Holy Writ, must protect the faithful from erroneous teachings that come from bad or false translations. The Church has forbidden the use of various translations that could not hold up under the scrutiny of bishops, who are charged by Christ to care for the souls of their flocks. Resulting from a historical misunderstanding of the most prudent action on the part of bishops, the charge that Catholics are forbidden to read Scripture is born. It is utterly false. Echoing the Second Vatican Council in its *Dei Verbum*, the *Catechism of the Catholic Church* states: "The Church 'forcefully and specifically exhorts all the Christian faithful ... to learn "the surpassing knowledge of Jesus Christ," by frequent reading of the divine Scriptures. "Ignorance of the Scriptures is ignorance of Christ" ' " (para. 133).

**623. Why do you Catholics arrogantly claim that your Pope and Church are infallible?**

Before addressing this question we must first define what infallibility *is not*. Infallibility is not impecability. The former refers to an inability to be wrong. In this case, in matters of faith and morals. The latter means sinlessness. No member of the Catholic Church claims to be sinless.

When we claim the Church is infallible, we are saying that the Church is protected by the Holy Spirit from teaching error in matters of faith and morals. The Church alone represents Christ. She alone can carry on His work of redemption. Reason demands that the teacher of Christ's divine revelation must be infallible.

Would a good God, "who desires all men to be saved and to come to the knowledge of the truth" (I Timothy 2:4), fail to provide His revelation with a living, infallible teacher? Would a just God command us to believe under penalty of hell (Mark 16:16), but leave us to the mercy of every false or lying teacher? Would He tell us to follow Him or go to hell, and then fail to leave us a way to know the way to follow Him?

No, God could not be God if He left us on our own. He would be arbitrary and capricious, thus lacking in perfection. The New Testament portrays the Church founded by Christ as a divine, infallible teaching authority. He refers to it as a city founded on a rock foundation, and that hell could never defeat it (Matthew 16:18; 7:24-28).

The pope, who is the successor of St. Peter, is the Vicar of Christ. St. Peter was given the keys to the kingdom of heaven and promised infallibility for himself and all his successors (Matthew 16:18-19). For the same reasons the Church is infallible, so too is its visible head, the pope, infallible.

But in this there are limits. The pope is not infallible if he, say, predicts the winner of the World Series. The pope is only infallible:

1. When he speaks *ex cathedra*, that is, when he speaks officially as the Supreme Pastor of the universal Church. He is not infallible as supreme legislator, judge or ruler, but only as Supreme Teacher.

2. When he defines a doctrine regarding faith and morals. In other words, when he pronounces a doctrinal truth with the intention of settling it definitely, finally, and irrevocably.

3. When he speaks of faith or morals, which includes the whole content of divine revelation. This means the ordinary, daily teachings of the Church.

4. When he intends to bind the whole Church to believe an article of faith under pain of sin.

God alone is essentially infallible, but He can make the pope infallible as His earthly representative to safeguard the deposit of faith. That He has done so is proved by Sacred Scripture and Church history.

### 624. Does the Bible ever speak of the Catholic Church?

The Bible nowhere mentions the word Catholic as regards the Church. Catholic comes from a Greek word which means "universal," and the Church is certainly that. St. Ignatius of Antioch, in his letters to the Smyrnaeans around the year 107, wrote that "[w]here the bishop is, there let the multitude of believers be; even as where Jesus Christ is, there is the Catholic Church."

St. Ignatius was a disciple of St. Polycarp, who was a disciple of St. John the Apostle. It is likely that St. Ignatius knew St. John, especially since the two saints died only seven years apart. The point to this is that since St. Ignatius uses the word Catholic as though it is nothing new — that it has already been long in use — then it is even likely that St. John himself used the word Catholic to describe the Church.

### 625. What proof can you offer that Peter was ever in Rome?

The fact that Peter was in Rome is proved by Sacred Scripture. He indicated that he was writing his epistle from Babylon (I Peter 5:13). Babylon is the Old Testament city of iniquity, spoken of by the prophets (Isaiah 21:9). The name "Babylon" was used during apostolic times as a code word for Rome, as St. John shows us (Revelation 14:8; 16:19; 17:5; 18:21).

St. Jerome, who wrote the Vulgate in the fourth century, tells us that Peter was indicating Rome when he wrote his epistle. This was done because St. Peter was a hunted man throughout the Empire. Had his letter been intercepted and Rome specifically mentioned, he would have been in grave danger. St. Peter was certainly willing to die for Christ, as history bears out, but he still had the moral obligation to be prudently cautious.

The Christians of the first four centuries frequently write of Peter's labors and his martyrdom in Rome. Such early writers include St. Clement in 97, St. Ignatius in 107, St. Clement of Alexandria in 190, St. Irenaeus in 178, and Caius in 214. There are many others who can be listed. Also, archeologists believe the evidence is overwhelming that St. Peter was not only in Rome, but that he was executed and is buried there, beneath the main altar of St. Peter's Basilica at the Vatican.

**626. Is there any biblical proof that Peter was the first pope?**

The Catholic Church believes St. Peter was the chief Apostle, and that he exercised his supreme power to govern the Church via a direct appointment by Christ. On three different occasions Christ speaks of the primacy of St. Peter over the other apostles:

(1.) After Peter had acknowledged His divinity, Christ promised him a reward in the following words: "And I tell you, you are Peter, and on this rock I will build my church, and the powers of death shall not prevail against it. I will give you the keys to the kingdom of heaven, and whatever you bind on earth shall be bound in heaven, and whatever you loose on earth shall be loosed in heaven" (Matthew 16:18-19).

The metaphor of the rock is easily understood. Christ the Rock, the chief cornerstone of the Church (Ephesians 2:20), promises to make Peter the rock, on which His Church (I Corinthians 3:11) is to be built. He is addressing Peter alone, not the other Apostles. Jesus has in mind the wise man in His own parable in Matthew 7:24.

Then Jesus gives the reason why He intends to build His Church upon Peter the Rock when He says "the powers of death shall not prevail against it." The Church of Christ is to withstand the attacks of every enemy from within or without until the end of time.

The symbol of the keys implies power and authority, and the giving of keys is to transfer that authority. We even honor dignitaries today by giving them the keys to the city. When we sell a building we give the keys to the new owner on the day that ownership is transferred. Prisoners particularly understand the authority and power attached to keys, as it is the guard alone who possesses keys. At shift change, when one guard leaves and another takes his place, the keys transfer from the old guard to the new. Even then, the power of the keys lies ultimately with the prison warden. The guards merely act with the authority the warden has given them.

(2.) The night before He died Jesus told Peter: "Simon, Simon, behold, Satan demanded to have you, that he might sift you like wheat, but I have prayed for you that your faith may not fail; and when you have turned again, strengthen your brethren" (Luke 22:31). Satan had desired to try Peter, as he had once tried Job (Job 1:11-12). Although He prayed for all the Apostles, Jesus tells Peter that He prayed especially for him so that he would strengthen his brothers. Christ prophesies that Peter will deny knowing Him, but not that he will deny who Jesus is. Just as the Church is "the pillar and bulwark of truth" (I Timothy 3:15), so is Peter the strengthener of the other Apostles. Simon is the security of the Church against Satan and the powers of hell; he is the solid rock on which the Church is to be built.

(3.) After the resurrection, Christ granted St. Peter the primacy He had twice promised. Here is the scene: "When they had finished breakfast, Jesus said to Simon Peter, 'Simon, son of John, do you love me more than these?' He said to him, 'Yes, Lord; you know that I love you.' He said to him, 'Feed my lambs.' A second time he said to him, 'Simon, son of John, do you love me?' He said to him, 'Yes, Lord; you know that I love you.' He said to him, 'Tend my sheep.' He said to him the third time, 'Simon, son of John, do you love me?' Peter was grieved because he said to him the third time, 'Do you love me?' And he said to him, 'Lord, you know everything; you know that I love you.' Jesus said to him, 'Feed my sheep' " (John 21:15-17).

Jesus' three-fold question reminds Peter of his former presumption (Matthew 26:33), and his three-fold denial (Matthew 26:75), and lets the other Apostles know that Peter's love for Him is the greatest. It was because of this that Christ gave Peter the higher office. Peter doesn't boast about his love this time, but instead appeals to Christ's omniscience as evidence of its reality.

The symbolism is plain to any honest reader. Christ declared Himself the Good Shepherd (John 10:11-16) frequently spoken of by the prophets (cf. Ezekial 34:23; 37:24-26; Zacharias 10:7). As the divine Ruler of the whole flock, Jesus makes Peter the ruler in his place now that He has to return to the Father. Christ's supreme power of teaching, judging, and legislating are now delegated to St. Peter and his successors.

Peter's preeminence is suggested in many passages of the New Testament. His name is changed at his first meeting with Christ (John 1:42), thus indicating the office to be given him later. He is always listed first in the lists of Apostles (Matthew 10:2; Mark 3:16; Luke 6:14), and always indicated as their leader (Matthew 17:1; 17:24-

25; 26:37-40; Mark 5:37; Luke 5:2-10; 7:44). After the resurrection Peter presides over the election of Matthias (Acts 1:15-26); he is the first to preach the gospel (Acts 2:14-47); he is the first to work miracles (Acts 3:6-7); it is he who judges Ananias and Saphira (Acts 5:3-10); he is the first to make a pagan convert (Acts 10); and he presides over the Council of Jerusalem (Acts 15).

### 627. Doesn't the rock refer to Christ in Matthew 16:18?

As many honest Protestant scholars admit, the word rock refers to Peter in Matthew 16:18. The early Christians frequently speak of Peter as the rock. Tertullian writes: "Peter, who is called the rock whereon the Church was to be built, and who obtained the keys to the kingdom of heaven...."[1] St. Cyprian writes: "Peter, whom the Lord chose as first, and upon whom He built His Church...."[2]

The great apologist Karl Keating tells us that people who refuse to accept the Catholic interpretation of Matthew 16:18 "note that in the Greek text the name of the apostle is *Petros*, a masculine noun, while rock is rendered as *petra*, which is feminine. The first means a small stone, the second a massive rock. If Peter was meant to be the massive rock, the steady foundation of the Church here below, why is his name not *Petra*? As Loraine Boettner puts it in *Roman Catholicism*, 'The Greek *petros* is commonly used of a small, movable stone, a mere pebble, as it were. But *petra* means an immovable foundation, in this instance, the basic truth that Peter had just confessed, the deity of Christ.'

---

[1] Tertullian, *De Praes.*, 22.
[2] St. Cyprian, *Ad Quintum*, Epistle 71.

"Boettner continues by saying, 'Had Christ intended to say that the Church would be founded on Peter, it would have been ridiculous for Him to have shifted to the feminine form of the word in the middle of the statement, saying, if we may translate literally and somewhat whimsically, "And I say unto thee, that thou art Mr. Rock, and upon this, the Miss Rock, I will build my Church...." He made two complete, distinct statements. He said, "Thou art Peter," and "upon this rock (change of gender indicating change of subject) I will build my church." ' Boettner's 'whimsy' obscures the straight forward solution to this problem.

"The first thing to note is that Christ did not speak to the disciples in Greek. (And not Hebrew, either, which was reserved as a sacred language and was not in common use, somewhat analogously to the way Latin, in the recent past, was the sacred language of Catholics, but was not used by them in everyday speech.) Christ spoke Aramaic, the common language of Palestine at the time. In that language the word for rock is *kepha*. What was said was thus: 'Thou art *Kepha*, and upon this *kepha* I will build my Church.' When Matthew's Gospel was translated from the original Aramaic to Greek, there arose a problem that did not confront the evangelist when he first composed his account of Christ's life in his native tongue.

"In Aramaic the word *kepha* has the same ending whether it refers to a rock or is used as a man's name. In Greek, though, the word for rock, *petra*, is feminine in gender. The translator could use it for the second appearance of *kepha* in the sentence, but not for the first, because it would be inappropriate to give a man a feminine name. So he put a masculine ending on it, and there was *Petros*, which happened to be a preexisting word meaning a small stone. Some of the effect of the play on words was lost, but that was the best that could be done in Greek.

In English, as in Aramaic, there is no problem with the endings, so an English rendering could read: 'Thou Art Rock, and upon this rock I will build my church.' In modern French Bibles, the word *pierre* appears in both places. The real meaning is hard to miss."[3]

**628. Doesn't the Bible require faith and repentance for baptism? How can babies be baptized?**

Space does not permit the extensive answer this question deserves, so we recommend that readers obtain a copy of Karl Keating's book *Catholicism and Fundamentalism*, in which Mr. Keating devotes an entire chapter to this question. Still, we will attempt an adequate defense of the Church's teaching on this subject of infant baptism.

The early Christians unanimously insist that infants are to be baptized, basing it on the universal command of Christ to baptize all (Matthew 28:19; John 3:5), and on its divine power to cleanse the soul of original sin. St. Iranaeus (140-205) writes: "He came to save all who through Him are born again unto God; infants, and children, boys and youths, and elders."[4] Origen (185-255) declares infant baptism an apostolic institution,[5] and necessary to cleanse the infant of original sin.[6] St. Cyprian and the bishops at the Third Council of Carthage (253) taught that children should be baptized as soon as possible after birth. Their baptism was not to be deferred until the eighth day, as some had maintained.

---

[3] Karl Keating, *Catholicism and Fundamentalism*, 209-210.

[4] St. Iranaeus, *Adv. Haer.* : 2:22.

[5] Origen, *Epis. ad. Rom.*; 5:9.

[6] Origen, *In Lev.*, 8:3.

# Appendix Two

## *Basic Prayers*

### Sign of the Cross
In the name of the Father, and of the Son, and of the Holy Spirit. Amen.

### Morning Offering
O my God, in union with the Immaculate Heart of Mary (*here kiss your Brown Scapular as a sign of your consecration*), I offer Thee the Precious Blood of Jesus from all the altars throughout the world, joining with It the offering of my every thought, word and action of this day.

O my Jesus, I desire today to gain every indulgence and merit I can, and I offer them, together with myself, to Mary Immaculate — that she may apply them to the interests of Thy most Sacred Heart. Precious Blood of Jesus, save us! Immaculate Heart of Mary, pray for us! Sacred Heart of Jesus, have mercy on us!

### In the Morning
I adore You, my God, and I love you with all my heart. I thank you for having created me, made me a Christian, and kept me this night. I offer You my actions of this day: grant that they all may be according to Your holy will and for Your greater glory. Keep me from all sin and evil. May Your grace be always with me and with my dear ones. Amen.

### The Our Father
Our Father, who art in heaven, hallowed be Thy name; Thy kingdom come, Thy will be done on earth as it is in heaven. Give us this day our daily bread; and forgive us our trespasses as we forgive those who trespass against us; and lead us not into temptation, but deliver us from evil. Amen.

## Hail Mary

Hail Mary, full of grace! The Lord is with thee. Blessed art thou among women and blessed is the fruit of thy womb, Jesus.

Holy Mary mother of God pray for us sinners now, and at the hour of our death. Amen.

## Glory Be to the Father

Glory be to the Father, and to the Son, and to the Holy Spirit. As it was in the beginning, is now, and ever shall be, world without end. Amen.

## The Apostles' Creed

I believe in God, the Father Almighty, Creator of heaven and earth; and in Jesus Christ, His only Son, our Lord; who was conceived by the Holy Spirit, born of the Virgin Mary, suffered under Pontius Pilate, was crucified, died and was buried. He descended into hell; the third day He arose again from the dead; He ascended into heaven, sits at the right hand of God, the Father Almighty; from thence He shall come to judge the living and the dead.

I believe in the Holy Spirit, the holy Catholic Church, the communion of saints, the forgiveness of sins, the resurrection of the body, and life everlasting. Amen.

## An Act of Faith

O my God, I firmly believe that you are one God in three Divine Persons, Father, Son, and Holy Spirit; I believe that Your Divine Son became man and died for our sins, and that He will come to judge the living and the dead. I believe these and all the truths which the holy Catholic Church teaches, because You revealed them, who can neither deceive nor be deceived.

## An Act of Hope
O my God, relying on Your infinite goodness and promises, I hope to obtain pardon of my sins, the help of your grace, and life everlasting, through the merits of Jesus Christ, my Lord and Redeemer.

## An Act of Love
O my God, I love You above all things, with my whole heart and soul, because You are all good and worthy of all love. I love my neighbor as myself for love of You. I forgive all who have injured me, and I ask pardon of all whom I have injured.

## For the Pope
Lord, cover with Your protection, our Holy Father, the Pope; be his light, his strength, his consolation.

## Hail Holy Queen
Hail, Holy Queen, Mother of Mercy, our life, our sweetness, and our hope! To you do we cry, poor banished children of Eve; to you do we send up our sighs, mourning and weeping in this vale of tears. Turn then, most gracious advocate, your eyes of mercy toward us, and after this our exile, show unto us the blessed fruit of your womb, Jesus. O clement, O loving, O sweet Virgin Mary.

## Angel of God
Angel of God, my guardian dear, to whom God's love entrusts me here, ever this day be at my side to light and guard, to rule and guide. Amen.

## An Act of Contrition
O, my God, I am heartily sorry for having offended Thee, and I detest all my sins, because of Thy just punishments, but most of all because they offend Thee, my God, who are all-

good and deserving of all my love. I firmly resolve, with the help of Thy grace, to sin no more and to avoid the near occasions of sin.

## Grace Before Meals

Bless us, O Lord, and these Thy gifts, which we are about to receive from Thy bounty, through Christ our Lord. Amen.

## Grace After Meals

We give Thee thanks for all Thy benefits, O almighty God, who lives and reigns forever; and may the souls of all the faithful departed, through the mercy of God, rest in peace. Amen.

## Prayer Before a Crucifix

Behold, my beloved and good Jesus, I cast myself upon my knees in Your sight, and with the most fervent desire of my soul I pray and beseech You to impress upon my heart lively sentiments of faith, hope and charity, with true repentance of my sins and a most firm desire of amendment; while with deep affection and grief of soul I consider within myself and mentally contemplate Your five most precious wounds, having before my eyes that which David, the prophet, long ago spoke about You, my Jesus: "They have pierced my hands and my feet; I can count all my bones."

## Soul of Christ

Soul of Christ, sanctify me.
Body of Christ, save me.
Blood of Christ, inebriate me.
Water from the side of Christ, wash me.
Passion of Christ, strengthen me.
O good Jesus, hear me.
Within Your wounds hide me.
Permit me not to be separated from You.

From the malignant enemy defend me.
In the hour of my death call me.
And bid me come to You,
That with Your saints I may praise You
For ever and ever. Amen.

## Litany of the Sacred Heart

Lord, have mercy on us.
Christ, have mercy on us.
Lord, have mercy on us.
Christ, hear us.
Christ, graciously hear us.
      (Repeat "have mercy on us" after each invocation.)
God, the Father of heaven,
God the Son, Redeemer of the World,
God the Holy Spirit,
Holy Trinity one God,
Heart of Jesus, formed by the Holy Spirit in the womb of the Virgin Mother,
Heart of Jesus, substantially united to the Word of God,
Heart of Jesus, of infinite majesty,
Heart of Jesus, sacred temple of God,
Heart of Jesus, tabernacle of the Most High,
Heart of Jesus, house of God and gate of heaven,
Heart of Jesus, burning furnace of charity,
Heart of Jesus, abode of justice and love,
Heart of Jesus, full of goodness and love,
Heart of Jesus, abyss of all virtues,
Heart of Jesus, most worthy of all praises,
Heart of Jesus, King and center of all hearts,
Heart of Jesus, in Whom are all the treasures of wisdom and knowledge,
Heart of Jesus, in Whom dwells the fullness of divinity,
Heart of Jesus, in Whom the Father was well pleased,
Heart of Jesus, of Whose fullness we have all received,

Heart of Jesus, desire of the everlasting hills,
Heart of Jesus, patient and most merciful,
Heart of Jesus, enriching all who invoke You,
Heart of Jesus, fountain of life and holiness,
Heart of Jesus, propitiation for our sins,
Heart of Jesus, loaded down with opprobrium,
Heart of Jesus, bruised for our offenses,
Heart of Jesus, obedient unto death,
Heart of Jesus, pierced with a lance,
Heart of Jesus, source of all consolation,
Heart of Jesus, our life and resurrection,
Heart of Jesus, our peace and reconciliation,
Heart of Jesus, victim for sins,
Heart of Jesus, salvation of those who trust in You,
Heart of Jesus, hope of those who die in You,
Heart of Jesus, delight of all the saints,

Lamb of God, who take away the sins of the world, spare us,
O Lord.
Lamb of God, who take away the sins of the world, graciously hear us, O Lord.
Lamb of God, who take away the sins of the world, have mercy on us.

V. Jesus, meek and humble of Heart,
R. Make our hearts like Yours.

### Let Us Pray

O almighty and everlasting God, look upon the heart of Your well-beloved Son, and the praise and satisfaction He offers You in the name of sinners and for those who seek Your mercy. Be appeased, and grant us pardon in the name of the same Jesus Christ, Your Son, who lives and reigns with You in the unity of the Holy Spirit, world without end. Amen.

## The Mysteries of the Rosary

*Joyful Mysteries*
(Monday and Thursday)
The Annunciation of the Angel to Mary.
The Visitation of Mary to Her Cousin Elizabeth.
The Nativity.
The Presentation of Jesus in the Temple.
The Finding of Jesus in the Temple.

*Sorrowful Mysteries*
(Tuesday and Friday)
The Agony in the Garden.
The Scourging at the Pillar.
The Crowning with Thorns.
The Carrying of the Cross.
The Crucifixion and Death.

*Glorious Mysteries*
(Wednesday, Saturday, Sunday)
The Resurrection.
The Ascension.
The Descent of the Holy Spirit.
The Assumption of the Blessed Virgin.
The Coronation of Mary as Queen of Heaven.

### Memorare

Remember, O most gracious Virgin Mary, that never was it known that anyone who fled to thy protection, implored thy assistance, or sought thy intercession was left unaided. Inspired with this confidence, we fly to thee, O Virgin of virgins, our Mother; to thee we come; before thee we stand sinful and sorrowful. O Mother of the Word Incarnate, despise not our petitions, but in thy mercy hear and answer them. Amen.

## Litany of the Blessed Virgin Mary

Lord, have mercy on us.
Christ, have mercy on us.
Lord, have mercy on us.
Christ, hear us.
Christ, graciously hear us.
God the Father of heaven, have mercy on us.
God the Son, Redeemer of the world, have mercy on us.
God the Holy Spirit, have mercy on us.
Holy Trinity, one God, have mercy on us.

(Repeat "pray for us" after each invocation.)

Holy Mary,
Holy Mother of God,
Holy Virgin of virgins,
Mother of Christ,
Mother of divine grace,
Mother most pure,
Mother most chaste,
Mother inviolate,
Mother undefiled,
Mother most amiable,
Mother most admirable,
Mother of good counsel,
Mother of our Creator,
Mother of our Redeemer,
Virgin most prudent,
Virgin most venerable,
Virgin most renowned,
Virgin most powerful,
Virgin most merciful,
Virgin most faithful,
Mirror of justice,
Seat of wisdom,
Cause of our joy,
Spiritual Vessel,

Vessel of honor,
Singular vessel of devotion,
Mystical rose,
Tower of David,
Tower of Ivory,
House of gold,
Ark of the covenant,
Gate of Heaven,
Morning star,
Refuge of sinners,
Comforter of the afflicted,
Help of Christians,
Queen of Angels,
Queen of Patriarchs,
Queen of Prophets,
Queen of Apostles,
Queen of Martyrs,
Queen of Confessors,
Queen of Virgins,
Queen of all Saints,
Queen conceived without original sin,
Queen assumed into heaven,
Queen of the Most Holy Rosary,
Queen of Peace,

Lamb of God, who take away the sins of the world, spare us, O Lord.
Lamb of God, who take away the sins of the world, graciously hear us, O Lord.
Lamb of God, who take away the sins of the world, have mercy on us.

### Let Us Pray

O God, whose only begotten Son by His life, death, and resurrection, has purchased for us the rewards of eternal salvation, grant, we pray, that meditating on these mysteries in the most holy rosary of the Blessed Virgin Mary, we may imitate what they contain and obtain what they promise. Amen.

### Prayer to the Holy Spirit

Come, Holy Spirit, fill the hearts of Your faithful and kindle within them the fire of Your love.

V. Send forth Your Spirit and they shall be created,

R. And You shall review the face of the earth.

### Let Us Pray

O God, who has taught the hearts of Your faithful by the light of the Holy Spirit, grant that by the gift of the same Spirit, we may be truly wise and ever rejoice in His consolations. Through Christ our Lord. Amen.

### Prayer to St. Joseph for Purity

St Joseph, father and guardian of virgins, to whose faithful care Christ Jesus, Innocence itself, and Mary, Virgin of Virgins, were committed, I pray and beg of you by these dear pledges, Jesus and Mary, free me from all uncleanness, and make me with spotless mind, pure heart and chaste body, ever more chastely to serve Jesus and Mary, all the days of my life. Amen.

# Appendix Three

## *Preparation for the Sacrament of Penance*[7]

*Preparation for confession should be thoughtful, not routine. It is important to ask the Lord for light:*

"O Lord, may I know myself; may I know you!" (St. Augustine) May I know my selfishness, ignorance and weakness, and know, too, that you are ready to lift me up and sustain me as I climb toward the spiritual heights you call me to attain. May I distrust myself and trust in you! Enlighten my mind, that I may see all my sins clearly. Soften my heart, that I may be truly sorry for them. Give me the grace and courage to confess them sincerely, and thus obtain your pardon; through Jesus Christ my Lord and Savior. Amen.

### Examination of Conscience

How long has it been since my last confession? Did I receive absolution? Did I purposely omit a mortal sin or make a false statement regarding a mortal sin? Was I sorry for my sins? Did I perform the penance the priest asked of me? (*Try to determine the number of times you committed each sin, especially serious sins. Also mention circumstances that may have changed the nature of the sins confessed.*)

---

[7] The totality of this *Preparation for the Sacrament of Penance* is reprinted from *Queen of Apostles Prayerbook* compiled by the Daughters of St. Paul, with permission of copyright holder, St. Paul Books & Media, 50 St. Paul's Avenue, Boston, MA 02130.

**First Commandment:** *I am the Lord your God; you shall not have strange gods before me.*

Have I doubted God's existence without trying to resolve my doubt?

Have I denied that I was a Catholic?

Have I refused to believe anything the Catholic Church teaches?

Have I formed close friendships with anyone who might endanger my faith?

Have I exposed my faith to danger by unnecessarily going to places where Catholic belief was attacked, or by frequently associating with anti-Catholics, or by reading books, articles, etc., that attack or speak disrespectfully about God, the Church, or Christian practices? Was I ashamed of my faith?

Have I omitted my prayers or other Christian practices because of the presence of others?

If I succeeded at something, did I glory in the success without any recognition of God's gifts to help me and His help?

Have I boasted of sin? Despaired of God's mercy, or doubted it? Murmured against God? Have I neglected to seek instruction about my faith when I knew that I needed it?

Have I willfully neglected my prayers? Is this a habit? Have I omitted all my prayers for some time?

Have I believed in superstitions — that is, believed in fortunetelling, charms, omens, lucky numbers, etc.?

Have I gone to spiritistic seances?

Have I treated disrespectfully things and places consecrated to God?

Have I received Communion in the state of mortal sin, or made an unworthy confession?

Have I willfully retained rebellious thoughts against God?

*Second Commandment:* You shall not take the name of the Lord your God in vain.

Have I used the name of God thoughtlessly, or in cursing, or in blasphemy?

Have I spoken irreverently about the saints or holy things, about the Church or its practices, customs, ceremonies?

Have I committed perjury or sworn by God's name in a trivial matter?

If I have made a vow, have I failed to fulfill it, or deferred its fulfillment for a long time without a sufficient reason?

Have I been a member of a forbidden society?

*Third Commandment:* Remember to keep holy the Lord's day.

Have I failed to attend Mass on Sundays/Saturday evenings or holy days of obligation without a sufficient reason? Was I late? Very late through my own fault? Did I leave before the end of Mass? Is this a habit?

During Mass or other religious services, have I acted disrespectfully, talked unnecessarily, or been willfully distracted? Have I distracted others?

Have I performed unnecessary hard or heavy work on Sundays or holy days of obligation? If so, for several hours?

*Fourth Commandment:* Honor your father and your mother.

Have I disobeyed my parents or other lawful superiors?

Have I insulted, grieved or ridiculed them?

Have I willfully done things to make them unhappy?

Have I struck them?

Have I failed to help them when they needed my help?

Have I failed to pray for them?

Have I failed to have Masses celebrated for them after they were dead?

Have I shown contempt for the laws of the Church or civil laws that are just and proper?

***Fifth Commandment:*** *You shall not kill.*

Have I caused or contributed to the death of another by willful neglect or a deliberate act, such as abortion?

Have I unjustly wounded or struck another?

Have I endangered another's life or health?

Have I endangered my own life?

Have I given vent to anger through explosive words or actions rather than controlled assertiveness and harmless physical outlets?

Have I allowed anger to turn into resentful brooding?

Have I hated someone? Wished someone evil? Desired revenge, or refused to forgive injuries?

Have I shown aversion or contempt toward others?

Have I refused to show the ordinary signs of friendship to my relatives and friends? Refused to speak to others?

Have I ridiculed or insulted others? Have I fought or quarreled?

Have I led others into sin? Taught others to commit sin?

Have I been intemperate in eating or drinking?

Have I been intoxicated?

Have I used medical drugs to such an extent as to injure my health?

Have I used drugs for pleasure?

Have I sold drugs?

**Sixth and Ninth Commandments**: *You shall not commit adultery. You shall not covet your neighbor's wife.*

Have I willfully entertained impure thoughts? Have I taken pleasure in them?

Have I had impure desires? Desired to do impure things? If so, with whom, that is, with relatives, persons of the same or opposite sex, married or religious persons?

Have I willfully listened to impure talk or songs, or shown pleasure in them and thus encouraged them?

Have I spoken of impure things? If so, in the presence of children or the opposite sex?

Have I desired to see impure things?

Have I willfully looked at impure pictures?

Have I read impure books, papers, or magazines, or given them to others to read?

Have I told impure or double-meaning jokes?

Have I touched myself or others impurely?

Have I committed an impure act with myself or others? What act? With persons of the same or opposite sex, children, relatives, or married persons? With animals?

Have I willingly been an occasion of sin to another by dressing immodestly?

Have I willfully and without necessity endangered my virtue by associating with questionable persons or by frequenting questionable places?

Am I dating someone whom I cannot lawfully marry, or am I permitting myself to fall in love with such a person?

If I am dating, am I guarding myself against all unnecessary occasions of sin? Have I been guilty of passionate kissing or love-making?

***Seventh and Tenth Commandments:*** *You shall not steal.*
*You shall not covet your neighbor's goods.*

Have I taken anything that was not my own?

Have I injured another's property or interests?

Have I charged exorbitant prices or adulterated something I sold?

Have I made restitution — that is, have I restored what I took or paid the owner its value?

Have I cheated in any other way?

Have I unjustly kept things that were not my own, when I knew the owner?

Have I failed to guard the property of others, or their person, when it was my duty to do so?

Have I failed to do sufficient work for my wages?

Have I failed to pay a just wage to my employees?

If I have failed in this, have I made restitution?

Did I commit an injustice against the Church?

Have I desired to do something unjust?

Have I sinned against justice in any other way?

***Eighth Commandment:*** *You shall not bear false witness against your neighbor.*

Have I unjustly injured the reputation of another by lying, or exposing that person's faults without necessity? Have I thereby caused grave harm?

Have I revealed the secrets of another? Professional secrets?

Have I read the letters of others when I had no right to read them?

Have I listened with pleasure to the exposure of the faults of others, or to lies told about them?

Have I rashly misjudged others, or falsely suspected them?

Have I lied?

### Commandments of the Church:

Have I failed to fast and abstain when I was not excused by a sufficient reason?

Have I confessed my sins at least once a year?

Have I received holy Communion at least once a year, during Easter time?

Have I failed to contribute to the support of my parish and diocese, the Holy Father and the missions, according to my means?

Have I attempted to contract marriage without the blessing of the Church?

### For Parents and Married People:

Have I had my children baptized as soon as convenient?

Have I taught them their prayers in due time?

Have I provided as best I could for their religious instruction and Christian formation?

Have I seen to it that they receive the sacraments frequently?

Have I watched over their companions, their reading matter, their viewing habits, etc.?

Have I done anything contrary to the love-giving, life-giving purpose of marriage — such as practicing artificial birth control?

## Resolution and Prayer after the
## Examination of Conscience

*Sincerely detest your sins. Resolve not to sin again, and to avoid anything that might lead you into sin.*

*Sorrow and resolution are essential for the reception for the sacrament of reconciliation.*

O holy Mary, my mother and the refuge of sinners, pray for me that I may make a good confession, that I may obtain forgiveness of my sins and never offend your Son again. Amen.

# Appendix Four

## Catholic Resource Guide

We have compiled this appendix so the reader may grow in knowledge, prayer, and soul by using some of these resources. We list books, magazines, newspapers, audio's, videos, and publishers with which we are personally familiar; however, this is by no means exhaustive, and we suggest that readers search for additional resources independently.

### Newspapers

*National Catholic Register* (33 Rossotto Drive, Hamden, CT 06514). Weekly newspaper of general interest to Catholics.

*The Wanderer* (201 Ohio St., St. Paul, MN 55107). This hard hitting weekly is a staunch defender of the Catholic faith.

### Magazines

*Catholic Digest* (P. O. Box 64090, St. Paul, MN 55164). A monthly of general interest to Catholics.

*The Catholic Faith* (P.O. Box 591090, San Francisco, CA 94159-1090). Bi-monthly Catechesis.

*The Catholic World Report* (2515 McAllister St., San Francisco, CA 94118). A beautifully done monthly news magazine that views world and U.S. events from a Catholic perspective.

*Communio* (P. O. Box 4557, Washington, DC 20017). A quarterly on Catholic thought and theology.

*The Family* (50 St. Paul's Ave., Boston, MA 02130). This monthly is a wholesome Catholic family magazine.

*Homiletic and Pastoral Review* (P.O. Box 591810, San Francisco, CA 94159-1810). A monthly journal designed for priests, but an excellent resource for people who wish to learn more about the Catholic faith, or who wish to share the faith.

*This Rock* (P. O. Box 17490, San Diego, CA 92177). A monthly magazine that teaches the reader how to defend the faith against attacks from non-Catholics, and promotes evangelization. This magazine gets our strongest endorsement.

### Books

For this section, not all of the information is complete due to our limited resources. We will provide all of the information on the following books that we can, but publishers' or authors' name may be absent. Virtually all of these books can be ordered through the publisher or through Magnificat Institute Press.

*A Warning is Given*, by John F. Downs, et. al.; published by Apostolatus Uniti, Woodstock, VA.

*A Handbook of Catholic Sacramentals*, by Ann Ball; published by Our Sunday Visitor Publishing, Huntington, IN.

*Orthodoxy*, by G. K. Chesterton; published by Ignatius Press, San Francisco, CA.

*The Incorruptibles*, by Joan Carroll Cruz; published by TAN Books and Publishers, Rockford, IL.

*Everything You Ever Wanted to Know About Heaven*, by Dr. Peter Kreeft; published by Ignatius Press, San Francisco, CA.

*The Sermon on the Mount*, by Anton Morgenroth; published by Trinity Communications, Manassas, VA.

*Our Father's Plan*, by Fr. William G. Most; published by Trinity Communications, Manassas, VA.

*Crossing the Threshold of Hope*, by Pope John Paul II; published by Knopf, NY.

*Purgatory*, by F. X. Schouppe; published by TAN Books and Publishers, Rockford, IL.

*Theology for Beginners*, by Frank Sheed; published by Ignatius Press, San Francisco, CA.

*Charity, Morality, Sex, and Young People*, by Fr. Robert J. Fox; published by Trinity Communications, Manassas, VA.

*Back to Virtue*, by Dr. Peter Kreeft; published by Ignatius Press, San Francisco, CA.

*Catholic Sexual Ethics*, by Fr. Ron Lawler, Joseph Boyle, and William May; published by Our Sunday Visitor Publishing, Huntington, IN.

*An Introduction to Moral Theology*, by Dr. William May; published by Our Sunday Visitor Publishing, Huntington, IN.

*Love and Responsibility*, by Karol Wojtyla (now Pope John Paul II); published by Farrar, Straus, Giroux, New York, NY.

*Eucharistic Miracles*, by Joan Carrol Cruz; published by TAN Books and Publishers, Rockford, IL.

*The World's Greatest Secret*, by John M. Haffert; published by AMI Press, Washington, NJ.

*Marriage is for Keeps,* by John F. Kippley; published by the Foundation for the Family, Cincinnati, OH.

*Annulment*, by Joseph Zwack; published by Harper and Row, New York, NY.

*A Doctor at Calvary*, by Pierre Barbet, M.D.; published by Image Books, Garden City, NY.

*To Know Christ Jesus,* by Frank Sheed; published by Ignatius Press, San Francisco, CA.

*The Mary Book,* by Fr. Robert J. Fox; published by the Fatima Family Apostolate, Alexandia, SD.

*The Sign of Her Heart,* by John M. Haffert; published by AMI Press, Washington, NJ.

*Our Lady of Fatima,* by William Thomas Walsh; published by Image Books, New York, NY.

*Church History,* by Fr. John Laux; published by TAN Books and Publishers, Rockford, IL.

*Evidence for Our Faith,* by Joseph Cavanaugh; published by University of Notre Dame Press, Notre Dame, IN.

*Protestant Fundamentalism and the Born Again Catholic,* by Fr. Robert J. Fox; published by Fatima Family Apostolate, Alexandria, SD.

*Rome Sweet Home,* by Scott and Kimberly Hahn; published by Ignatius Press, San Francisco, CA.

*Catholicism and Fundamentalism,* by Karl Keating; published by Ignatius Press, San Francisco, CA.

*Surprised by Truth,* by Patrick Madrid; published by Basilica Press, San Diego, CA.

*Radio Replies,* by Fathers Leslie Rumble and Charles Carty; published by TAN Books and Publishers, Rockford, IL. (3 volumes).

*Fundamentals of Catholic Dogma* by Ludwig Ott; published by TAN Books and Publishers, Rockford, IL.

*The Imitation of Christ,* by Thomas A'Kempis

*Saint Bernadette Soubirous,* by Abbe Francios Trochu; published by TAN Books and Publishers, Rockford, IL.

*The Sinner's Guide,* by Ven. Louis of Granada; published by TAN Books and Publishers, Rockford, IL.

*The Divine Romance* by Archbishop Fulton J. Sheen.

*10 Good Reasons to be a Catholic,* by Jim Aver.

*City of God,* by St. Augustine.

*Trojan Horse in the City of God*, by Dietrich Von Hildebrand.

*True Devotion to Mary*, by St. Louis De Montfort.

*The Confessions*, by St. Augustine.

*The 12 Steps to Holiness and Salvation*, by St. Alphonsus Liguori.

*Facts About Luther*, by Patrick O'Hare; published by TAN Books and Publishers, Rockford, IL.

*Summa Theologica*, by St. Thomas Aquinas. (5 volumes).

*The Fire Within*, by Fr. Thomas Dubar; published by Ignatius Press, San Francisco, CA.

*Vatican Council II: The Conciliar and Post Conciliar Documents*, edited by Austin Flannery.

## The Following May Be Obtained From Magnificat Institute Press

*Dominican Laity and the Year 2000*, by Anthony Dao Quang Chinh.

*About Happiness,* by Fr. William A. Kaschmitter, M.M.

*About Living*, by Fr. Victor Brezik.

*Rafael Cardinal Merry del Val* by Marie C. Buehrle.

*The Enemy Within the Gate* by John McKee.

*A Martyr Bishop: The Life Story of Oliver Plunkett* by John McKee.

*The Spirituality of the Catholic Church* by Rev. William A. Kaschmitter.

*Augustin Cardinal Bea: Spiritual Profile* by Stephen Schmidt, S.J.

*The New St. Joseph Baltimore Catechism*, Official Revised Edition Explained by Fr. Bennet, C.P.

*In Human Touch*, by Janina Babris.

*About Being A Priest* by Fr. Fedrico Suarez.

*Original Sin in the Light of Modern Science* by Rev. Patrick O'Connell, B.D.

*Stages of Simplicity* by Francis Florand, O.P.

*Marriage: A Path to Sanctity* by Javier Abad Eugenio Fenoy.

*The Catechetical Instruction of St. Thomas Acquinas.*

*Conscience & Freedom*, by Cormac Burke, second edition.

*Question & Answer Catechism* by Fr. M. Guzman and Fr. M. Castillo.

*Contraception and the Family*, by Fr. Roberto A. Latorre.

*The Children's Bible*, by Juan Marques Surinach.

*The Faith Explained*, by Leo J. Tresc.

*A Spiritual Retreat at Home*, by Fr. Ignatius R. Segarra.

*Jesus As Friend - Meditations*, by Salvatore Canals.

*Guadalupe What Her Eyes Say*, by Francis Anson.

*God and Children*, by Fr. Jesus Urteaga.

*Mary of Nazareth*, by Fredrico Suarez.

*The Leaven of the Gospel in Secular Society*, by Fr. Joseph M. De Torre.

*Will It Liberate: Questions About Liberation Theology*, by Michael Novak.

*Guidebook for Baptism*, by Fr. Luis Esteban Latorre.

### The Following May Be Obtained From Igantius Press

*Angels and Demons*, by Dr. Peter Kreeft.

*Living the Catechism of the Catholic Church*, by Bishop Christoph Schonborn.

*Marriage: The Rock on Which the Family is Built*, by Dr. William May.

*A Book of Angels*, by Marigold Hunt.

*A Moment of Grace*, by John Cardinal O'Connor.

*The Treasury of Catholic Wisdom*, by Fr. John A. Hardon.

*The Case for Clerical Celibacy*, by Alfons Cardinal Stickler.

*Catechism of the Catholic Church.*

*Introduction to the Catechism of the Catholic Church*, by Joseph Cardinal Ratzinger.
*A Companion to the Catechism of the Catholic Church.*
*Ignatius Bible - Catholic Edition of the RSV.*
*Theology and Sanity*, by Frank Sheed.
*The Jeweler's Shop*, by Karol Wojtyla (now Pope John Paul II).

## The Following Audio Cassettes May Be Obtained Through Leaflet Missal Company

*Gregorian Latin Classics*, by Jack Heinzl.
*The Bible and Mary*, by Steve Wood.
*Becoming a Catholic Even if You Happen to be One*, by Scott and Kimberly Hahn, Peter Kreeft, and Thomas Howard.
*The Gospel of St. John: A Scott Hahn Bible Study.*
*Romanism in Romans: A Scott Hahn Bible Study.*
*Becoming a Catholic Family*, by Scott and Kimberly Hahn, Peter Kreeft, and Thomas Howard.
*A New Look at Our Lady: A Biblical Understanding of Mary*, by Scott Hahn.
*The Answers to Seven Burdens of Life*, by Archbishop Fulton J. Sheen.
*Christ: His Passion and Death*, by Archbishop Fulton J. Sheen.
*Renewal and Reconciliation*, by Archbishop Fulton J. Sheen.
*Answering Common Objections*, by Scott Hahn.
*Baize: Veni Sanete Spiritus* (Spiritual music).
*Life is Worth Living*, by Archbishop Fulton J. Sheen.
*Covenant of Love and Life*, by Msgr. William Smith.
*An Ignatian Retreat*, by Fr. Donald McGuire.
*What Now America?*, by Archbishop Fulton J. Sheen.
*More Precious Than Jewels: How to be a Godly Wife and Mother*, by Kimberly Hahn.

*Cor Ad Cor Loquitur*, by Archbishop Fulton J. Sheen.

## The Following Audio Cassettes May Be Obtained From Ignatius Press

**Books on Tape**

*Theology for Beginners*, read by Paul Rogers.

*Catholicism and Fundamentalism*, read by Al Covaia.

*The Everlasting Man*, read by Al Covaia.

*A Popular History of the Catholic Church*, read by Mark Teheny.

*Abandonment to Divine Providence*, read by Mark Teheny.

**Standard Recordings**

*The Catholic Gospel,* by Scott Hahn.

*Hamanae Vitae: Making Happier, Healthier People*, by Janet Smith.

## The Following Videos May Be Obtained From Ignatius Press

*Come to the Stable*, with Loretta Young and Celeste Holm.

*The Seven Virtues*, with Fr. Benedict Groeschel.

*Contemplation*, with Fr. Thomas Dubay (2 tapes).

*A Celebration of Padre Pio.*

**The Chronicles of Narnia:**

*The Lion, the Witch, and the Wardrobe*

*Prince Caspian and the Voyage of the Dawn Trader*

*The Silver Chair*

*Patrick: Brave Shepherd of the Emerald Isle*, (animated).

*My Secret Friend: A Guardian Angel Story*, (animated).

*The Day the Sun Danced: The True Story of Fatima*, (animated).

*Nicholas: The Boy Who Became Santa*, (animated).

*The Bells of St. Mary's*, with Bing Crosby and Ingrid Bergman.

*Going My Way*, with Bing Crosby and Barry Fitzgerald.

*The Ten Commandments*, with Charlton Heston.

*Time for Mercy*, with Joseph Campanella.

*A Retreat with Fulton Sheen.*

*Becket*, with Richard Burton and Peter O'Toole.

*Sex and Love: What's a Teen to Do?*, with Mary Beth Bonacci.

*Fatima*, with Richardo Montalban.

*The Silent Witness*, (a documentary on the Shroud of Turin).

*The Agony and the Ecstasy*, with Charlton Heston and Rex Harrison.

*The Assisi Underground*, with Ben Cross, James Mason, and Irene Papas.

*Don Bosco*, with Ben Gazzarra.

*The Jeweler's Shop*, with Burt Lancaster, Ben Cross, and Olivia Hussey.

*A Man for All Seasons*, with Paul Scofield and Robert Shaw.

*Joan of Arc*, with Ingrid Bergman.

*The Detective*, with Alex Guiness.

*The Miracle of Marcelino*, with Fernando Rey.

*Jesus of Nazareth*, with Robert Powell, Olivia Hussey, Laurence Olivier, James Mason, and Anthony Quinn, (3 tapes).

*The Fourth Wise Man*, with Martin Sheen and Alan Arkin.

*The Miracle of Our Lady of Fatima*, with Gilbert Roland.

*The Song of Bernadette*, with Vincent Price, Lee J. Cobb, and Jennifer Jones.

*The Scarlet and the Black*, with Gregory Peck and Christopher Plummer.

*Pope John Paul II*, with Albert Finney as the Pope.

*A Time for Miracles*, with Kate Mulgrew.

*Fighting Father Dunne*, with Pat O'Brien.

*Mission*, with Robert DeNiro.

*This Is My Body, This Is My Blood: Miracles of the Eucharist*, with Bob and Penny Lord.
*Boys Town*, with Spencer Tracy and Mickey Rooney.
*A Time to Remember*, with Donald O'Connor.
*The Miracle of the Bells*, with Frank Sinatra and Fred MacMurry.

Papal encyclicals and other church documents can be obtained from:

St. Paul Editions
Daughters of St. Paul
50 St. Paul's Ave.
Boston, MA 02130

# Appendix Five

## First Article of the Creed

### *Examination*

### *True or False*

1. We are created by the angels.
2. We know God exists because our reason tells us so.
3. Tacitus was a pagan historian.
4. Jospehus was a pagan historian.
5. God has a body as we do.
6. God changes, becoming more perfect each day.
7. Omnipotence means God is everywhere.
8. Omnipotence means God is all-knowing.
9. Omnipotence means God is all-powerful.
10. God created the angels.
11. It is called Divine Providence when God takes loving care of us.
12. God is as equally capable of evil as He is of good.
13. The Blessed Trinity is three distinct Gods.
14. Our inability to understand the Trinity is called a mystery of Faith.
15. The angels have heavenly bodies.
16. God created all the angels good.
17. The angels assigned to take care of us are called archangels.
18. Man is a creature.
19. God created us because He was lonely.
20. God did not give us free will, but predestined our entire lives.
21. God created Adam and Eve as the first humans.
22. The greatest gift God gave Adam and Eve was freedom from death.

23.  Original sin is the first sin we each commit.
24.  Original sin is ordinarily removed by Baptism.
25.  The Immaculate Conception refers to Mary's pregnancy with Jesus.

## Second Article of the Creed

*Examination*

### True or False

1. The Incarnation is when God became man.
2. The name "Jesus" means Son of God.
3. Jesus is one Person.
4. Jesus is two Persons.
5. Jesus is three Persons.
6. Jesus has one nature.
7. Jesus has two natures.
8. Jesus has three natures.
9. Jesus is true God and true man.
10. Jesus has a human body and a human soul as we do.
11. Jesus has a human nature.
12. Jesus has a divine nature.
13. Jesus is a human Person.
14. Jesus is a divine Person.
15. Jesus has always existed.
16. The Son of God has always existed.
17. Jesus is the second God of the Blessed Trinity.
18. Jesus is the second Person of the Blessed Trinity.
19. Mary is the Mother of God because she gave birth to a divine nature.
20. Mary is the Mother of God because she gave birth to a divine Person.

## Third Article of the Creed

*Examination*

**True or False**

1. The Incarnation is when God became man.
2. The Incarnation is when the angel Gabriel asked Mary to become the Mother of God.
3. The Incarnation is when Mary was conceived.
4. The Annunciation is when God became man.
5. The Annunciation is when the angel Gabriel asked Mary to become the Mother of God.
6. The Annunciation is when Mary was conceived.
7. The father of Jesus is St. Joseph.
8. The father of Jesus is God the Holy Spirit.
9. The father of Jesus is God the Father.
10. Jesus chose to be born poor to teach us to be detached from earthly goods.
11. Mary was a virgin before she conceived Jesus.
12. Mary was a virgin during her pregnancy with Jesus.
13. Mary was a virgin after she gave birth to Jesus.
14. Jesus had brothers.
15. Mary is the Mother of God.
16. Mary became the Mother of the Church when Jesus gave her to John.
17. Devotion to Mary diminishes devotion to Christ.
18. Jesus only gradually realized He was God.
19. Jesus knew all things from the moment of His conception.
20. Jesus never said He was God.

## Fourth, Fifth, and Sixth Articles of the Creed

### Examination

**True or False**

1. Jesus is our Redeemer because He shed all His blood for the forgiveness of our sins.
2. Jesus' only suffering was His death on the cross.
3. Jesus died in a Roman torture chamber.
4. Jesus died on Calvary.
5. Jesus died on Golgotha.
6. Jesus died on Holy Thursday.
7. Jesus died as God.
8. Jesus died only for Christians.
9. Jesus did not have to die, because His smallest suffering would have redeemed us.
10. Jesus' soul descended into the limbo of the Fathers while His body lay in the tomb.
11. Jesus preached to the souls in "prison" after He died.
12. Jesus proved He is God by rising from the dead by His own power.
13. After the resurrection, Jesus spent forty days wandering around Palestine.
14. Jesus ascended into heaven to prepare a place for us.
15. Jesus ascended into heaven to be our Mediator with the Father.
16. Jesus ascended into heaven to send the Holy Spirit.
17. Jesus ascended into heaven alone.
18. That Jesus "sits at the right hand of God" means that His throne is next to the Father's.
19. Jesus is now only in heaven.
20. Jesus is King over all creation.

## Seventh and Eighth Articles of the Creed

### Examination

**True or False**

1. There will be three judgments.
2. The particular judgment takes place immediately after death.
3. The particular judgment takes place at the end of the world.
4. The general judgment takes place at the end of the world.
5. The general judgment takes place immediately after death.
6. Jesus specified the criteria for the particular judgment in the Bible.
7. Jesus specified the criteria for the general judgment in the Bible.
8. The criteria for the end of the world judgment is found in John 25.
9. The criteria for the end of the world judgment is found in Luke 25.
10. The criteria for the end of the world judgment is found in Mark 25.
11. The criteria for the end of the world judgment is found in Matthew 25.
12. When we feed the hungry, the Church teaches we are feeding Jesus literally.
13. The harsh treatment of prisoners is approved by Jesus and His Church.
14. The Holy Spirit is Jesus' created messenger.
15. The word "Paraclete" refers to Jesus.
16. The Holy Spirit came upon the Apostles during Passover.

17. The Holy Spirit came upon the Apostles on Passion Sunday.
18. The Holy Spirit came upon the Apostles on Pentecost Sunday.
19. The Holy Spirit is the Soul of Jesus.
20. The Holy Spirit is the Soul of the Church.

## Ninth Article of the Creed

*Examination*

**True or False**

1. St. Peter founded the Catholic Church.
2. Jesus founded the Catholic Church.
3. Jesus is the visible head of the Catholic Church.
4. Jesus founded the Church on St. Peter.
5. St. Peter's name, before Christ changed it, was Simon Bar Jona.
6. The Pope is the successor of Jesus.
7. The hierarchy of the Church includes the laity.
8. Bishops are successors of the Apostles.
9. The order of authority in the Church is the Pope, bishops, deacons, and priests.
10. Bishops are the authentic teachers of the Faith who share equal power with the Pope.
11. The priesthood is a means by which Christ unceasingly builds up and leads His Church.
12. Deacon comes from an Aramaic word meaning "kicking up dust."
13. There are two types of deacons.
14. A transitional deacon later becomes a priest.
15. A transitional deacon is a deacon for life.
16. Religious are any people who are pious.
17. The laity run the Church.
18. The earliest record of the word "catholic" being used as a name for the Church is found in a letter from St. Iraeneus in AD 107.
19. Another name for the Church is Mystical Body of Christ.
20. St. Paul's theology regarding the Mystical Body of Christ was formed by his conversion on the road to Damascus.

21. Jesus is the Soul of the Church.
22. The Church's mission is Jesus' own mission.
23. The obligation to advance the Church's mission is restricted solely to the Pope, bishops, priests, and deacons.
24. The Bible is the sole source of Divine Revelation.
25. Sacred Scripture is the written Word of God.
26. Sacred Tradition consists of customs, such as priestly dress.
27. The Magisterium is the living teaching authority of the Church.
28. There are two forms of the Magisterium.
29. The two forms of the Magisterium are *solemn* and *extraordinary*.
30. The Bible proves that Jesus founded the Catholic Church.
31. The word "catholic" is in the Bible.
32. The Church has two marks, or characteristics given by Christ.
33. To say the Church is universal is to say it is catholic.
34. The Catholic Church is holy because its founder, St. Peter, is holy.
35. The Catholic Church is holy because its founder, Jesus Christ, is holy.
36. To say the Church is indefectible is to say it can never err in its teaching on matters of faith and morals.
37. To say the Church is indefectible is to say it will last until the end of time.
38. To say the Church is infallible is to say it can never err in teaching on matters of faith and morals.
39. To say the Church is infallible is to say it will last until the end of time.

40. The Pope is infallible in his governance of the Church.
41. The Pope is infallible when teaching Church doctrine as universal pastor.
42. The Pope is infallible when speaking *ex cathedra*.
43. The Pope is infallible when acting as supreme law maker.
44. The bishops are infallible when teaching in union with the Pope.
45. The bishops are infallible when, with the Pope's approval, they teach by way of an ecumenical council.
46. Infallibility also means the Pope is sinless.
47. Jesus made His Church infallible so it would not compromise with the ideas of changing times.
48. Catholics are to love, respect, and obey the Church.
49. Heresy is the deliberate denial of one or more truths of the Catholic faith.
50. Heresy is the deliberate refusal to submit to the authority of the Pope.
51. Heresy is the complete rejection of one's Catholic faith.
52. Schism is the deliberate denial of one or more truths of the Catholic faith.
53. Schism is the deliberate refusal to submit to the authority of the Pope.
54. Schism is the complete rejection of one's Catholic faith.
55. Apostasy is the deliberate denial of one or more truths of the Catholic faith.
56. Apostasy is the deliberate refusal to submit to the authority of the Pope.
57. Apostasy is the complete rejection of one's Catholic faith.

58. All are obliged to belong to the Catholic Church.
59. The Church Suffering consists of Church members on earth.
60. The Church Suffering consists of Church members in purgatory.

## Tenth Article of the Creed

### *Examination*

**True or False**

1. The Church has the power to forgive all sin.
2. Blasphemy against the Holy Spirit is unforgivable.
3. Personal sin is the same as original sin.
4. There are two types of actual sin.
5. The worst of the types of actual sin is deadly, meaning it causes us to lose sanctifying grace.
6. For sin to be venial, thus causing loss of sanctifying grace, three elements must be present:  serious matter, sufficient reflection, and full consent of a free will.
7. For a sin to be mortal, thus causing loss of sanctifying grace, three elements must be present:  serious matter, sufficient reflection, and full consent of a free will.
8. A mortal sin can send us to hell.
9. Venial sin lacks one or more of the three elements of mortal sin.
10. Mortal sin lacks one or more of the three elements of venial sin.
11. The main sources of sin are the eight capital sins.
12. Persons, places, or things which lead one to commit sin are called sloth.
13. We must avoid all near occasions of sin.
14. Temptations are inclinations to sin.
15. "Situation ethics" and "fundamental option" are acceptable schools of thought under Catholic moral theology.

## Eleventh and Twelfth Articles of the Creed

### Examination

**True or False**

1. Both the good and evil will rise from the dead at the end of the world.
2. Our resurrected bodies will be new and different.
3. Mary ascended into heaven.
4. The Assumption is when Mary was taken body and soul to heaven.
5. Reincarnation is a false teaching.
6. The soul is mortal, it will one day die.
7. The worst torment of hell is eternal separation from God.
8. It is our decision alone whether we go to heaven or hell.
9. Purgatory is a place where we get a second chance if we die with mortal sin on our souls.
10. Purgatory is not explicitly mentioned in the Bible.
11. Jesus refers to purgatory on several occasions in the Bible.
12. Purgatory will last forever.
13. Purgatory will end after the general judgment.
14. A scriptural basis for praying for the dead is found in II Maccabees.
15. Heaven is where we will see God forever.

## Grace

### Examination

**True or False**

1.  Grace is a supernatural gift.
2.  All grace comes from Mary.
3.  There are four types of grace.
4.  Sanctifying grace is God's life in us.
5.  Sanctifying grace is the grace which allows us to choose good and avoid evil.
6.  Actual grace is God's life in us.
7.  Actual grace is the grace which allows us to choose good and avoid evil.
8.  Sanctifying grace is necessary for salvation.
9.  Actual grace is necessary for salvation.
10. To be in a state of grace means that our soul is worthy of heaven.
11. Sanctifying grace cannot be lost.
12. There are eight gifts of the Holy Spirit.
13. Actual grace is not necessary for acts of virtue.
14. God's grace is irresistible.
15. We dispose ourselves to react positively to actual grace by constant prayer.

## The Sacraments in General

### Examination

**True or False**

1. An example of a sacrament is the Rosary.
2. There are eight sacraments.
3. All the sacraments were instituted by Christ.
4. All the sacraments give both sanctifying and sacramental graces.
5. Sacramental grace is the special grace proper to a particular sacrament which gives us the right to those actual graces that will help us attain the sacrament's purpose.
6. The sacraments are divided into three groups.
7. The sacraments of initiation are Penance and Anointing of the Sick.
8. The sacraments of initiation are Holy Orders and Matrimony.
9. The sacraments of initiation are Baptism, Confirmation, and Eucharist.
10. The sacraments of reconciliation are Penance and Anointing of the Sick.
11. The sacraments of reconciliation are Holy Orders and Matrimony.
12. The sacraments of reconciliation are Baptism, Confirmation, and Eucharist.
13. The sacraments of vocation are Penance and Anointing of the Sick.
14. The sacraments of vocation are Baptism, Confirmation, and Eucharist.
15. The sacraments of vocation are Holy Orders and Matrimony.
16. Baptism, Confirmation, Holy Orders, and Matrimony can be received only once.

17. Two elements are necessary to constitute a true sacrament.
18. Matter is some sensible, concrete thing or action.
19. Matter refers to the essential words used by the minister of a sacrament.
20. Form is some sensible, concrete thing or action.
21. Form refers to the essential words used by the minister of a sacrament.
22. The matter and form must be united to make a sacrament valid.
23. The minister of a sacrament is always a priest or deacon.
24. A sacrament is only valid if the minister is in a state of grace.
25. A state of grace is necessary in order to receive all the sacraments.

## Baptism

### Examination

**True or False**

1. Baptism is the sacrament of regeneration through water in the word.
2. Baptism is not obligatory.
3. Baptism removes only original sin.
4. Baptism confers a permanent character on the soul.
5. The ordinary minister of Baptism is a priest or deacon.
6. Anyone can baptize in case of emergency.
7. Baptism is necessary for salvation.
8. Infant baptism is unacceptable.
9. Baptism of desire is the term applied to one who is not Catholic but suffers martyrdom for the Faith.
10. The position of godparent is merely honorable.

## Confirmation

### Examination

**True or False**

1. Confirmation makes us witnesses of Christ.
2. Confirmation is nowhere demonstrated in Sacred Scripture.
3. The ordinary minister of Confirmation is a deacon.
4. Confirmation is still valid if received in mortal sin.
5. All Catholics are obliged to be confirmed.

## *Holy Eucharist*

### *Examination*

**True or False**

1. The Holy Eucharist is a representation of the Body and Blood of Christ.
2. The Holy Eucharist was instituted on Ascension Thursday.
3. Accidentals are those elements which affect the five senses.
4. Jesus promised the Eucharist in the second chapter of St. John.
5. Jesus becomes present in the Eucharist by a change called consubstantiation.
6. Jesus becomes present in the Eucharist by a change called transubstantiation.
7. The correct term mentioned in one of the two previous statements is the change of the entire substance of the bread and wine into the Body and Blood of Christ.
8. "Consubstantiation" as a term was invented in 1215.
9. "Transubstantiation" as a term was invented in 1215.
10. Jesus is wholly and truly present in the Eucharist, His Body, Blood, Soul, and Divinity.
11. The Mass is Jesus sacrificing Himself again.
12. A deacon can celebrate Mass.
13. A priest can celebrate Mass.
14. A bishop can celebrate Mass.
15. A nun can celebrate Mass.
16. A lay person can celebrate Mass.
17. The first Mass was celebrated at the Last Supper.
18. The sacrifice of the Mass and the sacrifice of the cross are the same sacrifice.
19. The Mass is the highest form of divine worship.

20.  The Mass is offered to either God or the saints.
21.  The Mass can only be offered for the intention of worship.
22.  The Mass forgives venial sins.
23.  The Mass forgives mortal sins.
24.  The wine for Mass can be substituted with grape juice.
25.  The bread for Mass must be made of wheat flour, salt, and water.
26.  The Mass is divided into three parts.
27.  The Liturgy of the Word precedes the Liturgy of the Eucharist.
28.  The Liturgy of the Eucharist precedes the Liturgy of the Word.
29.  Holy Communion is nourishment for our souls.
30.  To receive Holy Communion we must have the right intention and be in a state of grace.
31.  To be in a state of grace is to be free of venial sin.
32.  Jesus is not received in Communion if the person is in mortal sin.
33.  Sacrilege is committed if Communion is received by one in mortal sin.
34.  One must fast for ten hours before receiving Communion.
35.  One must fast for one hour before receiving Communion.
36.  The Church commands us to receive Communion once a year, during the Easter time.
37.  The Real Presence ceases after Mass.
38.  A parish Eucharistic devotion is the Forty Hours.
39.  A parish Eucharistic devotion is Benediction.
40.  A parish Eucharistic devotion is *Anima Christi*.

## Penance

### Examination

**True or False**

1. Penance is the means of forgiveness after Baptism.
2. God breathed on the Apostles when He instituted Penance.
3. Pope Innocent III invented Penance in 1215.
4. Only Jesus forgives our sins, not the priest.
5. The priest merely represents Christ in Penance.
6. The priest acts in the person of Christ in Penance.
7. The priest can only forgive sins if he hears them.
8. The matter of Penance is the rite spoken by the priest.
9. The matter of Penance is contrition, confession of sins, and acceptance of the penance given by the priest.
10. The Sacrament of Penance must be received by any Catholic who has committed a mortal sin since Baptism.
11. There are seven elements necessary for us to make a good confession.
12. An examination of conscience is sorrow for our sins.
13. There are two types of contrition.
14. Imperfect contrition is sorrow motivated by the punishment we deserve.
15. Perfect contrition is sorrow motivated by love of God alone.
16. Imperfect contrition is sufficient to make a good confession.
17. A firm purpose of amendment is the resolve to make a good confession.
18. We must confess *all* sins, mortal and venial.
19. We must confess all venial sins.

20. We must confess all mortal sins.
21. Blasphemy of the Holy Spirit is unforgivable.
22. The seal of confession binds the priest to be willing to die rather than tell what he has heard in confession.
23. A priest can refuse to give absolution.
24. Deliberately omitting a mortal sin in confession adds the mortal sin of sacrilege to the charge of the soul.
25. Sacrilege is committed if we forget to confess a mortal sin.
26. The priest assigns a penance to make at least some satisfaction for our sins.
27. Temporal punishment due for forgiven sin can only be satisfied in purgatory.
28. Children should begin regular confession at about age seven.
29. An indulgence is the remission of temporal punishment due to forgiven sin.
30. One must be in a state of grace to receive an indulgence.

## Anointing of the Sick

### Examination

**True or False**

1. The Anointing of the Sick can heal us spiritually and physically.
2. The biblical proof of this sacrament is found in James 5.
3. The Anointing of the Sick remits venial sins.
4. The Anointing of the Sick cannot remit mortal sin.
5. One must be at the point of death to receive the Anointing of the Sick.
6. In order to receive the Anointing of the Sick, one must be in danger of death from sickness, old age, or injury.
7. A bishop may give the Anointing of the Sick.
8. A priest may give the Anointing of the Sick.
9. A deacon may give the Anointing of the Sick.
10. A lay person may give the Anointing of the Sick.
11. The proximate matter of this sacrament is the anointing itself.
12. The proximate matter of this sacrament is the oil used in the anointing.
13. A person may not receive the Anointing of the Sick more than once.
14. One should, if possible, make a good confession before receiving the Anointing of the Sick.
15. One about to undergo surgery may receive this sacrament.

## Holy Orders

*Examination*

**True or False**

1.  Holy Orders is the sacrament instituted by Christ that gives us the brothers and nuns of Religious Orders.
2.  Holy Orders includes three degrees.
3.  A deacon can administer Holy Orders.
4.  A priest can administer Holy Orders.
5.  A bishop may administer Holy Orders.
6.  Women may receive Holy Orders.
7.  All Catholics have a right to receive Holy Orders.
8.  All male Catholics have a right to receive Holy Orders.
9.  Holy Orders, like Baptism and Confirmation, gives an indelible character to the soul.
10. Those Catholics who call their priests "Father" violate Christ's mandate in Matthew 23:9.

## Matrimony

### Examination

**True or False**

1. The two-fold purpose of Matrimony is unity and procreation.
2. The bond of Matrimony lasts until the death of both spouses.
3. The priest is the minister of Matrimony.
4. Prior to the teachings of Christ, Matrimony was merely a sacred contract.
5. The ordinary marriage law of the Church is that a couple must be married in the presence of a priest, deacon, or magistrate and two witnesses.
6. A Nuptial Mass is absolutely necessary to validate a marriage.
7. A mixed marriage, strictly speaking, is a marriage between a Catholic and a non-baptized person.
8. One must be in a state of grace to receive Matrimony.
9. Children of a nullified marriage are illegitimate.
10. The bishop's permission must be granted for a separation.
11. The bishop's permission must be granted for a civil divorce.
12. Each party of a divorced couple is free to remarry.
13. To enter into a marriage with the intention of not having children renders the marriage invalid.
14. Childlessness renders a marriage invalid.
15. A husband's special duties are to exercise his God-given authority with love, kindness, and respect toward his wife and children.

## Conscience and the Ten Commandments

### Examination

**True or False**

1. Conscience is a judgment of emotion.
2. We must follow our conscience.
3. Conscience comes from the brain.
4. We are not necessarily responsible for all our actions.
5. A right conscience is upright and truthful.
6. A right conscience cannot decide for or against the morality of an act.
7. A right conscience is constantly in doubt.
8. A right conscience judges by convenience.
9. A "white lie" is acceptable if the outcome is a moral good.
10. There are four "great commandments."
11. The ten commandments were "written with the finger of God."
12. God gave us the ten commandments through Abraham.
13. The first three commandments deal with man's relationship to God.
14. The last seven commandments deal with man's relationship to man.
15. The first commandment obliges us to worship God alone.
16. The second commandment obliges us to rest on the Lord's day.
17. The third commandment obliges us to speak respectfully of God.
18. The fourth commandment obliges us to respect our parents.

19. The fifth commandment forbids the unjust taking of human life.
20. The sixth commandment forbids theft.
21. The seventh commandment forbids adultery.
22. The eighth commandment forbids false witness.
23. The ninth commandment forbids coveting your neighbor's goods.
24. The tenth commandment forbids coveting your neighbor's wife.
25. We can always keep the commandments.

## First Commandment

### Examination

**True or False**
1. Public prayer (prayer with others) is the only right way to pray to God.
2. The highest form of worship is the Mass.
3. Spiritism and divination are often the same thing.
4. The first commandment forbids honoring the saints.
5. Dulia is the honor given to God alone.
6. Hyperdulia is the honor given to God alone.
7. Latria is the honor given to God alone.
8. Dulia is the honor given to Mary alone.
9. Hyperdulia is the honor given to Mary alone.
10. Latria is the honor given to Mary alone.
11. We give dulia to the angels.
12. By honoring the saints we honor God Himself.
13. Participating in non-Catholic Communion is acceptable under the first commandment.
14. Catholics pray to relics and images.
15. God has permitted some saints' bodies to not know decay after death.

## *Second Commandment*

### *Examination*

**True or False**

1. The second commandment teaches us to be reverent in speech.
2. We must speak reverently of the angels, saints, and the Blessed Virgin Mary.
3. Profanity is the same as cursing.
4. Profanity is the same as vulgar language.
5. Profanity is the abuse of God's name.
6. Cursing is the same as vulgar language.
7. Cursing is invoking evil upon a person, place, or thing.
8. An oath is calling upon God to witness the truthfulness of what we say.
9. Perjury is illegal, but not sinful.
10. A vow is a promise made to God.

## Third Commandment

*Examination*

**True or False**

1. We must attend Mass on Sundays and holy days of obligation.
2. Televised Masses fulfill our Sunday obligation.
3. The obligation to attend Mass begins at age twelve.
4. It is a mortal sin to miss Mass on Sundays and holy days of obligation without a sufficient reason.
5. We are permitted to, say, paint the house or wash the car on Sunday.

## Fourth Commandment

### Examination

**True or False**

1. The fourth commandment obliges us to obey our parents, even if their demands are sinful.
2. The source of parental authority was the creation of Adam.
3. Children are obliged to respect their parents even after they are grown.
4. Parents are obliged to provide only for the spiritual needs of children.
5. Parents are expected to leave the education of their children to the Church by enrolling them in parochial school.
6. The fourth commandment obliges us to obey all lawful authority.
7. Workers are obliged to serve employers faithfully.
8. Employers are obliged to treat workers respectfully.
9. A citizen must obey just laws, but is not obliged to pay taxes.
10. A citizen is obliged to defend his country.
11. Catholic citizens may vote only for Catholic politicians.
12. Catholics are permitted to vote for politicians who favor legalized abortion.
13. Political authorities are obliged to respect the fundamental rights of the human person.
14. We are obliged to obey laws that contradict God's law.
15. Grown children are obliged to care for their parents when they can no longer care for themselves.

## Fifth Commandment

### Examination

**True or False**
1.   The fifth commandment allows for "mercy killing".
2.   Direct abortion is a mortal sin.
3.   Indirect abortion is a mortal sin.
4.   Excommunication could be imposed upon Catholic politicians who are "pro-choice" in their legislative voting and public support.
5.   Self defense can be a morally acceptable means of taking human life.
6.   The Church condemns the death penalty under the fifth commandment.
7.   Direct sterilization is a moral means of birth control.
8.   The recreational use of drugs is a grave offense.
9.   Scandal is the public exposure of a person's wrong doing.
10.   Soldiers who throw themselves on grenades to save their fellow soldiers commit culpable suicide.

## Sixth and Ninth Commandments

### Examination

**True or False**

1. The sixth commandment deals with external sexual purity.
2. The sixth commandment deals with interior sexual purity.
3. The ninth commandment deals with external sexual purity.
4. The ninth commandment deals with interior sexual purity.
5. Fornication is sexual relations between two people, at least one of whom is married.
6. The "Pill" is evil morally, ethically, and medically as a contraceptive.
7. Since married Catholics are obliged to procreate, *in vitro* fertilization is morally acceptable.
8. Since married Catholics are obliged to procreate, fertility drugs are morally acceptable.
9. Since married Catholics are obliged to procreate, the use of sperm or ovum from a third party is morally acceptable.
10. If used rightly, Natural Family Planning is a morally acceptable means of birth control.
11. It is evil to be a homosexual.
12. Homosexual activity is evil.
13. Premarital sex is sexual intercourse between future spouses prior to marriage.
14. Masturbation is the deliberate stimulation of the genital organs for sexual pleasure.
15. Since it involves only one person, masturbation is morally acceptable.
16. Masturbation is a gravely disordered action.

17. Since we cannot have sexual relations outside of marriage, it is at least acceptable to imagine and think about it.
18. Impure temptations are sinful in themselves.
19. Laziness and immodest dress are two dangers to chastity.
20. Couples dating should be especially careful about guarding chastity.

## Seventh and Tenth Commandments

### Examination

**True or False**

1. These commandments treat of Church authority.
2. Not everyone has a right to private ownership.
3. The seventh commandment obliges us to pay our debts.
4. We may purchase stolen goods.
5. A thief must return stolen goods.
6. We may ask a priest to return property we have stolen.
7. If we discover we have purchased stolen goods, we may ask the rightful owner to reimburse us.
8. It is a form of theft to keep what we have borrowed beyond the period agreed to by the owner.
9. Cheating is a form of theft.
10. Negligence in working is a form of cheating.
11. It is morally acceptable for a super market worker to treat himself to lunch from the market's stock without asking his employer.
12. Workers may strike.
13. Workers may use violence in a strike.
14. Employers are not obliged to provide safe working conditions for workers.
15. Politicians may not accept bribes.
16. Usury is the interest charged on a legal bank loan.
17. Usury is excessive interest charged on money loaned.
18. One may be absolved of stealing although he does not intend to make restitution.
19. Gambling, in and of itself, is not sinful.
20. We may not desire what belongs to another.

## Eighth Commandment

### Examination

**True or False**

1.   Lies are forbidden by the eighth commandment.
2.   We may tell a "white lie" for a good end.
3.   A jocose lie is the worst sort of lie.
4.   Hypocrisy is a lie.
5.   Detraction is exposing the faults of others without good cause.
6.   Tale bearing is the uncharitable telling of the truth.
7.   Calumny is showing contempt for another person.
8.   Calumny is damaging a person's reputation in print.
9.   Calumny is telling a lie that hurts a person's reputation.
10.  Contumely is showing contempt for another person.
11.  Contumely is damaging a person's reputation in print.
12.  Contumely is telling a lie that hurts a person's reputation.
13.  Libel is showing contempt for another person.
14.  Libel is damaging another person's reputation in print.
15.  Libel is telling a lie that hurts a person's reputation.
16.  We are obliged to keep the secrets of others.
17.  We may read the private writings of others.
18.  We owe reparation to the offended party if we sin against the eighth commandment.
19.  If we somehow acquire knowledge of someone's matter for confession, we may never reveal it.
20.  Reparation to an offended party may sometimes include material reparation.

## The Precepts of the Church
## and
## The Life of Virtue

*Examination*

**True or False**

1.   The Church has the authority of Christ to make laws.
2.   Catholics may decide for themselves to keep the precepts.
3.   It is a venial sin to miss Mass on Sundays and holy days of obligation.
4.   Mass obligation may be fulfilled at an anticipated Mass on the evening before.
5.   The Church recommends confession at least once a year.
6.   The Church recommends Communion at least once a year.
7.   Fast days fall on all the Fridays of Lent.
8.   We may eat snacks between meals on fast days.
9.   Seafood is permitted on days of abstinence.
10.  A virtue is the habit of doing good.
11.  A vice is the habit of doing good.
12.  Supernatural virtues are acquired by repeating naturally good acts.
13.  The most important virtues are the theological virtues.
14.  There are seven theological virtues.
15.  The theological virtues are faith, hope, and charity.
16.  We are justified by faith alone.
17.  Presumption and despair are sins against faith.
18.  Presumption and despair are sins against hope.
19.  Presumption and despair are sins against charity.
20.  Cardinal virtues are moral virtues.
21.  There are four cardinal virtues.

22.  There are ten beatitudes.
23.  The works of mercy are corporal and spiritual.
24.  The spiritual works of mercy are found in Matthew
     25 and Tobit.
25.  The corporal works of mercy are found in Matthew
     25 and Tobit.

## *Life of Prayer*

### *Examination*

**True or False**

1. Prayer is raising our hearts and minds to God in loving conversation.
2. We are obliged to pray for everyone.
3. God answers all prayers.
4. An aspiration and an ejaculation are the same thing.
5. Catholics are not permitted to use impromptu prayers.
6. The Our Father is not as good as the Lord's Prayer.
7. The Lord's Prayer is truly the summary of the whole gospel.
8. The main enemies of the spiritual life are the world, the flesh, and the devil.
9. Jesus promised those who follow Him a life free of suffering.
10. Meditation should be a daily part of our prayer life.
11. We should spend at least 15 minutes a day reading the Bible.
12. The Bible is made up of two testaments of the "lost books".
13. The Old Testament has twenty-seven books.
14. The New Testament has twenty-seven books.
15. Catholics are encouraged to interpret the Bible on their own.

## First Article of the Creed Examination Answers

| | | | | |
|---|---|---|---|---|
| 1. F | 6. F | 11. T | 16. T | 21. T |
| 2. T | 7. F | 12. F | 17. F | 22. F |
| 3. T | 8. F | 13. F | 18. T | 23. F |
| 4. F | 9. T | 14. T | 19. F | 24. T |
| 5. F | 10. T | 15. F | 20. F | 25. F |

## Second Article Exam Answers

| | | | | |
|---|---|---|---|---|
| 1. T | 5. F | 9. T | 13. F | 17. F |
| 2. F | 6. F | 10. T | 14. T | 18. T |
| 3. T | 7. T | 11. T | 15. F | 19. F |
| 4. F | 8. F | 12. T | 16. T | 20. T |

## Third Article Exam Answers

| | | | | |
|---|---|---|---|---|
| 1. T | 5. T | 9. T | 13. T | 17. F |
| 2. F | 6. F | 10. T | 14. F | 18. F |
| 3. F | 7. F | 11. T | 15. T | 19. T |
| 4. F | 8. F | 12. T | 16. T | 20. F |

## Fourth, Fifth, and Sixth Articles Exam Answers

| | | | | |
|---|---|---|---|---|
| 1. T | 5. T | 9. T | 13. F | 17. F |
| 2. F | 6. F | 10. T | 14. T | 18. F |
| 3. F | 7. F | 11. T | 15. T | 19. F |
| 4. T | 8. F | 12. T | 16. T | 20. T |

## Seventh and Eighth Articles Exam Answers

| | | | | |
|---|---|---|---|---|
| 1. F | 5. F | 9. F | 13. F | 17. F |
| 2. T | 6. F | 10. F | 14. F | 18. T |
| 3. F | 7. T | 11. T | 15. F | 19. F |
| 4. T | 8. F | 12. T | 16. F | 20. T |

## Ninth Article Exam Answers

| | | | | | |
|---|---|---|---|---|---|
| 1. F | 11. T | 21. F | 31. F | 41. T | 51. F |
| 2. T | 12. F | 22. T | 32. F | 42. T | 52. F |
| 3. F | 13. T | 23. F | 33. T | 43. F | 53. T |
| 4. T | 14. T | 24. F | 34. F | 44. T | 54. F |
| 5. T | 15. F | 25. T | 35. T | 45. T | 55. F |
| 6. F | 16. F | 26. F | 36. F | 46. F | 56. F |
| 7. F | 17. F | 27. T | 37. T | 47. T | 57. T |
| 8. T | 18. F | 28. T | 38. T | 48. T | 58. T |
| 9. F | 19. T | 29. F | 39. F | 49. T | 59. F |
| 10. F | 20. T | 30. T | 40. F | 50. F | 60. T |

## Tenth Article Exam Answers

| | | | | |
|---|---|---|---|---|
| 1. T | 4. T | 7. T | 10. F | 13. T |
| 2. F | 5. T | 8. T | 11. F | 14. T |
| 3. F | 6. F | 9. T | 12. F | 15. F |

## Eleventh and Twelfth Articles Exam Answers

| | | | | |
|---|---|---|---|---|
| 1. T | 4. T | 7. T | 10. T | 13. T |
| 2. F | 5. T | 8. T | 11. T | 14. T |
| 3. F | 6. F | 9. F | 12. F | 15. T |

## Grace Exam Answers

| | | | | |
|---|---|---|---|---|
| 1. T | 4. T | 7. T | 10. T | 13. F |
| 2. F | 5. F | 8. T | 11. F | 14. F |
| 3. F | 6. F | 9. F | 12. F | 15. T |

## Sacraments in General Exam Answers

| | | | | |
|---|---|---|---|---|
| 1. F | 6. T | 11. F | 16. F | 21. T |
| 2. F | 7. F | 12. F | 17. T | 22. T |
| 3. T | 8. F | 13. F | 18. T | 23. F |
| 4. T | 9. T | 14. F | 19. F | 24. F |
| 5. T | 10. T | 15. T | 20. F | 25. F |

## Baptism Exam Answers

| | | | | |
|---|---|---|---|---|
| 1. T | 3. F | 5. T | 7. T | 9. F |
| 2. F | 4. T | 6. T | 8. F | 10. F |

## Confirmation Exam Answers

| | | | | |
|---|---|---|---|---|
| 1. T | 2. F | 3. F | 4. T | 5. T |

## Holy Eucharist Exam Answers

| | | | | | |
|---|---|---|---|---|---|
| 1. F | 8. F | 15. F | 22. T | 29. T | 36. T |
| 2. F | 9. T | 16. F | 23. F | 30. T | 37. F |
| 3. T | 10. T | 17. T | 24. F | 31. F | 38. T |
| 4. F | 11. F | 18. T | 25. F | 32. F | 39. T |
| 5. F | 12. F | 19. T | 26. F | 33. T | 40. F |
| 6. T | 13. T | 20. F | 27. T | 34. F | |
| 7. T | 14. T | 21. F | 28. F | 35. T | |

## Penance Exam Answers

| | | | | | |
|---|---|---|---|---|---|
| 1. T | 6. T | 11. F | 16. T | 21. F | 26. T |
| 2. T | 7. T | 12. F | 17. F | 22. T | 27. F |
| 3. F | 8. F | 13. T | 18. F | 23. T | 28. T |
| 4. F | 9. T | 14. T | 19. F | 24. T | 29. T |
| 5. F | 10. T | 15. T | 20. T | 25. F | 30. T |

## Anointing of the Sick Exam Answers

| | | | | |
|---|---|---|---|---|
| 1. T | 4. F | 7. T | 10. F | 13. F |
| 2. T | 5. F | 8. T | 11. T | 14. T |
| 3. T | 6. T | 9. F | 12. F | 15. T |

## Holy Orders Exam Answers

| | | | | |
|---|---|---|---|---|
| 1. F | 3. F | 5. T | 7. F | 9. T |
| 2. T | 4. F | 6. F | 8. F | 10. F |

## Matrimony Exam Answers

| | | | | |
|---|---|---|---|---|
| 1. T | 4. T | 7. T | 10. T | 13. T |
| 2. F | 5. F | 8. T | 11. T | 14. F |
| 3. F | 6. F | 9. F | 12. F | 15. T |

## Conscience and Ten Commandments Exam Answers

| | | | | |
|---|---|---|---|---|
| 1. F | 6. F | 11. T | 16. F | 21. F |
| 2. T | 7. F | 12. F | 17. F | 22. T |
| 3. F | 8. F | 13. T | 18. T | 23. F |
| 4. F | 9. F | 14. T | 19. T | 24. F |
| 5. T | 10. F | 15. T | 20. F | 25. T |

## First Commandment Exam Answers

| | | | | |
|---|---|---|---|---|
| 1. F | 4. F | 7. T | 10. F | 13. F |
| 2. T | 5. F | 8. F | 11. T | 14. F |
| 3. T | 6. F | 9. T | 12. T | 15. T |

## Second Commandment Exam Answers

| | | | | |
|---|---|---|---|---|
| 1. T | 3. F | 5. T | 7. T | 9. F |
| 2. T | 4. F | 6. F | 8. T | 10. T |

### Third Commandment Exam Answers

1. T    2. F    3. F    4. T    5. F

### Fourth Commandment Exam Answers

| 1. F | 4. F | 7. T | 10. T | 13. T |
| 2. F | 5. F | 8. T | 11. F | 14. F |
| 3. T | 6. T | 9. F | 12. F | 15. T |

### Fifth Commandment Exam Answers

| 1. F | 3. F | 5. T | 7. F | 9. F |
| 2.T | 4. T | 6. F | 8. T | 10. F |

### Sixth and Ninth Commandments Exam Answers

| 1. T | 5. F | 9. F | 13. T | 17. F |
| 2. F | 6. T | 10. T | 14. T | 18. F |
| 3. F | 7. F | 11. F | 15. F | 19. T |
| 4. T | 8. T | 12. T | 16. T | 20. F |

### Seventh and Tenth Commandments Exam Answers

| 1. F | 5. T | 9. T | 13. F | 17. T |
| 2. F | 6. T | 10. T | 14. F | 18. F |
| 3. T | 7. F | 11. F | 15. T | 19. T |
| 4. F | 8. T | 12. T | 16. F | 20. F |

### Eighth Commandment Exam Answers

| 1. T | 5. T | 9. T | 13. F | 17. F |
| 2. F | 6. T | 10. T | 14. T | 18. T |
| 3. F | 7. F | 11. F | 15. F | 19. T |
| 4. T | 8. F | 12. F | 16. T | 20. T |

## The Precepts and Virtues Exam Answers

| | | | | |
|---|---|---|---|---|
| 1. T | 6. F | 11. F | 16. F | 21. T |
| 2. F | 7. F | 12. F | 17. F | 22. F |
| 3. F | 8. F | 13. T | 18. T | 23. T |
| 4. T | 9. T | 14. F | 19. F | 24. F |
| 5. F | 10. T | 15. T | 20. T | 25. T |

## Life of Prayer Exam Answers

| | | | | |
|---|---|---|---|---|
| 1. T | 4. T | 7. T | 10. T | 13. F |
| 2. T | 5. F | 8. T | 11. T | 14. T |
| 3. T | 6. F | 9. F | 12. F | 15. F |

# Index[1]

[1] The numbers next to the topical headings in this index refer to the question rather than the page.

# Acknowledgements

ACKNOWLEDGEMENTS are, to my way of thinking, recognition of those persons who make possible the opera of writers; however, when writers reflect upon the list of those to whom they owe thanks and are deserving of recognition, the list grows longer with each reflective movement. Consequently, not every deserving soul gets mentioned, except by way of an *et alia* type statement. I trust that those persons to whom I wish to give thanks for this opus *in pectore* will realize who they are, and will bask in the gift of humility God has given them. They have my heart and devotion.

On that most glorious plane of eternal discovery of God which we call heaven, I have dedicated this book to The Blessed Trinity: our heavenly Father, who has taught me to cry Daddy; His Son, who has caused love to infiltrate the void of this sinner's heart; and the Holy Spirit, who is teaching me to appreciate silent conversion. The Mother of God was the one human person to love me when I was at my most unlovable; St. Herbie, my angel, who protects me from myself; St. Bartholemew, who won for me the graces to fall passionately in love with our Eucharistic King; St. John Bosco, who has been a dear friend and the inspiration for my meager attempts at evangelization; Blessed Josemaria Escriva, who is helping me to learn how to live our holy and ancient faith; and the late Fr. Killian Mooney, S.T., who nurtured my infant soul and gave me a zeal to evangelize.

There are quite literally scores of persons in the Church Militant without whose help this book would not have been possible, and the following is a representation: Mom, who chose to give me life; Angi Smith, who labored constantly with love and in suffering to process the manuscript; Michael Mayola, the friend, godfather, and teacher who urged, argued, counseled, and lectured me through most of this book; John Finnegan, whose love and prayers sustained me during those times when my faith was the most costly; Sr. Mary Lelia, D.C.J., who truly loves the sinner while hating the sin; Fr. Gerard Santora, whose Masses and prayers have had a happy and noticeable effect in my life; Fr. Robert J. Fox, whose love for Mary is contagious (thanks be to God!), and who first encouraged me to write; Karl Keating, who taught me to love apologetics and gave me many opportunities to teach others on the pages of his magazine, *This Rock*; Dr. Joseph Strada, who has edified and inspired me by lived Catholicism; Sterling and Roianne Frith, Marty and Irene Barrack, Paul, Junie, Kelly and Michael O'Connell, Tom Burk and Mary Grace, who have very charitably overlooked my faults, shown immense patience with me, and loved Jesus in me; the Alabama prison officials who have strengthened my faith through persecution; and to all those souls who have come to know Christ's True Church through *The Missionary's Catechism.*

### How To Order

# The Missionary's Catechism

If you enjoyed <u>The Missionary's Catechism</u> (ISBN 0-9657125-1-6), you may order them from Magnificat Institute Press for $12.95. Shipping and Handling are $3.00 for one copy, $4.00 for two copies, and $5.00 for three copies. (For shipping and handling on larger quantities or for foreign orders, please contact us toll free at 1-800-370-8201.) We accept **Visa, Master Card, American Express,** and **Discover Card.** Texas residents add 8.25% sales tax. Send check or money order (U.S. Funds Only) to address listed on the order form below.

### ATTENTION BOOKSTORES

*The Missionary's Catechism* is available to bookstores at trade discount. Please contact us via telephone at **800-370-8201** or via e-mail at **mipress@earthlink.net**

# Order Form

Name: _____

Street: _____

City _____ State _____ Zip _____

Please send ____ copies of *The Missionary's Catechism* @ $12.95.

Please make checks payable to:  Magnificat Institute Press
P.O. Box 60591
Houston, TX 77205-0591

**We are on the web at: www.magnificatpress.com**

# Dominican Laity and the Year 2000

Anthony Dao Quang Chinh, O.P.

Everything you ever wanted to know about the Dominican Laity but were afraid to ask.
Written by Father Anthony Dao, O.P., Dominican Laity explains how the third order works, who they are, what they do, how they pray, how they minister, and how they receive St. Dominic's charism of preaching, 120 pages.

Available from Magnificat Institute Press for
$9.95 plus $2.00 shipping and handling.

Foreword by Rev. John A. Hardon, S.J.
Foreword by Rev. William Most, Ph.D.

## SECOND EXODUS

by Martin K. Barrack

The roots of the Catholic Church are Jewish and this
book shows them better than anything else written since the
Second Vatican Council.

With forewords by two holy priest-scholars, this book is
must reading for anyone interested in the connection between
Judaism and Christianity, 388 pages.

Available from Magnificat Institute Press for
$14.95 plus $3.00 shipping and handling.